Prince Lichnowsky and the Great War

Prince Lichnowsky
and the
Great War

Harry F. Young

The University of Georgia Press
Athens

Library of Congress Catalog Card Number: 75-11448
International Standard Book Number: 0-8203-0385-2

The University of Georgia Press, Athens 30602

Set in 11 on 13 pt. Linotype Baskerville
Printed in the United States of America

Contents

ℭreface

The history of European diplomacy in the twentieth century presents no more tragic figure than imperial Germany's last ambassador in London, Prince Karl Max Lichnowsky (1860–1928). As the son of a rich and historied family he seemed destined for a distinguished career. He had joined the diplomatic corps at the age of twenty-three, and when he left the service some twenty years later to attend to his inherited properties he was recognized as a man of goodwill who had faith in the international system and the values of Western civilization. He had just married a beautiful woman who was a writer of considerable gifts. And he could have led a life of honorable ease if in the fall of 1912 his sovereign Wilhelm II had not called upon him to be his representative at the Court of St. James's.

Lichnowsky anticipated a happy and successful mission. London was the most important post in the German service, but it was not at this time an easy one. As Germany rose to a position of world power Anglo-German relations had become strained. Lichnowsky was convinced that he could reverse this trend. For years he had argued that the naval rivalry, which was the symbol of Anglo-German conflict, need not lead to permanent estrangement or, as some predicted, to war. Chancellor Bethmann Hollweg concurred in his belief that the atmosphere would improve if Germany sought agreement on outstanding minor questions. But the prince also warned that it was necessary to accept the Continental balance of power. "People in Great Britain have grown too comfort-loving to *want* a war," he wrote in one of his early dispatches. "The nation loves peace and does not care to be disturbed in the routine of its daily life. A war with us would therefore not be popular, but in spite of all this the English *would* wage such a war if France were threatened by us, for the opinion is general here that France would not be able to stand up against the superior might of Germany without British help."

The danger, therefore, lay on the Continent. When Lichnowsky became ambassador the most acute of Continental rivalries was the Austro-Serbian. Here he recognized a danger to his own mission, for he knew that an Austrian attack upon the smaller country would result inevitably in war between Germany and England. Hence his horror in the summer of 1914 when, after the murder of the Austrian archduke, Berlin decided to support Vienna's plan to eliminate "the hotbed of criminal agitation in Belgrade." He was the only German official to counsel against this plan and to urge that Austria submit the dispute to arbitration. But his arguments were discounted and his mounting fears dismissed as unworthy. Suddenly, on the day Germany declared war on Russia, he seemed to take hope. He reported an English offer of neutrality (which it appeared he had misunderstood), and even though the cabinet had reached the decision to intervene he seemed to think England was hesitating to commit her forces. And so when the hostilities began as he had predicted, it was he who could be said to have misjudged the situation and to have failed.

The outbreak of the war in 1914 is the event that dominates Lichnowsky's life. It put an end to successful endeavors that were of benefit to the entire European community, and it robbed him of his good name. The remainder of his life he spent in vain attempts to clear his record and to explain to himself why the German leaders in 1914 had persisted on the obviously fatal course. In the fifth month of war he wrote to a friend that "only he who knows the truly fabulous incompetence of our leading statesmen will understand that such a policy was indeed possible *without* their desiring war!" He was slow to adopt the phrase "preventive war." He did not use it in the account of his ambassadorship written in 1916 and entitled *My London Mission, 1912–1914* where he averred that his mission had failed "not because of the wiles (*Tücken*) of British policy but because of the defects (*Lücken*) of our own," and where he said that in view of the evidence it was no wonder that "the whole of the civilized world outside Germany places the entire responsibility for the world war on our shoulders." In 1918 the Allies acquired a copy of this memoir, which the prince had distributed to members of his family and to friends, and broadcast it in multiple editions all over the globe. And this brought down upon his head a storm that did not abate when the empire collapsed and Germany became a republic.

He could not dispel the shadow that events had cast upon his life. Nor could he provide a convincing explanation of what had occurred in 1914. Respect for the national interest impeded his efforts, for he wished to be a loyal citizen of the fledgling republic burdened with reparations that were justified on the grounds that Germany alone was responsible for the war. So when he published his collected papers in 1927 he suppressed in essays he had written earlier the most serious of his accusations against the imperial statesmen, emphasized the deeper roots of the catastrophe (notably Bismarck's turning away from Russia), and concluded that the leaders of 1914 had "blundered into the war by mistake." His book was a total disaster. He failed to note that he had made textual changes in the essays and that he had also modified the wording in some of the official dispatches already available in their original form. The advocates of Germany's innocence in 1914 seized the opportunity to complete his disgrace. They were in full attack when, in February 1928, he died.

There has been need for a just account of Lichnowsky's career. General knowledge of his role in the coming of the Great War is dependent upon the few more extensive accounts of his life which are flawed by considerable inaccuracies or distorted by partisan intent. Edward F. Willis, *Prince Lichnowsky: Ambassador of Peace*, the only book-length study of his career, was out-of-date even before it was published in 1942. It is a worthy effort, but its sources are limited to published materials available in the early 1930s and it concentrates narrowly on the diplomacy of the years 1912–1914. Most of the German historians who between the wars examined Lichnowsky's record were looking for flaws in order to discredit his testimony against Bethmann and his advisors in the Foreign Ministry. In recent years the climate of opinion in German historiography has taken a radical turn in his favor. A critical attitude toward the commanding figures in 1914 has supplanted the former tendency to defend them. But, as to Lichnowsky, the false interpretations persist and there are many misunderstandings and inaccuracies in works that are on the whole favorable to him. The result is that after four decades of research on the origins of the war of 1914–1918 knowledge of this central figure is in many ways less advanced than it was when the first phalanx of war-guilt scholars had completed their minute examination of the evidence.

The present work attempts to provide a unified account of Lichnowsky's life and career. It is based on a variety of sources. Records in official documents collections and other published works are joined with previously unknown or unused materials in official files and private papers, including the remnants of the prince's own archives, and information from his family. The story concentrates on Lichnowsky's ambassadorship and his struggle to explain the reasons for the catastrophe. To see his diplomatic career in its natural setting it is necessary to review his family origins and describe his position in the social and political system. As no other diplomat had so personal a connection with the events leading to the outbreak of war in 1914 and the emotional debate concerning its origins, this is mainly a contribution to the study of World War I. But it is hoped that the unhappy history of an aristocrat who was a man of goodwill and sensibility and the perfect choice for a mission in London will illumine the general condition of Wilhelminian Germany.

The question of responsibility for the war has become in recent years once more a matter of acute interest. Fritz Fischer's 1961 book on Germany's war aims (*Griff nach der Weltmacht*) revived a discussion that had lost its vigor. His original thesis that Germany bore chief responsibility for the outbreak of the war because her plan of action was the aggressive one is now generally accepted by Western historians. But the discussion has moved on from that beginning. Increasingly the debate has become centered upon the motives and calculations behind the fateful decisions initiating the chain of events that led to hostilities. While Fischer's adherents believe that Germany consciously sought a general European war and indeed will conclude that this was an aggressive war instead of a defensive or preventive one, Karl Dietrich Erdmann concludes from the evidence in the diaries of Chancellor Bethmann's close advisor Kurt Riezler that Bethmann, though accepting the risk of war, was not bent upon bringing it about.

Lichnowsky's experience will not solve this problem for us—at least not in the terms in which we are accustomed to present it. There is no doubt that Lichnowsky always held Germany responsible for the war and recognized both its hegemonial and preventive aspects. The historian who reviews the period from 1912 to 1914 in the light of Lichnowsky's career can scarcely fail to see that Berlin did not share his respect for the balance of power and his desire for an entente with England in order to bring about a general understanding among the powers. Although Lichnowsky was kept in ignorance of the actual counsel Berlin took, he knew what currents of thought ebbed and flowed, what idées fixes and infatuations moved the military and civilian advisors. And still he could never settle upon a simple explanation of Berlin's purpose or of what determined the crucial decisions in 1914. There was a circumstance to which he was particularly alive—the personal animosity in the Wilhelmstrasse toward him. That this existed and that it affected the conduct of affairs during his embassy is clear from the record. How important it was in the resistance to his ideas in July 1914 is difficult to assess. But since he himself saw this animosity as the stable and in the end determining element in the chemistry of that summer, it is an aspect that we, considering Lichnowsky's biography, cannot ignore.

I wish to acknowledge the many debts I incurred while writing this book. The research I conducted abroad was made possible by grants from the International Affairs Center of Indiana University and the American Philosophical Society. Ohio University provided funds to help defray the expense of typing. Robert H. Ferrell and Ian MacKenzie gave me the advantage of their experience and skill in matters of format and organization. For assistance in obtaining source materials I am indebted to Wilhelm Carlgren, Fritz T. Epstein, Fritz Fischer, Holger Fliessbach, Imanuel Geiss, Günter Moltmann, Annelise Thimme, and Therese, Countess Arco-Zinneberg. The late novelist August Scholtis, who as a youth served as a clerk-typist in the prince's private office and typed *My London Mission* from manuscript, let me see his unpublished essay and other materials he had collected concerning Lichnowsky and his memorandum. To my wife I owe encouragement and intelligent criticism as well as help with the physical labor involved in preparing the manuscript.

I am deeply grateful for the support I have received from the prince's children—the late Prince Wilhelm, Count Michael, and

Countess Leonore Lichnowsky. Without their remembrances and careful comments on questions I raised I could not have hoped to achieve any authenticity in my presentation of their father's career. My obligations to Countess Lichnowsky are especially great. In conversation and correspondence she gave me full advantage of her personal and scholarly knowledge. She also placed at my disposal an excellent selection of family photographs from which the illustrations were chosen.

None of the persons whose aid I gratefully acknowledge bears any responsibility for the errors and imperfections of which I might be guilty.

Prince Lichnowsky and the Great War

Chapter I

𝔇rigins

Prince Karl Max Lichnowsky was born in the manor house at Kreuzenort, Upper Silesia, on 8 March 1860.[1] For more than a century this originally Slavic territory, long ruled by Austria, had been subject to the king of Prussia. In 1860 Bismarck was Prussian ambassador in Saint Petersburg, and the Hohenzollern prince Friedrich Wilhelm Victor Albert, the later emperor Wilhelm II, was one year old. The struggle between Austria and Prussia for mastery in Germany had not yet come to a head, and ten years were to pass before Bismarck would create the new German Reich.

The child's parents were Karl, the fifth prince Lichnowsky, and Marie, princess of Croy-Dülmen. The Croys originated in Picardy but had split into several branches, and since the eighteenth century the branch to which Princess Marie belonged had been settled in a Catholic region of northwestern Germany. The young prince, their first child, was named Carl Maximilian (later commonly written as Karl Max) in honor of the Lichnowsky ancestor who in the seventeenth century had gathered his family's scattered and encumbered possessions and laid the basis for the flourishing domains of 1860. He was baptized by his uncle Mons. Robert Lichnowsky,[2] papal prelate and canon at the cathedral chapter at Olmütz in Moravia.

Karl Max was educated mostly at home but not in the fashion of his time. His father was a willful man who was pronouncedly in favor of practical subjects. Strongly resenting the classical education to which he had been subjected and like Bismarck seeing no utility in dead languages, he would not let his son be trained in Greek and Latin. At the age of nine the young prince was sent to Neuchâtel in Switzerland to improve the French he had already acquired from his mother and French governesses. There he lived with his tutor, a Protestant scholar and historian who was director of the local schools. In the remnants of the family archives there are fragments of letters he wrote his mother at that time expressing in good French the normal concerns of a young boy. It was not until he was in his teens that his father grudgingly recognized that without the ancient languages his son could not complete his secondary education and would be permanently excluded from a gentleman's career in the civil service. After some tutoring at home, Karl Max entered the Vitzthum Gymnasium in Dresden, graduating at the age of twenty.[3]

The prince did not attend a university but went into military service. "It was a tradition in aristocratic families," wrote Count Johann Bernstorff, Lichnowsky's contemporary and diplomatic colleague, "that the eldest son, who was to succeed to the family estate, should prepare himself by a period of service in a guard cavalry regiment, or enter the civil service."[4] Prince Lichnowsky was twenty-two years old when he joined the *Leibgardehusaren-regiment*,[5] a costly unit that was entirely aristocratic in membership and that a few years later came under the direct personal command of Prince Wilhelm of Prussia. As the junior member of this corps, Lichnowsky was subjected to some good-natured hazing. Once his comrades, knowing that he had ordered a fine mount from England, sent him to the railroad yards to take delivery on a spavined cab horse.[6]

In appearance and manner young Lichnowsky had nothing about him of the soldier. He was of medium height and not particularly robust. His face was strong boned, with a sensitive mouth, and grey eyes that could be alternately penetrating and introspective. Black hair and a slightly aquiline nose gave evidence of the Hungarian strain that had entered the family with his paternal grandmother. He had been a studious child—to the regret of his energetic father who once said that his son took only after his mother's side and was "all Croy."[7] But he was also expansive and at times high spirited. As a young man he once lost a large sum of money gambling. His father, who was glad to see his son pursuing manly pastimes, paid his debts without a murmur. But the prince never gambled again.[8]

Prince Lichnowsky was neither a Junker nor a typical Prussian, but the product of a cultural and political frontier. His family's estates lay largely in the angle formed where the River Oppa flows into the Oder. In this fertile soil grains, beets, and potatoes flourish. At the tip of the wedge where the rivers meet, outside the Lichnowsky properties, a deposit of coal betokens the industrial region that begins a few kilometers away. Kreuzenort lay at the edge of the Czech enclave on Prussian territory which the Germans called Hultschiner Ländchen. At the center of the enclave stood the family's main residence, Kuchelna. The late novelist August Scholtis, whose native village was surrounded by Lichnowsky properties, remembers that from a vantage point on the road to Kuchelna where as a boy he tended his father's cows, he could survey "all that the earth had to offer in the way of park-like forests, fruitful fields, cozy villages, proud castles, manors, church towers, ponds, and flowing waters."[9] Eight kilometers to the south, beyond the Oppa, and on Austrian territory, was another Lichnowsky residence, Grätz (Hradec in Czech), where a well-proportioned chateau set in gardens commanded a romantic view of the countryside. This was a region blending industry and agriculture, Slav and German, Austria and Prussia.

The Lichnowskys had not always been German, nor Catholic. Their line can be be traced back to the nobles of Woszczyc in the indubitably Polish region north of Pless. The family's direct progenitor, who lived at the end of the fifteenth century, is Hanus of Woszczyc. Some time during the 1490s he acquired by marriage the domain at Lichnov, some fifty miles to the west in present-day Czechoslovakia, and began calling himself the man from Lichnov, or Lichnovský, as it is spelled in Czech. Lichnov was sold in the seventeeth century and the heirs chose to live in near-by Kuchelna. Kreuzenort (Germanized from the original Polish Krzyżanowice by Karl Max's father) was added to the properties in 1775. The land here belonged originally to the Margravate of Moravia but was joined to Silesia when the Czech kings acquired that province. In 1526 all the Czech lands fell to Austria. While the townsmen of this region were largely German, the landed nobility preferred to speak Czech, the language of their charters and a mark of social distinction. These noblemen had become Protestants (the Lichnowskys were at first Lutheran and then Calvinist); and it was not until the end of the seventeenth century that religious and political pressures could turn them all into Catholics and Germans.[10]

Karl Max often said that his family had made its splash in the eighteenth century. As Catholics they could now take advantage of opportunities formerly closed to them. First they advanced from the local knighthood into the local order of lords. In 1702 Franz Bernhard Lichnowsky was made baron and a member of the old Bohemian peerage (*alter Herrenstand* [*böhmischer*]), and in 1727, count. His son added through marriage the title count of Werdenberg; and his grandson advanced to high positions in the Habsburg bureaucracy in Vienna.

The Lichnowskys had transcended their provincial bounds and become members of an international aristocracy centered in the Austrian capital when, as a result of the War of Austrian Succession, the bulk of their properties passed under Prussian rule. As subjects of the Hohenzollerns they continued to prosper. At first Frederick the Great confiscated their properties because the head of the family continued his service in Vienna. But he restored them later upon payment of a heavy fine; and then he forgot his pique entirely.[11] In 1773 he raised the Lichnowskys to the titular rank of prince (*Fürst*) and in 1778 permitted them to entail their lands under a *Majorat*, by which all the property devolved intact upon the oldest son.[12] These favors did not, however, reorient the Lichnowskys toward Berlin. Although Maria Theresia refused their request to entail the properties that remained under her jurisdiction, they bought the estate at Grätz and a house in the city of Vienna.

It is in Austria that the most notable chapter in the cultural history of the family is set; it concerns their patronage of Beethoven. His association with the Lichnowskys, which was intimate and involved the entire family, lasted from 1794 until his death. Prince Karl Lichnowsky (1761–1814) was Beethoven's most generous patron. For two years after his arrival in Vienna from Bonn, the young musician lodged with the Lichnowskys who gave him the comforts of family life. Later Prince Karl granted him an annual pension of six hundred florins. Beethoven was twice in residence at Grätz, where there is still a large collection of Beethoven memorabilia. Most of the Master's early Vienna works were first heard at the Lichnowsky Friday evening musicales, and many of his compositions were dedicated to Prince Karl or other members of the family.[13]

The Lichnowskys were tolerant of Beethoven's fits of rage. A famous incident occurred in Grätz in 1806. One evening the prince had invited French officers from the nearby Napoleonic garrison. In the presence of these soldiers Beethoven suddenly fell into a fury, barricaded himself in his room, threatened to crown the prince with a chair, and then, cramming the Appassionata under his arm, stalked through pouring rain to Troppau, some fifteen kilometers distant, where he found shelter with Prince Karl's brother, Count Moritz, who was his most intimate friend among the Lichnowskys.[14]

The family's preference for Austria continued well into the nineteenth century. Under Prince Eduard Marie (1789–1845) their attachment to the Habsburgs assumed an explicit ideology. While his father had read philosophical literature and joined the Freemasons, Eduard, having experienced Jacobin terror and Bonaparte's tyranny, was a dedicated supporter of all that was legitimate and established. He was the first Lichnowsky to acquire a reputation as a writer, and his works, varied in form, are all romantic in temper. They include a gloomy tragedy, a translation of Lamennais's essay on religious indifference, and a thesaurus of Austrian artistic monuments. His chef d'oeuvre is *Geschichte des Hauses Habsburg*, an eight-volume celebration of Austrian medieval history. Although he polemicizes in the preface against a shallow rationalism that would alienate man from the natural Christian and historical order, it is a work of meticulous scholarship (Emperor Franz ordered him "to bring forth what is true and to suppress nothing at all")[15] and it has not been replaced or surpassed by any subsequent work.

Eduard's short-lived successor was Prince Felix (1814–1848), called by one of his contemporaries "the last of the knights." He was at first an ardent supporter of Catholic legitimacy. His personal stationery was decorated with the Bourbon lily, and at the age of twenty-two he went into battle at the side of the Spanish pretender Don Carlos. Yet he was the first Lichnowsky to aspire to a political career in Prussia and to sit in a representative assembly. In the first Prussian parliament of 1847, where he sat among the lords, he was considered very much to the left. But as representative to the revolutionary German National Assembly in 1848 the black-bearded Felix, the *bel-homme* of the assembly (as Karl Marx said), was the most picturesque and exasperating of the conservative blades and the very symbol of reaction. When in September democrats rose against the provisional government, he was one of the deputies singled out for attack. One afternoon he set out on horseback to meet the artillery summoned for use against the barricades. He fell into the hands of a mob. He was shot and then beaten so severely that by nightfall he was dead.[16]

It was under Prince Karl (1820–1901), Felix's brother and successor, that the Lichnowskys became definitively Prussian. Prince Karl lacked his father's romanticism and his brother's knight-errantry and was concerned to manage and develop the inherited properties. This he did with great success in spite of an almost ruinous hobby of building Gothic castles (he reared a huge donjon before the chateau at Grätz). In an age of parliaments and political debate he was obliged to look to his interests where his properties were concentrated—and this was Prussia. After 1852 he held, by virtue of the *Majorat*, a hereditary seat in the Prussian Upper Chamber, the *Herrenhaus*. By tradition and his estate in life he was a conservative. But when Prussia in 1866 defeated Austria and destroyed the German Confederation, he helped to form the Union of Free Conservatives to support Bismarck's program of a limited Germany and compromise with liberalism. As a Free Conservative he was elected to the North German Constituent Diet, and later served for four years as a member of the German Reichstag. Thus he accepted Austria's exclusion from Germany, a national parliament elected by universal male suffrage, the supremacy of politics over religion, the equality of all citizens before the law. But he also accepted the system of elections to the Prussian House of Representatives which divided voters into three income classes and gave advantage to those who were richest. And he benefited by the social and political dominance of the Protestant gentry, the Junkers, whose economic interests he, as an agriculturist, shared.[17]

In later years it was said that Prince Karl had conceived a hatred for Austria. It is true that he associated Austria with the classical education he had endured there in a Jesuit school. And in 1866 he was in serious trouble with the Austrian police after fighting a duel with the Hungarian Count Nemes, whom he had accused of cheating at cards. Unfortunately he killed his opponent.[18] But these experiences were not so overwhelming as to destroy the family's traditions and long-established ties. Grätz was still the most beautiful of the estates; Karl's brother Othenio was an officer in the imperial army; his two sisters were married to Austro-Hungarian noblemen; and his younger daughter would marry the Austro-Polish magnate Count Karl Lanckoroński and become lady-in-waiting to the empress Elisabeth.

Karl Max was the heir of his father's wealth and his family's accumulated distinctions which marked him from birth for a career in his sovereign's service. His active military duty was very brief. Joining the guards in 1882, in October 1883 he was commandeered to the Foreign Ministry. In the two decades following unification Bismarck often resorted to the army for suitably educated young men to eke out a short supply of diplomats.[19] Although the circumstances of Lichnowsky's transfer are unknown, we may assume that Bismarck or the secretary of state for foreign affairs in the Wilhelmstrasse had asked the regiment to recommend candidates for the diplomatic service. It is not inconceivable that Karl Max Lichnowsky owed his entry into the foreign service to the favor of his fellow officer, the prince who in five years would become Emperor Wilhelm II.

Chapter II

Diplomacy and Society

> There is no doubt that a land-owning class such as existed in England and constituted the nucleus of the early Roman senatorial nobility is for the state an inimitable source of political tradition, education, and moderation. But where is ours? How many men of such established position are there in Germany, or, more especially, in Prussia? Where is their political tradition? Politically they have practically no influence, and least of all in Prussia.
>
> Max Weber, "Wahlrecht and Demokratie in Deutschland," 1917

Prince Lichnowsky was a second lieutenant when in 1883 he left the guards to join the Wilhelmstrasse. He was still dependent upon his father, for probationers in the foreign service received no salary. His first assignment was a year's tour as attaché at the embassy in London, where thirty years later he was to be the chief. At twenty-three he had something of the subaltern's prankish nature. He once told his children about an incident that occurred early in his tour of duty. The councillor of embassy, Baron von Plessen, reluctantly let him go on a week-end leave, ordering him to report to him immediately upon his return. It was very late Sunday night when he burst into Plessen's bedroom and, bending over his sleeping superior, announced, "Here I am, here I am!" Seventeen years later when Lichnowsky was chief of personnel and had access to his own file, he discovered that Plessen had written home that he was "brash and disorderly." But he and Plessen were very good friends.[1]

In London the prince decided that he should make his career in diplomacy. He was dropped from the active military rolls in 1886, and in 1887 passed the foreign service examination to become a full-fledged diplomat qualified for appointment to a salaried position. His first assignments were to relatively minor posts—Stockholm, Constantinople, Dresden, and Bucharest. Count Bernstorff, who was with him in Constantinople, recalls that the secretaries and attachés had little to do:

I usually did my work with the second secretary, Carl Max Lichnowsky, with whom I remained on terms of friendship until his death. It was his duty to keep the political diary, and this he commonly left to me; in itself a mechanical and monotonous task, but it had the advantage of involving a knowledge of all political matters that entered and left the embassy. We often rode together in the lovely Belgrade woods on the Bosporous, and as far as Kilia on the Black Sea. Life in Constantinople was otherwise rather devoid of interest, except for political activities and these were monopolized by the ambassador and the first dragoman.[2]

In Bucharest, his next post, where at the age of thirty he was still a second secretary, Lichnowsky struck the Rumanian Take Ionescu as "intelligent, merry, witty, and withal a *grand seigneur.*"[3]

It was in Bucharest that Lichnowsky attracted the attention of a man whose opinion of him was to follow him for the rest of his life and even beyond the grave. Bernhard von Bülow, who was the minister in Bucharest, was at that time regarded as Germany's leading diplomat and a man of great promise. It is recorded that when he was serving in Saint Petersburg, the junior officers, impressed by his knowledge, would bone up on abstruse subjects which they would then casually introduce in social conversation, hoping some day to stump their colleague—but always to no avail, for he knew more about every subject than they and was an accomplished casuist.[4] His social mark was affability: he was charming, flattering, courteous—*un ami de tout le monde.* In the 1890s, during the decade of weak chancellors following Bismarck's dismissal, he was in close touch with Friedrich von Holstein, the most knowledgeable and experienced official in the Foreign Ministry, and with Philipp zu Eulenburg-Hertefeld, the kaiser's intimate. These three belonged to the small circle of men who were the true governors of the German Reich. Bülow became foreign secretary in 1897, and in 1900 was made chancellor.

The prince was too young and too junior in rank to participate in Bülow's factional intrigues, but between them there was some affinity in manners. They were amiable, unprejudiced (this, at any rate, was the impression Bülow wished to give), and liberal in their choice of company—characteristics that were thought to constitute a peculiar Bülovian approach to diplomacy and society. Their closeness was taken for granted. Colleagues who were fond of devising nicknames for one another chose to call Lichnowsky the "sorcerer's apprentice" (*Zauberlehrling*), for Bülow was known as the sorcerer. Bülow seemed to have a genuine liking for Lichnowsky, and once praised him to Eulenburg as "all heart and true as gold."[5]

There is an element in this relationship about which we can only speculate. It was commonly believed that Prince Lichnowsky was Princess Bülow's lover, and some suspected that this was with Bülow's knowledge and consent.[6] Maria Bülow was the daughter of a Principe di Camporeale and of Donna Laura Minghetti, widow by a second marriage of Marco Minghetti, the one-time premier of Italy. Bülow had married Maria against the advice of Herbert Bismarck, as she was a foreign Catholic divorced from another German diplomat and the subject of much gossip;[7] but the choice was much to his benefit. Maria Bülow was very attractive. She had soft eyes in an oval face, was petite and youthful in appearance and had an easy sincerity that charmed women and fascinated men of all ages. With the help of her handsome and knowing mother, who was still a power in Italian affairs, she presided over an intimate salon known fondly as the "casa Bülow," surrounding herself "with young diplomats who shared her literary and artistic interests and were devoted to her husband."[8] So common was the suspicion that Bülow's wife and mother-in-law influenced his diplomatic appointments that the kaiser once jokingly said that he had a foreign office with women waiting table.[9]

Whatever the nature of Princess Bülow's relationship with Lichnowsky, it is plain that she was very fond of him.[10] After his marriage they continued to exchange letters. Little of what she wrote still exists, but there is a letter she sent him in 1918 in a moment of deep concern for him, when she reminded him that they had met twenty-seven years ago and that he should know that she was a true friend who had always followed his life's path with affectionate interest.[11]

Bülow's hand is evident in Lichnowsky's advancement to his first post of responsibility, councillor of embassy in Vienna.[12] This occurred in January 1895 after three years of service in

Vienna as second secretary. There were good reasons for his promotion. In 1894 Eulenburg had been chosen as ambassador with the mission of improving the atmosphere of Austro-German exchanges. "It was a well-known fact," Lichnowsky later wrote, "that the dislike of the leading Viennese circles for everything Prussian continued even after the conclusion of our fatal treaty of alliance."[13] And although Bismarck had in 1879 committed Germany to Austria's defense, his complicated diplomacy was often disconcerting to the Austrians. Bismarck's successors wished to solidify the alliance and remove all doubts about Berlin's intentions.[14] Wilhelm II told the Austrian ambassador that he was sending his "best friend" to Vienna to demonstrate the importance he attached to "friendly and more intimate relations between the two realms."[15] Eulenburg knew that if he wished to represent Germany's interests firmly but without giving offense he would have to ingratiate himself with the Austrian aristocracy.[16] And Lichnowsky, as Bülow wrote Eulenburg in 1893, had achieved "an excellent social position [as he is] related to most of this country's upper nobility."[17]

Lichnowsky's close connections with Austria did not imply any sympathy for the Austrian regime. The editors of the *Berliner Neueste Nachrichten* were far from the mark when in July 1895 they doubted whether a diplomat whose family owned property in the host country would observe the proper objectivity toward that country's affairs.[18] Lichnowsky leaned in quite the opposite direction, for in Austrian matters history had destined him to be a judge of uncommon severity. Not a generation had passed since his family had turned away from the Habsburgs and their monarchical conglomerate. Like his father he was a Catholic rallier to the Protestant German national state and very much alive to the historical conflict with the Austrian clerical and feudal system. Austria (he wrote in one of his dispatches in 1895) would continue to be governed by a "caste of counts and princes" who "neither loved nor understood the new German Empire." And in 1898 he wrote Berlin that politically Austria was a concept devoid of life-giving blood and symbolized by a "pitiable old man and his unruly nephew and a Roman-Slavic priesthood." Because of his own experience he felt the full weight of the Austrian nationality struggles. "A confrontation between the Germans and the Slavs of Austria," he wrote in 1897, "had become inevitable when Austria was separated from Germany because of the irresistible awakening of the former 'servant peoples' to national consciousness and their rise to cultural significance." And he recognized that the struggle created problems for which there were only temporary solutions.[19]

Lichnowsky's skepticism about Austria deeply affected his reporting from Vienna, which was marked by surface conformity and more or less implicit dissent. It was only in later years that the ideas he formed about Germany's relations with Austria were to prove to be essentially contrary to the official policy. His thought centered upon the nature of Germany's commitment under the alliance of 1879. He did not doubt that Germany had basic and unique obligations toward the historic ally. For him, as for all German diplomats, this dual alliance, if not the Triple Alliance (which extended the Austro-German union to Italy), was the starting point for all thought about Germany's position among the powers. For better or for worse, this union would continue. But there was room for opinion on how Germany should interpret or in actual diplomacy manage the commitment to defend Austria's integrity against attack by a third power. In practice it was a question of German support for Austria's policies in the Balkans, where there was always the danger of conflict with Russia. It had been Bismarck's policy to shun involvement in oriental questions, in the Balkans and in Turkey, and to preserve Germany's right to decide when Austria's position was so threatened that Germany must provide assistance. In spite of the alliance it was his practice to pursue a policy of the free hand. This seemed less possible in the 1890s after Germany dropped the reinsurance treaty with Russia and in 1894 the Tsarist monarchy became allied with republican France. But it was nevertheless the policy that Lichowsky championed and justified in his reporting.

Lichnowsky's views on the alliance with Austria emerged from extensive political analysis. His responsibility as councillor was to follow internal developments in the Austrian half of the dual monarchy. It was not that these affairs were by themselves of such importance: but since 1879 it had been the imperative duty of German diplomacy to beware of any signs of defection or chang-

ing attitudes toward the alliance. In a series of dispatches he
wrote in his first year as deputy Lichnowsky examined the domestic sources of Austrian foreign policy. His analysis began with
the groups and parties that seemed to prefer an anti-German
orientation. These groups, as Berlin knew, were formidable.
There were the Czech nationalists, growing ever stronger, who
would abrogate the alliance if they came to power; the church-
men and their political followers, who begrudged, as Lichnowsky
said, all governments they believed had obstructed "the ambitions of the Roman universal theocracy"; and the feudalists, who,
if of German origin, nevertheless preferred Slavs and clericals for
political bedfellows. These groups held their position of strength
because the Austro-German liberals, once the pillars of the alliance, had been torn apart by anti-Semitism and the Catholic
political movement. They could not be replaced by the Pan-
German nationalists, who, though they were vociferous supporters
of the alliance and therefore of some potential service to Berlin,
were unacceptable allies because the dynasty regarded them as
traitors.[20]

This, however, as Lichnowsky emphasized, was only part of the
story. For a broader analysis extended to both halves of the
monarchy would show that the alliance would continue to at-
tract more support than opposition. The significant fact about
the political system in the Austrian half of the monarchy was that
the decisive influence belonged to the Polish gentry. As a class
these Slavic squires were no friends of the Germans; but they
supported the Austrian alliance with its powerful neighbor because they feared that Russian conquest would destroy their dominant position in the nationally mixed province of Galicia. More
important still was the attitude of the Magyar ruling classes. For
they had the truly decisive voice in the monarchy as a whole, and
as they too feared the loss of their privileged position in a world
of Slavic populations, they would force the government to abide
by the alliance with Germany. And there was additional pressure
from an Italy that coveted Austrian territory. "Encompassed by
the German, the Italian, and the Magyar national states," Lichnowsky wrote, "Austria can give us nothing to fear. She can move
neither against us nor away from us."[21]

Lichnowsky's conviction as to Austria's dependency was connected with his view of German's attitude toward Russia. He consistently favored a policy of friendship and concession. In later years he would maintain that in the 1870s Germany had the opportunity to make a partner of Russia and that Bismarck's decision to go with Austria instead was a mistake of catastrophic proportions. This is not what he proposed in the 1890s; perhaps he did not yet perceive that the alternative had existed as he later thought; and in any case as a member of the German diplomatic corps he had to accept the alliance with Austria and to judge relations with Russia by their effect upon that arrangement. But he did not see the dual alliance as an obstacle to good relations between the only two Continental powers who were strong enough to pursue an independent policy and make arrangements for themselves. While it was clear to him that Austria could not condone complete Russian dominance in the Balkans, that, he thought, as Balkan history showed, was scarcely conceivable. The important conclusion he reached was that Germany's interest in maintaining the alliance with Austria was well served by a friendly policy toward Russia. For this would discourage the anti-German elements who themselves hoped to reorient policy toward France and Russia. An amicable relation between Berlin and Saint Petersburg would only increase Austria's dependency upon Germany.[22]

It is in this conviction of Austria's dependency that we have the germs of a conflict between Lichnowsky and Holstein and those who followed the latter's lead. Holstein assumed that Austria had more freedom of action than Lichnowsky did, and he feared that Austria would abandon Germany if Germany refused her support on vital questions. Throughout the 1890s we can detect a slow trend toward modification of Bismarck's insistence that Germany's commitment toward Austria remain indefinite.[23] To be sure, Berlin did not abandon the right to judge herself when Austria was to be supported, and there is no lasting conflict between Lichnowsky and his superiors on this question. Only briefly in the fall of 1895 does the difference between Lichnowsky's and Holstein's perception become acute. The occasion was the Turkish massacre of the Armenians which had led to European intervention and to possible seizure of the Turkish Straits by Russia. In principle Germany was at that time not opposed to this extension of Russian power. But the Austrian emperor Franz Joseph and his foreign minister Count Agenor Gołuchowski could not bear the thought of Tsarist occupation in Constantinople. Gołuchowski, a Pole who had an instinctive dislike of the Russians, had since he became foreign minister that spring been pressuring the Germans to make their commitment to Austria more explicit.

At the height of the crisis Lichnowsky told the British ambassador that Germany would never abandon her position of passive neutrality. But Holstein found this formulation much too rigid. Fearing that "poets and dilettantes" (Eulenburg and Lichnowsky? or Bülow?) were dismantling the Triple Alliance while the Franco-Russian alliance remained intact, he rejected the notion that Germany "would never go into action on account of the Turkish Straits." For even if the Straits were in themselves unimportant any conflict that arose because of them and threatened Austria's position as a great power was of vital concern to Germany. Echoing Holstein's worry, the foreign secretary, Adolf Marschall von Bieberstein, wrote Bülow of the powerful elements in Austria who hoped for an opportunity to reverse the policy of alliance with Germany and said that if the Triple Alliance afforded no security in the Balkans Austria would inevitably come to an agreement with France and Russia.[24]

There was one other time when the Wilhelmstrasse seemed to doubt Lichnowsky's adherence to the basic principles of German policy. It was in November 1898 toward the end of Lichnowsky's tour. The occasion was one of the many and vivid dispatches that Lichnowsky wrote that year about the revival of German nationalism in Austria. This had been the unanticipated result of the language ordinances of 1897, in which the Vienna government had decreed that all state officials employed in Bohemia and Moravia must within a certain period of time be able to conduct business in Czech as well as German regardless of the tongue dominant in their locality. To the Austro-Germans this was an unreasonable concession to Czech nationalism; and there were outbursts of emotion, disorder, and violence that continued well into the following year. These developments are accurately reflected in Lichnowsky's reports, and both he and Eulenburg drew special attention to the sudden rise of German nationalism.

In a dispatch of June 1898, where he wrote that an ever-increasing number of German Austrians were losing their faith in the monarchy and taking comfort in the idea of *Anschluss,* or union with Germany, he deplored the tendency of Reich-German newspapers to criticize the Austrians for their disloyalty to the dynasty. Assuming that he wished to influence the German press in the opposite direction, Berlin reminded him that since Bismarck's time it was Germany's established policy to support the Habsburg dynasty and maintain Austria's position as a great power.

This reprimand reveals a total misunderstanding of Lichnowsky's message. He had never openly doubted the necessity of the monarchical alliance but had always pointed out that the divisions among the German population in Austria greatly weakened the domestic support for that arrangement. Now, as a result of the language ordinances, the trend was reversed. The Germans had reacquired their national feeling. While Berlin could not openly take sides in Austria's political struggles, it was wrong to discourage a movement that worked in Germany's favor. From the standpoint of Germany's established policy, the revival of German nationalism was the only bright spot in the gloomy picture that Austria presented in that year of tumults and disorder.[25]

Lichnowsky's divergence from the trend of thought in the Wilhelmstrasse was of no consequence in the 1890s. Policy had not become fixed on any course that would bring him into standing conflict with his superiors. When he wrote that the anti-German nobility would continue to wield considerable power in Austria, the kaiser remarked, "Quite so——for which reason we must try to cultivate relations with our eastern neighbor."[26] At a time when skepticism about Austria was the common coin of German diplomacy no one thought him particularly austrophobic, even though he expressed his feelings about the Habsburg monarchy in a manner that only intimacy breeds. He left this, his first post of responsibility, in good repute. He had worked very hard in Vienna. Frequently the whole burden of this important embassy had fallen upon his shoulders, for Eulenburg had pressing duties at the court in Berlin. His dispatches, lengthy and graphic as they were, had made a good impression.

It is in Vienna that we first encounter Lichnowsky as a writer. The literary talent displayed in the essays he wrote in later years is evident in his early diplomatic reporting. It was obvious that writing was an occupation that gave him great pleasure. He wrote a consciously literary dispatch, full of allusions and carefully modulated to achieve artistic effects, which nevertheless was precise and functional. His description of Gołuchowski is a good example of his reporting. "The son and foreign minister," he said, having spoken first of Gołuchowski's father,

has inherited in addition to an extensive fortune, which he has considerably enlarged, certain characteristics and predilections. He too is a competent, conscientious, and clear-headed bureaucrat. In spite of a pronounced conceitedness his manner is amiable and gentlemanly flexible. A visage framed by a Parisian hair style reminiscent of Metternich reveals the pleasure-loving man of the world. Though he does not give the impression of intellectual gifts or deep culture, he is plainly intelligent, experienced, artful, and adroit. He is not lacking in candor, but rather in calm in unpleasant situations.[27]

The descriptive and analytical pieces he wrote in the 1890s did not always conform to ideal standards of diplomatic reporting. His colors were often too vivid as his judgment of the host country was all too just and exact; and at times he indulged in ironic twists of expression that would not be acceptable in a more impersonal system of communication.[28] Referring to the new-found Czech sympathies of the Bohemian nobility, which he, belonging to that class, considered unbecoming, he wrote that "this nobility descends from those condottieri who went plundering and slaughtering through this land and, when the true Czech nobility had been banned or executed, were regaled with their property—for the greater honor of the Holy Roman Empire of the *Austrian* nation."[29] He ventured far from the path of straight reporting when Emperor Franz Joseph paid a visit to Saint Petersburg in 1897. This had encouraged the anti-German elements in Austria, and he reported that the Vienna press was indulging in "veritable orgies of peace" and singing hosannas "to the beginning of an age of idyllic brotherliness."[30]

But that was a different time; hyperbole was in fashion, and Lichnowsky's facile language enlightened and entertained his small and congenial audience (every member of which he knew personally). He made a good impression upon Wilhelm II, who would often note in the margins of a dispatch his approval of content or expression or scrawl at the end that it was "very well written."

In December 1899 Lichnowsky was reassigned to the Foreign Ministry in Berlin. He spent the first six months of that year on leave and took a trip around the world. While traveling he kept a diary which was among the papers destroyed at the end of World War II.[31] He traveled by sea to China, where he visited Canton, Macao, Hong Kong, Shanghai, Peking, and Kiaochow. After a month in Japan he sailed across the Pacific, returning to Europe after traversing the American continent. From Hong Kong he wrote Eulenburg that the tropical heat during the four-week voyage to China had exhausted him. But when he arrived there was "so much interesting and new, and the weather so marvelous, that there was no end of things to see and learn."[32] In Peking he stayed with the German minister von Heyking. Madame Heyking in her memoirs remembers his "extraordinarily shrewd countenance, with deep-set intelligent eyes and the brow of a thinker."[33]

The prince returned to Berlin at the beginning of the year 1900. He was now a councillor (*vortragender Rat*) in the Foreign Ministry's political division, the section concerned with diplomatic affairs. This, the heart of the Wilhelmstrasse, was a small establishment, consisting of six or seven councillors in addition to the foreign secretary. The British Foreign Office, by contrast, employed in 1914 seven senior clerks (comparable to the German councillors), a controller of commercial affairs, three assistant undersecretaries, the permanent undersecretary, and the parliamentary undersecretary (an office unknown in Germany, as the Foreign Ministry had no formal relations with the Reichstag).[34]

In 1900 the work of the Wilhelmstrasse's political section was dominated by one councillor, Friedrich von Holstein. His authority rested upon the knowledge and routine he had acquired in twenty-two years of uninterrupted service in the ministry itself. Although the chancellors who followed Bismarck—Caprivi, Hohenlohe, and Bülow—depended upon Holstein's advice, he never advanced beyond the rank of councillor and in form he was subordinate to the state secretary for foreign affairs. In England foreign policy was conducted in a more public manner, and actual authority was likely to correspond to the formal responsibility. There were of course certain British officials below the rank of secretary who might acquire a more than ordinary influence, as did Sir William Tyrrell as private secretary to Sir Edward Grey, the secretary of state after 1906. But they were subject to greater public control and scrutiny than in Germany.

The position that Lichnowsky now occupied also defied formal description. In rank he was rather in advance of most men at the age of forty, as upon his recall from Vienna he was promoted to minister and granted the title of envoy extraordinary. In 1912 when the kaiser had him appointed ambassador in London, the Wilhelmstrasse informed the British embassy that Lichnowsky had formerly held in the ministry the position of *chef de cabinet*.[36] The term usually designates a position on the order of that held by Tyrrell. In Lichnowsky's case the term referred to a special relationship to the chancellor which raised him somewhat above his peers. Like Holstein and Otto Hammann, director of the Foreign Ministry's press section, he had the right of direct access to the chief, bypassing the state secretary.[36] It was not his normal responsibilities—he was desk officer for England and head of the diplomatic appointments board—that granted him this preferment but various other not strictly definable services and duties. Documents in the subject files, some of which were published in the *Grosse Politik*, indicate that he was charged with liaison with the military services, and that it fell to him to interview visiting German and foreign diplomats and other persons of note. Bülow seems also to have employed him on delicate personnel matters not usually the responsibility of senior clerks or the head of the appointments board. It became Lichnowsky's duty to persuade Baron von Richthofen to accept the state secretaryship without the assurance (which he had demanded) that Holstein submit all correspondence to him.[37]

It was only as head of the appointments board that Lichnowsky, during his four years in the ministry, enjoyed some independence. His job was to choose and test candidates for the career service and to counsel the chancellor on the filling of vacancies in the legations and embassies. While the chancellor could ignore his advice and appoint anyone he thought suitable, the appointments chief was the major obstacle for most young candidates for a diplomatic career. In July 1900 Baroness Spitzemberg noted in her diary that Lichnowsky, whom she had seen privately and to whom she had warmly recommended a number of young men of her acquaintance who were already in the service, "seemed well-disposed toward his subordinates and concerned above all to introduce into the diplomatic corps persons of good family, a practice that of late had greatly fallen off."[38] This cannot mean that he intended to give preference to ancient lineage. As his closest friends in the corps had not even a recent patent of nobility, we may assume that he intended to make up for his predecessor's apparent infatuation with resounding titles.[39] Still, he accepted the dominance of the aristocracy in the diplomatic corps as a pragmatic necessity.

Lichnowsky described his work as personnel chief for the first time in an essay entitled "Diplomacy and Democracy," published during the war, when he realized that a reform of the foreign service was inescapable. But even at that time the influence of the established aristocracy seemed to him to be a disadvantage only where "birth has to make up for lack of brains." "The fact that most of our diplomats bear a title of nobility," he wrote, "is partly ascribable to the circumstances that out of social and financial considerations the choice of candidates for the foreign service is limited to the class of the optimates." "I found it no easy task to select young men who were satisfactory in all respects. I never troubled about pedigree or wealth. . . . I made it a practice to watch the candidate as he entered the room. Then I knew pretty well with whom I had to deal. The conversation that ensued soon showed what sort of intelligence he possessed."[40]

In the assignment of senior personnel Lichnowsky's role was quite different. From letters he received from the Princess of Pless and Elisabeth von Heyking, who were seeking preferment for their husbands, it was obvious that he was thought to have considerable influence. Daisy of Pless was peeved when her husband (who was not in the service but was enormously rich and well connected) did not receive an appointment as ambassador, and she blamed Lichnowsky for this. Lichnowsky doubtless had no influence on this level. He advised her to turn to Bülow; and he told the Baroness von Spitzemberg that it was very difficult "to resist the infatuations of the ambassadors and other high-placed gentlemen, not to mention the very highest of them all."[41] Of course, the kaiser had the right of appointment, but it was the chancellor who made the recommendation, and his source of advice on this as on other matters was Holstein.[42]

The prince probably first met Holstein when he was assigned to the ministry as a probationer in the 1880s. But it was not until he joined the staff in 1900 that he encountered the Grey Eminence as an equal. At first their relations reputedly were cordial, and we know that Holstein, himself an excellent draftsman, recognized the value of Lichnowsky's fluent pen.[43] In private, however, Holstein treated the younger man with affable condescension. "Though impulsive and easily influenced," he wrote an Italian friend who was also acquainted with Lichnowsky and the Bülow women, "he does no damage—quite the contrary." In 1909 Holstein told a visitor that although Lichnowsky was a good fellow, he was certainly no shining intellect. And in a discussion with Maximilian Harden he dismissed his colleague as a muddlehead.[44]

One can only guess at the reasons for this denigration. The diplomatic record shows no incidents between the two other than the feverish moment in 1895 when Holstein felt that Eulenburg and Lichnowsky were too zealously representing Berlin's disinterestedness in the fate of the Turkish Straits.[45] Perhaps Holstein resented Lichnowsky's presumption to an independent view of Austria's role as Germany's partner. The diplomat Friedrich Rosen has suggested that Holstein feared the prince's influence on the chancellor, and Harden, who was very close to Holstein for two years before his death, believed that the effect of Lichnowsky's intimacy with Bülow was to make Holstein jealous.[46]

It seems clear that Lichnowsky's hatred of Holstein, so apparent in his later publications, matured only after the prince left the ministry and perhaps only after the outbreak of the war. The record of his reaction to Holstein while they were together in the ministry is slim. Herbert von Hindenburg, who served as a

probationer under Lichnowsky at that time, recalls that when he
was about to resign because of ill-treatment by Holstein (who
had a grudge against the young man's grandfather), Lichnowsky
advised him to shrug the matter off, for, as he said, Holstein's
moods were unpredictable and quitting the service would only
be to do him a favor.[47]

By 1916 the prince's references to Holstein had lost all restraint. In *My London Mission* he wrote that after leaving Vienna there was no way to have any influence on political matters
"unless one was prepared to help a half-crazy chief in drafting his
crotchety orders with their crabbed instructions." In the following year, in the essay "Diplomacy and Democracy," referred to
above, he wrote, while contrasting the British system of diplomacy with the German, that in Germany control of foreign
policy rested in the hands of a single minister advised by "ir-
responsible and mostly incompetent, sometimes not even quite
normal, subordinates." And in his collected papers of 1927 he
wrote that he had retired in 1904 "having long since abandoned
all hope of being employed on any diplomatic task that did not
consist merely of dinner parties and receptions. My inadequacy
as a diplomat was obvious, at least in Herr von Holstein's
opinion."[48]

In 1904 Lichnowsky's career, it is true, had reached an impasse.
He had hoped to be appointed to one of the embassies; he
thought in fact that he had an understanding with Bülow that
eventually he would be sent to Rome.[49] But when that post became vacant in 1902 Bülow filled it with Count Anton Monts, an
early (but not constant) friend of the "casa Bülow." Vienna,
London, and Saint Petersburg were manned in 1901 and 1902
by older men. High positions outside diplomacy were of no interest to the prince; in 1903 he refused Bülow's offer of the provincial governorship in Posen.[50] Perhaps Holstein had used his
influence to prevent Lichnowsky's assignment to an embassy;
but there were other obstacles: the seniority of the men who were
appointed to the desirable posts; Bülow's use of him at home;
and of course, his coming into property and his decision to marry.
That would change his style of life and his relations with the
Bülows. All these factors caused him to request an indefinite

leave, which being granted, became effective on the first of July 1904.

In August 1904, a little more than a month after he left the Foreign Ministry, Lichnowsky, now forty-four years old, married Mechtilde, Countess Arco-Zinneberg. The Arcos were an ancient family whose original seat was a castle on the bluffs above the River Sarca where it enters the Lago di Garda. They had inter-married with the Borgias. Imperial service had taken them to Germany, and Mechtilde was a direct descendant of the empress Maria Theresia.[51] She had met her husband but a few months before their marriage. The bride's mother later told her grand-children that in the spring of 1904 Count Hugo Lerchenfeld (the Bavarian minister in Prussia) told the prince that it was high time he married; Berlin was no place to look for a bride, but in Munich he would find many nice Catholic girls—for instance, Lerchenfeld's own cousin, the gifted Mechtilde Arco.

On April 23, the prince was in Munich for the gala of the Bavarian Knights of Saint George. A striking girl entered the room. "Who is that?" he asked. When told, he exclaimed, "why that is the one I am supposed to meet!"[52] In June they were en-gaged in Florence, where the bride's sister lived with her hus-band, the painter Count Harrach. In July Mechtilde went to Paris with her mother to buy her trousseau. The prince joined them there, and on the eleventh they all went to Carlsbad to meet the prince's mother.[53] They were married in Munich in August. Their first child, a boy, was born in 1905. The prince intended to name him Felix, after his uncle, but as the kaiser insisted on being godfather, the young *Prinz* was named Wilhelm. A daugh-ter, Leonore, was born in 1906, and a second son, Michael, in 1909.[54]

Princess Lichnowsky was a colorful and independent woman who left no one with an indifferent impression. Daisy of Pless found her individual and very good looking and "nice," but feared the court would think her almost too natural, as "she doesn't care a hang for anyone or anything."[55] Mechtilde Lich-nowsky was physically adept, and gifted in all the arts. Had she not been a countess whose education was subject to nineteenth-century conventions, she might have attended a conservatory or an academy of art. As it was, literature was the only outlet compatible with her circumstances.

Her literary record consists of eighteen works published from 1912 to 1958, the year of her death. It is a lively and varied oeuvre, including plays, novels, a collection of limericks, reflections on manners, a philosophical account of a trip up the Nile, an autobiographical novel about her childhood, a study of usage, and books of remembrance. These works were well received by the critics. Harden detected the ghost of Heine in her first work, the book on the Nile, and saw in "this original woman" "an impulse to see things, to hear, to taste, to smell, to touch as if in the light of the first day of creation."[56] And Karl Kraus once said that she had more wit than all other German writers put together.[57]

After his marriage, Prince Lichnowsky lived the life of a landed gentlemen. "I passed my time," he wrote in *My London Mission*, "between flax and turnips, among horses and meadows, read extensively and occasionally published political essays."[58] He had retained the studious habits of his childhood, and enjoyed the advantages of an excellent library. The main Lichnowsky collection, housed at Grätz, contained over fifteen thousand volumes. It was both a collector's library and a practical one, for there were Italian and German renaissance editions of Greek and Latin classics, works of the humanists, a good sampling of the philosophes and political and historical works of recent times, including Karl Marx.[59] The prince favored history and political biography, but he also read philosophy, novels, and poetry. Schopenhauer was his favorite philosopher.[60] Some might say that this misanthropic pessimist was the natural preference for an aristocrat who had retained his feudal privileges while accepting the bourgeois capitalist order. And perhaps there is a ready explanation for his poetic preference, Heinrich Heine, who had made fun of his uncle Felix, whom he called Schnapphahnski (*Schnapphahn* being a highwayman).[61]

The prince had become the epitome of the central European gentleman. Many have remarked his slow speech and rather nasal tones, typical of the Austrian aristocrat. Certainly there was an Austrian influence from his youth, and the Berlin court also affected a kind of Viennese style. He enjoyed the good life. As a connoisseur of good food he often quoted his uncle Mons. Robert Lichnowsky, a renaissance-style churchman who was famous for the carefully prepared meals he served in the refectory of the German church in the Vatican, whose motto was "small in quantity and simple in character, but perfect in quality."[62] For the rest, he adhered to the English model of the gentleman long preferred in central Europe. He ordered his clothes from a London tailor. "He pressed his monocle to his eye," wrote the novelist August Scholtis, who once worked in the prince's office, "and hung his walking stick in his pocket as Winston Churchill does."[63]

The *Majorat* inherited in 1901 afforded him important political rights and privileges. He held his family's seat in the Prussian *Herrenhaus*; he was a member of the curia for large landowners in the diet of the district of Ratibor; and as in Prussia the administrative bailiwicks were still coterminous with the noble estates, the captain of the bailiwick, the *Amtsvorsteher*, conducted all his business in a building on the grounds of the manor at Kuchelna and doubled as the prince's private secretary.[64]

Lichnowsky was commonly thought to belong to that group of rich noblemen known as the Upper Silesian magnates. Geographically and politically there was some justice in this, for they were typically Free-Conservative. But the true magnates whose property lay in the coal basin had turned their original feuds into industrial enterprises. The Lichnowsky holdings lay at the edge of this industrial region. Having no coal, the economy had remained agricultural. The properties compromised some 8,800 hectares in Prussia, centered on Kuchelna, and 4,432 hectares around Grätz in Austria. Over 60 percent of the economically useful land was devoted to acreage. Wheat, sugar beets, oats, barley, and potatoes were the main crops. To the dairy and the ceramic tile plant his father had constructed the prince added a profitable factory for processing flax. This was the largest of its kind in Germany. Before 1914 a large percentage of the flax fibers and the entire crop of barley (which was of high quality and suitable for brewing) were exported to Great Britain. The prince governed an efficient and socially exemplary enterprise. For the heads of families working on the estate he erected over one hundred two-family houses, and for the girls employed in the flax factory who lived some distance away he provided free board and lodging in a home run by a social worker who gave free instruction in domestic sciences.[65]

In 1910 Lichnowsky hired as general manager an agronomist named Paul Püschel, who in the 1920s after his dismissal by the prince helped the Bolsheviks draw up their plan for agricultural reform in the Soviet Union. Lichnowsky dismissed Püschel because he had caused serious damage to the fields by insisting on replanting flax in the same soil each year, claiming that with modern methods crop rotation was no longer necessary.[66]

Neither a magnate, nor a Protestant Junker, but allied to both, the prince belonged to a class that never quite achieved definition in Germany—the liberal aristocracy. There was a tolerant level of Wilhelminian society where literati, scholars, artists, and accomplished businessmen rubbed elbows with counts and princes. Wilhelm II himself furthered this mixture, for wealth and success meant a great deal to him, and Bülow and his wife Maria in the nine years he was chancellor consciously strove to reduce the social barriers. As a bachelor Lichnowsky had enjoyed stimulating company. "He often gave small breakfasts," his colleague Friedrich Rosen remembered, "where gradually I met all the most interesting personalities or renewed acquaintances I had already made, such as Herbert Bismarck, [the diplomat] Eckardstein and his beautiful English wife, Count Henckell-Donnersmarck [the richest of the Silesian magnates], Siegfried Wagner [son of the composer], Max Liebermann [the Berlin painter], and Adolf Harnack [the religious scholar]."[67]

Lichnowsky enjoyed excellent relations with a number of leading journalists. Some of the political essays written during his retirement he published in the progressive *Berliner Tageblatt*, edited by the talented essayist Theodor Wolff. After the turn of the century he became acquainted with Ludwig Stein, a professor of philosophy who loved journalism and fancied himself the mediator between the world of art and learning and the province of the politically prominent. In 1912 Stein introduced Lichnowsky to the eminent socialist Eduard Bernstein. Under Bismarck Bernstein had gone into exile in England and had remained there until Bülow eased his return to Germany. Lichnowsky wished to consult Bernstein on conditions in the country to which he had just been appointed ambassador.[68]

The prince's social liberality extended to the Foreign Ministry. His closest friends there were men of bourgeois origin—Friedrich Rosen, who was later German envoy in Portugal, and Wilhelm Solf, who became colonial secretary.[69] In this respect he differed completely from Hugo von Radolin, the rich and well-connected Pole from Posnania who was ambassador in Paris from 1900 to 1910. Radolin was enraged when Berlin chose to replace him in Paris with an ennobled bourgeois, von Schoen, whose ancestors had made their money selling the skins of hares and rabbits.[70]

After his marriage, the prince's society, if anything, expanded. The Lichnowskys divided their time between Berlin and the estates. In 1908 he bought a house on the Buchenstrasse, where he stayed during "the season" and while he was attending sessions of the *Herrenhaus*. With his wife he traveled to places of literary and historical interest—Spain, Greece, and Egypt. The observations the princess made on their trip up the Nile in 1911 formed her first book, *Götter, Könige und Tiere in Ägypten* (Gods, kings and animals in Egypt)—too long a title, she said later. Their taste in literature and the arts was advanced. They had one of the earliest collections of Picassos; the painter Fritz Ruf was in demand afer he painted the princess's portrait; the sculptor Georg Kolbe did busts of them in 1909.[71] Their estates and house in Berlin were open to a varied company. In 1910 Hugo von Hofmannsthal wrote Arthur Schnitzler that he had just left Grätz, "not on foot or by night or in anger, as Beethoven did, but in daylight, amiably, and in an automobile."[72]

The prince was also at home in the narrower world centering upon the court and its aristocratic retinue. Here the entertainment was lavish and the sports were bloody. Sometimes the Lichnowskys were guests at the castle of Fürstenstein, fifty miles east of Kuchelna, owned by Hans and Daisy of Pless—"fair and fairy princess," Lichnowsky called her in closing a letter to Daisy in 1901.[73] She once described a shoot on their properties. "We all sat in little built-up stands to which we climbed up by ladder, and which were hidden in Christmastree bushes. Three buffaloes

came close and would have passed between me and Prince Lichnowsky if I hadn't sneezed and coughed and frightened them
back on purpose."[74] Wilhelm II, on his meanderings from paladin to paladin, visited Pless once early in 1912. The noble ladies
provided the entertainment. "Betka Potocka recited in French
to piano accompaniment. May Larisch did a sort of Greek dance
to an altar of roses, just graceful poses. Mechtilde Lichnowsky
sang *en costume* and Hansie Larisch dressed up some of the
bandsmen as Neapolitans and sang in imitation Italian; Olivia
with castanets, and two other girls did chorus."[75] Wilhelm would
also bring his retinue to Kuchelna. "One more visit from the
kaiser," the prince reputedly said, "and I'll be bankrupt."[76]

The framework of Lichnowsky's political life was Free Conservatism. He resembled his father in very little else, but he had
followed him into the Free Conservative Union. At one time he
was a member of the party's national committee (on the national
level known as the *Reichspartei*) and of the Silesian provincial
committee.[77] Attempting to bridge the differences between conservatism and liberalism, the party enjoyed a large following
among the Catholic nobles of Upper Silesia who had given up
their Austrian sympathies, and among Prussian bureaucrats who
wished to signify in this combination their double adherence to
the conservative Protestant monarchy in Prussia and the liberal
constitution of the new German federation. For the Catholic ral-
liers Free Conservatism implied a rejection of Catholic-oriented
politics. The prince's father had imbibed none of the family's
earlier reverence for the Church, although he and Karl Max remained practicing Catholics. The prince's children were educated in schools run by religious orders; once he said he would
never have married a Protestant; and unlike most Free Conservative Catholics he believed Bismarck's struggle against the Church
in the 1870s was a political mistake. Yet his contemporaries considered him an anticlerical; and his daughter believes that in
many ways he was really a free thinker.[78]

The prince's reaction to specific political and social questions
reflects a typically Free Conservative mixture. In 1908 he rose in
the *Herrenhaus* to argue against a proposed reduction in hunting
fees for peasant householders. A proper social policy, he said,
should aim at improving the moral and intellectual condition of

the less fortunate and not encourage them, as hunting would do, to neglect the home, the family, and the job. He added that experience had shown that where hunting begins, poaching is not far behind.[79] This aristocratic view may not be incompatible with his paternalistic efforts to establish exemplary social conditions on his estates.

Party principles determined Lichnowsky's attitudes toward Polish nationalism in Prussia's eastern provinces. Supporting the national unity achieved by Bismarck, Free Conservatives were hostile to all regional or separatist movements. As he believed that Polish nationalism in Germany would necessarily adopt the goal of national independence,[80] he supported the government's germanizing program in the mixed districts and voted for the bill that permitted expropriation of Polish landowners.[81] Here there was an element of social Darwinism at work in his thought. He believed that German culture was the progressive one, superior to the Polish, and socially and intellectually liberating.

Until he was appointed ambassador in London, Lichnowsky's liberalism remained within the Free Conservative range. He approved of liberal forms of government and free exchange of ideas. "In Germany there is an insurmountable antipathy toward anything reactionary that would limit freedom of thought,"[82] he wrote to Philipp Eulenburg in 1895. As a social Darwinist he also recognized that political systems, as manifestations of life, were subject to evolution and obsolescence. When the Prussian government in 1910 proposed to liberalize the three-class electoral system he spoke of the urgent necessity to make timely concessions to democracy,[83] but he was not yet prepared to accept the democratic program himself. This is evident in a letter he wrote to Bülow in 1909 after listening to the new chancellor Bethmann Hollweg deliver his maiden speech. It was Theodor Wolff's opinion that the new chancellor had spoken like a simpleminded schoolmaster. "But of course every imperial chancellor will be attacked from these quarters," the prince remarked, "as long as the ideal of the great democracy, of pure parliamentarianism, and equal, direct, and secret suffrage are not realized in Prussia."[84]

Wolff, for his part, was disappointed in Lichnowsky. Free Conservatism was in Wolff's opinion no framework for a man

of liberal outlook. In the years preceding the war, the party lost
its popular support and was infested by Pan-German authori-
tarianism.[85] Wolff regretted that the Silesian magnates and other
grands seigneurs who had a potential for liberal action, wasted
their time "promoting the military and diplomatic careers of
their sons and grand-nephews."[86] In 1910 he addressed a public
letter to Lichnowsky. The prince had just voted for an electoral
reform law that Conservative amendments had rendered worthless. "Not one of them," was the headline above this letter. Not
a single aristocrat had found his way to the side of the people.

In this chamber consisting of those possessed of hereditary privileges
(and afflictions) you [Lichnowsky] are the one who follows an almost
modern and independent train of thought. Through your capacity
for general ideas and historical reflection you often transcend the outlook peculiar to your social sphere. . . . The inquisitive and flexible
intelligence shown by your sympathy for new developments in the
theater and in art surely must recognize that our anachronistic form
of government is absurd. If this were the eighteenth century, you
would no doubt attend with pleasure to Rousseau's *Social Contract*.
But like so many of your fellow nobles of that time, who were content to recognize abuses while resisting their timely removal, you
have failed to muster the necessary resolve. The measure you chose to
support will have the effect of debasing our electoral system even
more.[87]

Lichnowsky continued to cherish the hope that one day he would
be appointed to an embassy. For some years he had reason to believe that his wishes would eventually be fulfilled. Holstein, the
man he thought had obstructed his advancement, retired in 1906.
His relations with the kaiser continued to be excellent. Although
Bülow retired in 1909, his successor, Theobald von Bethmann
Hollweg, was a friend of long standing.

   Bethmann was a civil servant knowledgeable about domestic
matters but inexperienced in foreign affairs. To Lloyd George,
British chancellor of the exchequer, who visited Germany in
1908, Bethmann seemed "an intelligent, industrious and eminently sensible bureaucrat, but he did not leave in my mind an impression of having met a man of power who might one day shake
destiny."[88] By comparison with Bülow, Bethmann was decidedly

gauche and ponderous. "He takes everything so seriously," Lichnowsky wrote Bülow after attending "friend Theobald's" maiden speech as chancellor, "that I fear the gravity and the responsibility of his position will in time wear him down unless he should succeed in acquiring some of his predecessor's Olympian indifference."[89] In the spring of 1910 the prince wrote Bülow he thought Bethmann would retain his office. "But whether he is still pleasing to the highest instance I cannot judge. It is said that there he is considered boring. He simply can't tell any amusing stories, and when others recount an experience or an anecdote nothing ever occurs to him."[90] While Lichnowsky's relations with Bethmann were obviously not as intimate as with Bülow, the new chancellor was a Free Conservative of liberal inclinations. He belonged roughly to Lichnowsky's political circle, and he was among the guests invited to Grätz and Kuchelna.

Under Bethmann Lichnowsky's chances for a suitable appointment did not improve. Gradually his hopes dimmed. In a letter to Princess Bülow in 1910 he predicted that "in spite of the friendly disposition of the two decisive factors" the desirable positions would fall to other candidates. And, as he could foresee difficulties with regard to leave, he had lost for the time being all desire to "emigrate."[91] In truth he was overlooked when Paris became vacant in the fall of 1910 and von Schoen was chosen to replace Radolin, who was retiring from the service. Although Bethmann at the end of 1911 suggested in a note to Alfred von Kiderlen-Wächter, his foreign secretary, that the prince might be recalled for Vienna, that post was retained by its incumbent, Tschirschky.[92] At that time Lichnowsky no longer had any status in the corps. In 1904 he had gone on indefinite leave. In January 1911, despairing of suitable employment, he petitioned for and was granted formal and final release from His Majesty's service.[93]

Chapter III
An Ambassador for London

I will send only *My* ambassador to London, who has *My* trust, obeys *My* will, follows *My* orders, and with *My* instructions!

Minute by Wilhelm II, 3 October 1912

Lloyd George recalled a reception during his visit to Berlin in 1908 where Bethmann, then vice-chancellor, "embarked upon a discussion of the European situation, and was very bitter about what he called 'the encirclement of Germany with an iron ring by France, Russia, and England.'" "'An iron ring!' he repeated violently, shouting out the statement to the whole assembled company. 'England is embracing France. She is making friends with Russia. But it is not that you love each other; it is that you hate Germany.'"[1]

By this time England had become for Germany a source of immense frustration. Within a decade more and more Germans had come to see England in the same resentful light in which the kaiser viewed his mother's homeland. A real basis for conflict had scarcely existed until Wilhelm II and Bülow, when foreign secretary, inaugurated their program of *Weltpolitik*. Their intrusion into the affairs of the world at large complicated Britain's diplomacy, while the German battle fleet, taking shape after 1900, openly threatened her supremacy at sea. "Let him play with his fleet," the Prince of Wales, later King Edward VII, had said of his nephew's plans in 1899. But Germany's ambitions and growing power could not be ignored. In 1904 Wilhelm invited his uncle to Kiel where from the decks of the imperial yacht, decorated with banks of flowers, fountains, and waterfalls, he proudly displayed his powerful modern warships.[2] And so the English thought of counterbalances. They embarked themselves upon a program of naval expansion, building the dreadnoughts. They consolidated the Entente Cordiale with France begun in

1904 through an agreement on spheres of influence in North
Africa, and settled their colonial differences with Russia in 1907.
Nevertheless, England was prepared to deal with Germany too in
hope of arriving at a system of naval limitation.[3]

When Bethmann became chancellor in 1909, Admiral Alfred
von Tirpitz was head of the German Naval Ministry. "The kaiser
always demonstrated a good eye for men whose gifts might fulfill
his own wishes," writes Emil Ludwig in his biography of Wilhelm II. He "had fished out the most gifted man in his navy. . . .
In contrast to everyone who previously surrounded the kaiser,
here was a man whose flexibility never descended to flattery, who
was never disturbed by doubts or flawed by vices: for he was an
expert who combined great technical knowledge with a genuine
passion for his weaponry."[4] Tirpitz was the father of the high
seas fleet, and he had his own ideas about policy toward England
which he was determined to carry out. His navy was intended to
be a strategic political instrument. The "risk fleet" (as it was
called because when it was complete any attacker would invite
the danger of serious losses) would force England to recognize
Germany's equality as a world power. By his calculation twenty
years would be required to build it. That period he called the
"danger zone" (a time when Germany would have to reckon with
the possibility of British counteraction) during which Berlin
must pursue a cautious and nonprovocative foreign policy.[5]

Bethmann accepted the program of *Weltpolitik* and believed
in "the absolute necessity of a very strong navy for Germany," as
he told the British councillor of embassy in 1912.[6] But in order
to break the "iron ring" he was prepared to negotiate and to
come to some kind of an agreement with England.[7] He knew this
was difficult, for England would not willingly give up the position she had achieved as the world's arbiter through her naval
supremacy and the European balance of power. After the outbreak of the war he told the Reichstag he had considered it possible that "the growing power of Germany and the increasing
risk of a war might compel England to realize that the old principle had become impractical and prefer a friendly compromise
with Germany."[8] To this end he did in fact turn his efforts—
in ways that were not always acceptable to Tirpitz. For he was
willing to compromise on the size of the fleet in order to arrive

at a "political formula," an arrangement that in the event of a Continental war would remove England from the list of enemies and break the encirclement. Discussions with London in 1909 ended in a deadlock because the Germans refused to reduce the naval construction already planned. The attempt at a political formula in 1912, when the British secretary of war Lord Haldane visited Berlin, likewise failed, for neither power could obtain from the other a commitment that promised the security it desired. Bethmann wanted a convention "that would guarantee England's neutrality, one approaching the character of a defensive alliance."[9]

Lichnowsky left the ministry before England had achieved her understandings with France and Russia and the naval question had become so serious. As desk officer for England he had had no influence on these developments, for it was Bülow and Holstein who made policy and drew up the tactical directives. There is, however, a memorandum Lichnowsky wrote in April 1904 shortly after France and England had signed their agreement on Morocco. Here he comments on a suggestion by the German consul in Tangier that the time had come to demonstrate against the Moroccan government for misdeeds recently perpetrated upon German citizens. The consul proposed that as the French penetration of Morocco was proceeding slowly from the interior side, Germany might safely land a force somewhere on the Atlantic coast. Lichnowsky thought this proposal should be given serious consideration. "We need a success in foreign policy," he wrote in his commentary, "as the Anglo-French Entente and the Italo-French rapprochement are generally regarded as a defeat for us." Before taking any action, however, it would be necessary to sound out London and obtain English approval. Perhaps the English would welcome the venture, thinking that it might increase French dependency upon them.[10]

This short note indicates that at the beginning of the Moroccan crisis Lichnowsky had imagined a policy quite different from the one Holstein and Bülow later adopted. Their purpose, when they dispatched their kaiser to Tangier in April 1905 to demonstrate Germany's support for the sultan, was to force France to abandon England and to seek her advantages through friendship with Germany. Threatening war, forcing the dismissal of foreign

minister Delcassé, and insisting upon an international conference
to deal with the Moroccan question, Bülow and Holstein helped
England and France consolidate their Entente Cordiale and en-
visage the need for future military cooperation. Lichnowsky, on
the other hand, had no thought of breaking up the Entente or
forcing France into an agreement. He wished to solicit England's
help for a share in the colonial venture. As he thought it possible
to acquire a harbor and territory by peaceful means on the west
coast of Africa, he regretted the provocatory actions of 1905, for
then, as he noted in *My London Mission,* "such concessions were
impossible."[11]

Lichnowsky's opinions on Anglo-German relations are more
fully recorded for the period of his retirement. Now he would
occasionally write essays on current affairs for newspapers and
magazines. During the naval discussions in 1909 the *Berliner
Tageblatt* conducted a symposium to which he contributed an article entitled simply "Die deutsche Flotte und England." Here
too he sees a political question in a Darwinistic light. As a part of
life, politics was subject to natural forces, he said. In life there is
rise and fall and continuous development. Would it ever be
possible to ban from politics the natural element of competition
or prevent "the rise of the capable and the strong?" This being
the process that was at work in relations between England and
Germany, it was idle to ponder whether the fleet was the main
cause of Anglo-German estrangement. No doubt the expansion of
the German navy had deepened English suspicions of Germany,
and relations would doubtless improve if the two Powers could
agree to limit their naval construction. But this would not put
an end to all rivalry, for the fleet was only one manifestation of
Germany's rise, and with or without the fleet England would
have to reckon with the threat posed by this developing power.

It was quite wrong, however, to conclude that these competing
nations must inevitably go to war. Germany had nothing to gain
by hostilities, and it was certain that "even a victorious war
by those who would overcome us would entail for them very
heavy sacrifices." For that matter, a Continental war seemed more
and more improbable. Neither Russia nor France had aggressive
intentions toward Germany and Austria, and France was concerned lest Germany attack her. Therefore, the prince concluded,

the main object of German foreign policy should be "to prevent relations with England from deteriorating." And to that end Berlin "must avoid all actions that cause unnecessary mistrust while we enable our fleet to keep pace with our economic growth and overseas needs."[12]

These were not totally individualistic thoughts. Their Darwinistic essence bears a strong resemblance to the theory of international relations presented a few years later in the books by the young scholar Kurt Riezler, who worked for the Foreign Ministry and became Bethmann's factotum. And it is obvious that they could be taken as an apologia for Tirpitz's program. Did Lichnowsky not suggest that it would be risky to attack Germany, and propose a cautious diplomacy so long as the fleet was under construction? Yet, translated into practical diplomacy his general view will be quite different from the Riezler-Bethmann outline, as we shall see. And his acceptance of the fleet did not imply common navalist attitudes. For he tried to understand the foreign point of view; he did not believe Russia and France were closing an iron ring around Germany with England's help; he did not resent England nor encourage the distrust that had so poisoned the atmosphere.

As he would not condemn the fleet, but rather justified it, Lichnowsky was not in accord with the then ambassador in London, Count Paul Wolff Metternich zur Gracht. Appointed to London permanently in 1902, Metternich's position had grown increasingly unpleasant. He was an opponent of the fleet, as he was convinced that the British would match the Germans ship for ship and that this rivalry would in the end produce a war. He urged Berlin to accommodate England's concern for the balance of power, to accept her understandings with France and Russia, and to seek reconciliation on colonial matters where compromise was possible. As a result he was permanently in conflict with the naval attaché Captain Wilhelm Widenmann, whose reports, following the navalist line, attempted to demonstrate that although the English were intensely hostile toward Germany, Tirpitz's fleet would eventually bring them in line. The kaiser enjoyed Widenmann's pasquinades and would not condone Metternich's attempts to suppress them. As Bethmann would not stand behind his ambassador, in June 1912 the long-suffering Metternich took his leave.[13]

The British deplored this turn of affairs. Metternich was a notoriously unsociable bachelor, but he was commonly regarded as a great gentleman and as one of the few Germans one could trust. Germany had few friends in the British diplomatic establishment in 1912. A formidable anti-German phalanx had formed consisting of Sir Eyre Crowe (senior clerk from 1906 to 1912 and then temporary undersecretary), Sir Francis Bertie (ambassador in Paris from 1905), Sir Edward Goschen (ambassador in Berlin from 1908) and Sir Arthur Nicolson (ambassador in Saint Petersburg from 1906 to 1910 and then permanent undersecretary).[14] Although some British officials believed the German government was divided into a "peace party" and a "war party," and that Bethmann represented the former and Tirpitz the latter, this was not the opinion of Sir Eyre Crowe.

"No one who understands the working of the German government," he wrote in 1912, after reading examples of German navalist propaganda, "is . . . likely to have any doubt that the policy propagated in the manner reported in the present dispatch is the policy of the German government, and not that of an admiralty clique fighting in opposition to the emperor and the chancellor."[15] "I wonder what the German game is and why they are so fearfully keen about a political understanding," mused Goschen in October 1910. "We know the phrase 'balance of power' stinks in their nostrils," he continued. "In fact they have told me so. They want the hegemony of Europe and to neutralize the only thing which has prevented them from getting it—viz. England's naval strength. They want an understanding which would have that effect."[16]

The group that feared Germany influenced but did not dominate the foreign secretary Sir Edward Grey. Dealing with Germany presented special difficulties of which he was sadly aware. "For seven years," he wrote Goschen in 1913, "some of the Pan-Germans in Germany have been working upon the pro-Germans in this country. The Pan-Germans are chauvinists, our pro-Germans are pacifists; but the latter are nevertheless very subject to the influence of the former."[17] But he could not affront these sentiments, prevalent in his own Liberal party, however paradoxical they might be. Besides, not all the diplomatic officials favored a hard anti-German line. Ralph Paget, assistant undersecretary after 1913, and Grey's own private secretary, Sir William Tyrrell, provided a pro-German balance. The evidence supports Lichnowsky's perception that by 1914 Tyrrell possessed greater influence than the permanent undersecretary Sir Arthur Nicolson. "At first," wrote Lichnowsky in *My London Mission*, "he favored the anti-German policy, which was then in fashion among the younger British diplomatists, but later on he became a convinced advocate of the understanding. He influenced Sir Edward Grey, with whom he was very intimate, in this direction."[18]

The appointment of Baron Marschall von Bieberstein to succeed Metternich was (in Lichnowsky's retrospective opinion) "but one of many mistakes that characterized our foreign policy."[19] Marschall was seventy years old. Formerly state secretary for foreign affairs, he had represented Germany at Constantinople since 1897. He had a reputation as a clever and hard-minded negotiator. Apparently the kaiser expected him to bring the English to their senses, and Bethmann wrote Lichnowsky later that although he had not shared the widespread conviction that Marschall would have achieved great things in a short time, he did believe that his prestige "would have smoothed out the ground."[20] But in England, as the Austrian ambassador Mensdorff reported, the appointment aroused universal mistrust.[21] "Now they send us this 'great diplomat,' " said King George to Mensdorff. "I am afraid he will not be able to achieve anything now. Besides, he always worked against us—at Constantinople, at the Hague Conference and also as secretary of state at Berlin. . . . He comes here with all this flourish in the papers. If he begins playing with the press here he will make a great mistake."[22]

Marschall was in London less than a month. Arriving early in July, he immersed himself in the files. When he had completed his review of current business he seemed to approve his predecessor's policy, for he told Richard von Kühlmann, Metternich's deputy who had continued in that position, that they would proceed along the path followed before his arrival.[23]

Marschall left England on holiday on 5 August 1912, and died unexpectedly on 24 September. Who was to succeed him was a matter of great interest in the German ruling circles. "His death was a grave, an irreplaceable loss for our fatherland," wrote Baroness Spitzemberg in her diary. She thought the leading candidates for the vacancy were first Bernstorff, then Lichnowsky, Hatzfeldt (son of a previous ambassador in London), and Wilhelm von Stumm (former councillor of embassy in London and now director of the political division and desk officer for England) .[24]

The kaiser also had his candidates ready. On the day Marschall died, as we may deduce from the correspondence that followed, Wilhelm wrote Bethmann that the vacancy should be filled by Prince Lichnowsky or Prince Hatzfeldt.[25]

How Lichnowsky, after eight years of retirement and being overlooked on all previous occasions, should now have become the kaiser's candidate for the most important diplomatic post we can answer with some certainty. In July 1912 Lichnowsky published another article on Anglo-German relations in the magazine *Nord und Süd*. (That summer he also published an article on Franco-German relations in *Deutsche Revue*, in which once more he denied that France had aggressive intentions against Germany.) [26] *Nord und Süd*, a long-established journal, had recently come under the control of Prof. Ludwig Stein, an old acquaintance of Lichnowsky's who was an indefatigable promoter of good causes. To Goschen, who mentioned in a dispatch in October 1912 that Stein had visited him at the embassy, he was "the peacemaker and wirepuller of Europe, and on messenger mornings, a bore of the first water."[27] Stein had begun in *Nord und Süd* a series of symposia intended to improve relations between different pairs of antagonistic powers; the June and July issues were devoted to Germany and England.[28] In June various prominent Englishmen presented their views of Anglo-German relations, and in July there were rejoinders by prominent Germans.

Lichnowsky's contribution, entitled "Deutsch-englische Missverständnisse," answered an article by A. J. Balfour. Balfour's thesis was that a large fleet, though not a vital necessity for Germany, was a question of life and death for Britain. Lichnowsky's reply was reminiscent of the article he wrote for the *Berliner Tageblatt* in 1909. Although he agreed that England's special requirements called for a large navy, he countered that Germany could not be left totally defenseless against this superior power. Indeed, the German fleet was a fact of life which the British must accept. On the other hand, the Germans must accept the fact that England would remain attached to France. If England and Germany respected one another's needs, and recognized that their differences could not be eliminated by force, they might well reach an agreement delimiting their armaments. In any case, it was possible to arrive at a modus vivendi eliminating all danger of war.[29]

The kaiser read this article with keen interest. Stein, who had favored Lichnowsky over Marschall when Metternich withdrew from London, writes in his memoirs that he advised the prince to send his manuscript for review to the kaiser and Bethmann so that the piece would acquire a semiofficial character. It seems evident that Lichnowsky did not do this. The letter he wrote Stein accompanying his article, which Stein includes in his memoirs, has no reference to this proposal,[30] and it appears that the article had its effect after publication and not before. The biographical sketch of the prince the Wilhelmstrasse sent the British embassy, noting that it was the kaiser who had first suggested him, said that the kaiser's attention had been drawn to him afresh by the contribution in *Nord und Süd* (which he had apparently learned about from Admiral von Müller, his naval chief of staff).[31] The kaiser could see that Lichnowsky was no opponent of the fleet and therefore, if for no other reason, an acceptable candidate for the embassy in London. In any case, in the letter he sent Bethmann the day Marschall died he gave preference to Lichnowsky over Hatzfeldt.

Bethmann, however, politely rejected the kaiser's suggestions. First of all, Hatzfeldt was in financial difficulties which would prevent him from responding to His Majesty's call. And although Lichnowsky was himself "not unsuitable" and at one time had definitely wished to rejoin the service (though he had said nothing about it when Bethmann visited him a fortnight earlier),[32] his wife (who reportedly opposed his return to diplomacy) gave cause for serious doubts. "The Princess is unquestionably an excellent woman, for whom I have the highest personal regard," he said. "But she is consumed by her interests (almost exclusively art, music, and more especially the theater), has little understanding of her husband's social position, gives him no support in this direction and therefore has not known how to establish herself in either the Berlin or the Silesian society."[33]

Rather than Lichnowsky, Bethmann proposed Karl von Eisendecher, who was then Prussian representative to the Grand Duchy of Baden. Eisendecher had already served as German minister in Washington and Tokyo. Originally a naval officer, he had for years managed the kaiser's yacht at the Cowes Regatta, and had been rewarded for this with promotion to the rank of honorary admiral. He was seventy years old. That Bethmann regarded him as a temporary replacement for London is clear not only from his subsequent nomination of Wilhelm von Stumm but from the wording of his counterproposal to the kaiser. He told his sovereign that it was not possible to make "a really good proposal." Although there were some able men who were still too young who doubtless would perform as well in London as they had at their other posts, at this point it seemed important "to send to London a representative whose personality gives proof that it is Your Majesty's intention to make relations between England and Germany more cordial and confidential." Eisendecher was the right man to do that; he was acceptable to the king and had many English friends in high places. And, as a former naval officer, said Bethmann, obviously wishing to evoke bad memories of Metternich, Eisendecher understood "the barrenness of the disarmament idea." His age had to be borne in mind, of course. But "even if his service should be of limited duration," added Bethmann, "other capable men who were suitable for the position would have time to mature."[34]

Although the kaiser later said that he thought Eisendecher too old and frail,[35] he deferred to the chancellor and apparently himself first broke the news of the appointment to his old friend. On 27 September the kaiser answered Eisendecher's letter of condolence on Marschall's death, saying that this had been a complete catastrophe, for Marschall was "the only one of my civilian officials who was a statesman and possessed dash, bravery, and energy." He added in English: "Would you feel up to replacing him?"[36] Replying on 30 September, Eisendecher told the kaiser that in all honesty he felt he could not accept the offer. He indicated his wife's infirmity and his own advanced age and ill health.[37] He did however request permission (which was granted) to visit London to have a talk with Sir Edward Grey. (This greatly mystified the British. According to Kühlmann, the chargé in London, Grey asked him to repeat his explanation of the planned visit and then he repeated after Kühlmann: Eisendecher declined the post, the kaiser accepted his decision, and now Eisendecher wanted to have a discussion with him.) [38]

Now the kaiser wished to amend his proposal. Marschall's death afforded the opportunity to put Anglo-German exchanges on a basis of equality. Apparently Wilhelm had stuck at Bethmann's suggestion that they send an ambassador who would give evidence of his desire for improved relations. In a message to Bethmann on 30 September he complained that everyone seemed to think it was German's responsibility to keep up the friendship. The English had to be indulged. "Therefore the butler Metternich was quite acceptable and given a great sendoff," he wrote. "The butler Marschall was welcome and they expected a great deal from him—in servicing English whims and wishes—and now he is dead and they are waiting to see whether the agency will be able to find another good butler." England had not reciprocated Germany's gesture in sending the "great man" Marschall. "They simply left us Goschen, whose own countrymen describe as a darned ass[39] because we aren't worth anything more than that." It was time for England to show her good will by removing Goschen. Germany was not to hurry with Marschall's replacement but indicate to the British that they must send a "great man" to Berlin.[40]

Bethmann's reply of 3 October agreed with the kaiser's judgment of Goschen, and he too thought it best to delay the appointment of a new ambassador to London. Eisendecher's refusal now afforded Bethmann the opportunity to present the ministry's true candidate—Wilhelm von Stumm. Born in 1869 Stumm was a member of the recent nobility and had come to diplomacy as an army officer. After serving at a number of embassies and legations in subordinate capacities, he was assigned to London in 1908 as councillor. He was recalled to Berlin in 1909 because (according to Kühlmann) after the kaiser's indiscretions to the

Daily Telegraph the ministry saw that it was necessary to have an expert on English affairs stationed at home.[41] Mensdorff thought that for want of a better choice he would be acceptable in London.[42] But he did in fact make a very poor impression upon the English. In 1910 Goschen wrote Grey that Stumm was always "rather hot about Anglo-German relations; he says it is because his colleagues always throw the delinquencies of 'his friends the English' in his teeth. It is possible that he may be an anglophil, but he certainly takes every opportunity of reviling us —perhaps as the proverbial candid friend. Of one thing there is no doubt, which is that like most official Germans he is quite incapable of seeing two sides to a question."[43]

If we may believe Kühlmann, who had serious personal differences with him, Stumm made a still worse impression upon Sir William Tyrrell. In the summer of 1914, in the excitement of the Austro-Serbian crisis, Tyrrell complained to Kühlmann that the man who was giving the German chancellor his advice on England was mentally unstable. Tyrrell recalled a terrifying visit from Stumm in the course of which the latter progressively lost contact with his surroundings and finally, becoming immobile, assumed a fixed stare.[44]

Bethmann was slow in bringing his letter around to Stumm. He went over the ground again: it was regrettable, he said, that Eisendecher seemed unequal to the strain of even a temporary appointment, for after an interregnum when the high expectations Marschall had generated had subsided, His Majesty would have more freedom in making the definitive choice. Of the candidates the kaiser had named,[45] Bethmann was inclined to give preference to Lichnowsky. The princess was not necessarily a serious obstacle. "With her intelligence," he wrote, "she might become reconciled to the duties required of an ambassadress, and there is no people more willing than the English to condone the eccentricities of ambassadresses and princesses." But in the event His Majesty wished to have recourse to younger assets, the chancellor wished to call his attention to Wilhelm von Stumm. "He was councillor in London, speaks excellent English, has a large fortune, and is a patient and circumspect worker who would be able to judge English 'assurances' for what they are really worth."[46]

This letter put a stop to all further consideration of ambassadorial candidates and hastened the appointment of Lichnowsky. The ponderousness of Bethmann's communication enraged the kaiser. It gave no satisfaction to his complaint that Germany was expected to take all the conciliatory steps or his wish that Goschen be replaced. The kaiser saw a contradiction in Bethmann's suggestion that the Germans bring their wish (to have Goschen replaced) to British attention subtly and unofficially and the proposal he made that the message be carried by a prince of the blood or some other high nobleman. The reasons for delaying a permanent appointment to London struck him as insubstantial. "Holy Plato!" he exclaimed in the margin. He would not hear of Stumm. "Definitely not. He fears the English too much. And he hates my naval building program." The kaiser therefore wished no further delay but the appointment of someone who was responsive to German needs and not to British wishes.[47]

His displeasure with Bethmann's temporizing he summed up in a minute at the end of the letter. "What a tortured pro et contra preceded this letter and runs through the whole thing," he wrote.

Its whole object is to avoid a positive statement. I will send only *My* ambassador to London, who has *My* trust, obeys *My* will, follows *My* orders, and with *My* instructions! If after his arrival in London Grey should ask him: "What have you to offer?" Answer: "Nothing. I ought to hear what you have to offer." If Grey is astonished and dismayed, tell him: "Ask your ambassador in Berlin." If Grey says, "He doesn't know anything, reports nothing," answer as follows: "Then why don't you send someone else?" That's how you have to handle these Foreign Office big-wigs.[48]

The letter on which the kaiser made these remarks was dated 3 October. Within a week the Wilhelmstrasse settled upon Lichnowsky. The circumstances of the final decision are not clear, but it is highly probable that Lichnowsky had expressed his interest in the position when he sent Bethmann the antlers of a stag the chancellor had shot during a hunt at Grätz in mid-September. Bethmann, sending his thanks on 3 October, wrote that he and the kaiser had made no decision concerning the vacancy.[49] In the biographical sketch sent to the British embassy on 14 October, the Wilhelmstrasse, noting that the prince was first suggested by the kaiser, said that after careful consideration of all candidates they were unanimously in his favor.[50] The kaiser's letter informing the prince of his nomination has been lost, but Lichnowsky's letter of acceptance preserved in the Hohenzollern archives is dated 11 October.[51] His notification was sent to him at home. His older son recalls that he and his sister were having a grammar lesson when the prince suddenly entered their room and said, "Father has been appointed ambassador to London."[52]

Although the kaiser's letter has been lost, the two men who alleged they saw it agree upon its exuberant character. Emil Ludwig says that this message, written in pencil, which Lichnowsky showed him after the war, was "filled with the silliest expressions of hatred for England, and gave the new ambassador instructions it would have been impossible to follow."[53] Bülow reports in his memoirs that he saw the letter the night it was received at the Hotel Atlantic in Hamburg, where he and the prince had taken lodgings. Lichnowsky burst into his room waving the letter, exlaiming "Success!" (*Es ist erreicht!*) While the account of the circumstances is faulty, the prince having received notification at home, the contents of the letter Bülow remembered are quite plausible. The new ambassador was charged to remember that he owed his appointment to the kaiser himself, not to the councillors in the Wilhelmstrasse, and to be a "jolly good fellow" so as to be the screen behind which the kaiser could finish building his fleet. Whereupon world peace would be secured and the kaiser would have achieved his life's ambition.[54]

Lichnowsky's appointment met with substantial approval. The truly critical voices were limited to the Social Democrats and the Pan-Germans. The *Vorwärts* ridiculed the closing paragraphs of the article in *Nord und Süd* where the prince had facetiously asked why German borrowings from England should include tennis, polo and horseracing but not love of the fleet. The *Deutsche Tageszeitung*, organ of the Agrarian League, conservative and nationalistic, condemned his familiarity with Theodor Wolff's democratic *Berliner Tageblatt*. Wolff, for his part, writing a friendly and approving article, wished that the nominee had not

resisted the promptings of his natural liberalism. The Center
Party's *Germania* regretted that this obviously qualified man had
not seen fit to promote the interests of Catholicism. The Free
Conservative *Die Post* noted that he was a man of "reliably
patriotic opinion."[55] Equally favorable was the judgment of Admiral Holleben, head of the German Committee for Anglo-
German Understanding. He wrote Eisendecher that he had "always taken pleasure, particularly with regard to the debates in
the House of Lords, in [Prince Lichnowsky's] completely unprejudiced character and freedom from all partisanship."[56]

The response abroad was gratifying. Russian, French, Austrian, and English observers all thought Lichnowsky was a perfect
choice for London.[57] The king had desired a gentleman. (After
Marschall died, he told the Austrian ambassador Mensdorff that
there were two Germans he would not accept: Kiderlen-Wächter,
who was generally undesirable, and Count Bernstorff, ambassador in Washington, who was "an intrigant and had an undis-
tinguished American wife.")[58] Lichnowsky satisfied all but the
most inveterate of anti-Germans. Goschen wrote Tyrrell privately
that Lichnowsky was a man "with whom one can discuss things
and he is not so narrow minded as Prussians usually are: he has
not the charm of some Poles—but I think he means well and that
you will find him easy to get on with and well disposed. The
Princess is very nice in an unconventional way and I like her:
she is very artistic and musical and a bit 'sauvage.' "[59]

All might have been well if Lichowsky's debut at home had
been equally auspicious. In the nature of things this was scarcely
possible. German ambassadors occupied an institutionally in-
ferior position: in order to prevent conflicting policies toward
foreign countries, Bismarck had demanded strict compliance with
instructions drawn up in Berlin; and no ambassador (with the
possible exception of Marschall in Constantinople) had ever
achieved a position of independent authority. This desirable
centralization of command led, however, to a division between
the home office and its representatives abroad. As the councillors
in the Wilhelmstrasse were jealous of their prerogatives, the ambassadors were not generally consulted on policy nor were they
necessarily informed about the government's strategy. (Among
young diplomats it was a commonplace that to be successful one

should report only what Berlin wanted to hear.) [60] And the German diplomatic corps was not immune to that process natural to all services: when a man in the field changes his chancellery for a room in the ministry he will quickly adopt the disposition of his new surroundings. When Kiderlen-Wächter, after long years in a legation, became state secretary and was dissatisfied with two-thirds of the envoys (even the great man Marschall), he was reminded of Holstein's proposition that "the average ambassador will prefer to go along with the government with which he is sojourning and against the government that is paying him."[61]

Lichnowsky had a serious clash with Kiderlen before he left Berlin for London. The occasion was a newspaper article about his plans as ambassador, one of a series of interviews he had granted to German and British papers in which he repeated the ideas expressed in his *Nord und Süd* article. He told his interviewers that in spite of misconceptions and jingo agitation on both sides of the Channel, he intended to create an atmosphere of trust between the two countries; and in these efforts he hoped he could count on the support of the press. The clear implication was that he intended to pursue a program of his own. On the next day a probationer, hearing a great bellowing issuing from Kiderlen's room, discovered that it was Kiderlen himself confronting Lichnowsky with his interview.[62] The prince referred to this incident later in *My London Mission*, saying that Kiderlen "immediately manifested unmistakable illwill towards me, and endeavored to intimidate me by his incivility."[63]

It was to Eisendecher that Bethmann expressed his uneasiness about Lichnowsky's appointment. (He did not say that Eisendecher himself had been thought of as a stopgap only.) "BH again very much disappointed that I did not accept London," the old admiral told his diary (which he kept partly in English) after a farewell dinner for the prince, and "thinks me more likely to succeed there than Lichnowsky who is too oberflächlich talkative etc."[64]

Chapter IV

Concert and Conflict

> Prince Lichnowsky was a gallant man, full of good
> faith. . . . I knew him well, and I was always
> astonished by the unfavorable opinion that the Wil-
> helmstrasse had of him.
>
> Jules Cambon, in Preface, N. Schebeko,
> *Souvenirs,* 1936

Prince Lichnowsky arrived in London on 13 November 1912.
"Never has any foreign ambassador achieved such rapid or resounding popularity," wrote Harold Nicolson.

The rulers of England, at that time, had lost none of their reverence
for the territorial aristocracy, but they liked their patricians to be
decorative without becoming patronizing. The Lichnowskys completely fulfilled these requirements. They gave most sumptuous and
regal entertainments at which the footmen were arrayed in liveries
dating from the time of John Sobiesky. And next morning Princess
Lichnowsky, laughing and hatless, could be seen running races with
her dogs and children in the park. English people like that sort of
thing.[1]

Lichnowsky entered into cordial relations with the British
statesmen. In a short time the prince and his wife were on friendly terms with Prime Minister Asquith and his family, "and were
guests in his small country house on the Thames."[2] Although Sir
Arthur Nicolson "was no friend of Germany's," the prince
wrote, "his attitude towards me was scrupulously correct and
courteous. Our personal relations were excellent."[3] Lichnowsky
immediately conceived a genuine liking for the angular, calm,
modest, and in his opinion very English foreign secretary. Although Grey did "not know foreign countries at all," the prince
wrote in *My London Mission,* "and had never left England except for a short visit to Paris, he was fully conversant with all the
important questions owing to his long parliamentary experience
and his natural insight."[4]

In London Lichnowsky joined a corps of experienced diplomats. The senior representative was the ambassador of France, Paul Cambon, who had been appointed in 1898. (His brother Jules was the French ambassador in Berlin.) The only bourgeois among the European ambassadors, Paul Cambon was socially at a disadvantage with the imperial representatives, who had easy entrée in the highest circles and who spoke excellent English. But he was a man of rigorous education and wide intellectual interests, and no doubt he is the model for the distinguished southern European diplomat that Mechtilde Lichnowsky describes in her novel *Der Lauf der Asdur* as a man who thought a volume of thoughts for every line he read.[5] Considered in Paris to be the best of France's active diplomats, he was one of the principal authors of the Anglo-French rapprochement that had preceded the agreement of 1904.

The imperial ambassadors were all of one class—indeed, they were of a single family, being personally related. The Russian ambassador, Alexander Konstantinovich Benckendorff, the son of a princess of Croy, was Lichnowsky's cousin. This cosmopolitan who spent most of his youth in Germany spelled Russian so poorly that he needed a special dispensation to write his dispatches in French. He was not well liked in the Russian foreign ministry because he seemed to have fallen under English influence (he was a chamberlain of the king rather than a Russian official, said Count Witte), but he was a favorite of the tsar, who had assigned him to his mother's court in Copenhagen before sending him to London in 1903.[6] "Although not, perhaps, a very eminent personality," Lichnowsky wrote later, "Count Benckendorff is endowed with a number of qualifications that distinguish a good diplomat—tact, polished manners, experience, courtesy, and a natural eye for men and affairs."[7]

The Austrian representative was Count Albert Mensdorff-Pouilly-Dietrichstein. No envoy had ever come to London with greater social advantages. Related to the British royal house through his grandmother, a Coburg, he had been sent to London in 1904 at King Edward's personal request,[8] and to subordinates he seemed less a statesman than a courtier.[9] His role in London was that of peacemaker. Loyal to the Triple Alliance, he was constantly at pains to dispel English mistrust of Germany,[10] and as he was obsessed by fear of republican and socialist upheaval, he appealed to King George to lead the established powers together in defense of their common interests.[11] He was distantly related to Lichnowsky and had known the prince since boyhood.

The Prince was also well acquainted with the Italian ambassador, Marquis Imperiali di Francavilla, who had been transferred to London from Constantinople in 1910. Imperiali had been Italian councillor in Berlin while Lichnowsky was Bülow's assistant in the Foreign Ministry.

Throughout his stay in London Lichnowsky was assisted by a deputy who himself was a public figure—Richard von Kühlmann. Thirteen years Lichnowsky's junior, Kühlmann had followed Stumm as councillor in London in 1909. It was safe to predict that he would have a brilliant career. Early in the war he became chief of mission in The Hague, later in Constantinople. He was foreign secretary when the Bolsheviks sued for peace, and at Brest-Litovsk he personally matched wits with Trotsky. At war's end, however, he retired from public life. Self-assured and enterprising but of not totally transparent character, he could have sorely tried the patience of a chief whose views he did not share. As it was, he believed in Anglo-German reconciliation to be achieved by gradual elimination of differences on the negotiable questions. And thus he worked in perfect harmony with Lichnowsky. But for reasons not fully apparent in the disappointing memoirs he completed in the midst of the Second World War, he had personal as well as professional differences never resolved with his colleague, his wife's first cousin, Wilhelm von Stumm.

In social position Lichnowsky soon outstripped his colleagues. His rapid rise to popularity was due in part to a conscious effort, as he recognized that an ambassador had to establish a position at court and in society. "Although the British Constitution leaves only very limited powers to the Crown," he wrote in My London Mission, where he attempted to explain his emphasis on sociability, "yet the monarch, in virtue of his position, can exercise a considerable influence on opinion, both in society and in the government. The Crown is the apex of the social pyramid; it sets the fashion and gives the tone. Society, which is principally Unionist (Conservative), has always taken an active interest in politics, a habit which the ladies share." "An Englishman is either a member of society or would like to be one," he continued. "It is his constant endeavor to be a 'gentleman,' and even people of modest origin delight to mingle in society and in the company of beautiful and fashionable women." "In view of the close relationship between politics and society in England, it would be wrong," he believed, "to undervalue social relations, even when the majority of the upper ten thousand are in opposition to the government." "Hence the social adaptability of a representative nowhere plays a greater role than in England. A hospitable house run by pleasant hosts is worth more than the most profound special knowledge; a savant with provincial manners and limited means would gain no influence, in spite of all his learning. The Briton loathes a bore, a schemer and a prig; what he likes is a good fellow."[12]

As he accepted progress and change in all things, so the prince did not mourn after bygone conditions of diplomacy and recognized that in his time an ambassador must be something of a public figure. He carried his message of goodwill beyond the court and the country houses. He hoped to counteract the talk about commercial jealousy, which he considered pernicious because among the British the increase of trade with Germany had actually "given rise to the wish to maintain friendly relations with their best customer and business friend, and had driven all other considerations into the background." In order to get in touch with the business community he had accepted invitations from the United Chambers of Commerce and from the London and Bradford Chamber. He was the guest of the cities of Newcastle and Liverpool and spoke in Manchester, Glasgow, and Edinburgh. "As a matter of fact," he wrote, "nobody in these circles took any interest in the Russian, Italian, Austrian or even the French representative, despite the striking personality of the latter and despite his political successes. None but the German and American ambassadors attracted public attention."[13]

Lichnowsky's relations with the British statesmen and with the foreign ambassadors in London were far more harmonious than with his colleagues in Berlin. His confrontation with Kiderlen a few days after his appointment as ambassador was the first of a series of conflicts that lasted throughout his tour in London. On the surface the differences might seem to be accidental, because of a clash of style and personality, particularly Lichnowsky's attitude of independence; on general policy Lichnowsky and his government appeared to be in perfect accord. Bethmann agreed with him that relations with England would improve in spite of the naval rivalry; Anglo-German discussions on colonial questions, from which both partners expected a rapprochement, were already under way; and Berlin had agreed that the Great Power ambassadors in London should meet under Grey's leadership to deal in concert with the territorial problems presented by the Turkish collapse in the First Balkan War. It is during the exchanges on the Balkan question in 1912–1913, before and during the Conference of Ambassadors, that the peculiar temper of Lichnowsky's relations with the Wilhelmstrasse becomes evident.

The upset in the Balkans in the fall of 1912 ushered in a period of intense diplomacy. Events had occurred very rapidly. The fighting broke out on 8 October, three days before Lichnowsky's appointment to London, when Montenegro declared war on Turkey. Bulgaria, Greece, and Serbia joined their diminutive partner, and within a month the Turkish armies were everywhere defeated. The prospect of sweeping territorial changes was alarming to Austria and Russia. It was Serbia's advance that made the Austrians anxious. The Serbian armies seized lands Austria wished to keep out of Serbian hands and were progressing toward the Adriatic. Theatening to intervene, Vienna proposed that the Powers create an independent Albania that would block Serbia's way to the sea. For the Russians it was Bulgaria's advance on Constantinople that caused concern. Saint Petersburg feared that a change of regime on the Turkish Straits would endanger the free passage of goods to and from the Ukraine. Serbia's claim to a seaport was therefore of no interest to the Russians. But for reasons of prestige they could not wholly abandon the fellow Slavic state to Austrian and Italian pressures. In this Saint Petersburg was encouraged by Paris, who recognized in the concern over Constantinople the possibility of a Russo-German rapprochement.[14]

It was not Germany's intention, however, to seek an understanding with Russia. For Bethmann and Kiderlen soon recognized that the upset in the Balkans might facilitate the effort to arrive at an agreement with England. Conversations on colonial matters were already underway, and London seemed to agree that Germany and England, being the Powers least involved in the Balkan territorial questions, might act together as honest brokers for the states whose interests were affected more directly. Berlin hoped that if such cooperation produced satisfactory solutions England would be inclined to cooperate with Germany in some future Continental embroglio. At the same time Berlin was determined to defend Austria's position as a Great Power, for Anglo-German cooperation had no purpose if Germany's position on the Continent should on that account be weakened. Lacking a plan or firm ideas about what constituted Austria's legitimate interests, Berlin decided to espouse Vienna's proposal to create an independent Albania to prevent Serbian access to the sea.[15]

Lichnowsky, however, was very much alarmed by Austria's demands. He saw them as motivated by vague notions of prestige and feared that intervention against Serbia would bring about a general war. Nothing had occurred since the 1890s to change his conclusion that Austria was wholly dependent upon Germany and could not conduct a foreign policy of her own. He could not have agreed with Kiderlen when the latter on 28 November told the Bundesrat that "we leave to our ally any ultimate assertion of her claims"; and he would never have entertained the conclusion that Kiderlen volunteered, namely, that if Austria, in the process of asserting her claims, should find herself at war with Russia, Germany would fulfill her obligations as an ally.[16]

Lichnowsky had no intention of hiding his concern. He probably outlined his views to Bethmann before he left for London, for in December he wrote the chancellor that he thought their parting interview had left them in full agreement.[17] But surely he did not tell the chancellor that he had also urged his ideas upon the kaiser. This he had done in a letter of 6 November in which he informed his sovereign of a delay in his departure for London. Venturing to discuss political matters, he volunteered the opinion that Germany had done right in avoiding one-sided support for Turkey, for Turkey was crumbling and the spirit of history (that is, evolutionary progress) was working for the other side.

Under these circumstances [he continued] it would seem to me very regrettable if Vienna's imaginary needs should lead us to intercede in Old Serbia or Albania. A commitment so far-reaching accords with the spirit of the Triple Alliance (which primarily guarantees existing possessions) no more than it does with the truly vital interests of the Austro-Hungarian Monarchy.

As I know from long acquaintance with Austrian conditions, the policy of the Vienna cabinet is often determined by notions of political prestige and influence. From their standpoint these may have a certain justification. But the responsibility for defending such interests, and for the consequences this defense might entail, falls upon that state alone and not upon its ally.

While it is understandable that every expansion of Serbian territory, let alone its extension as far as the sea, should disturb Austro-Hungarian statesmen, it is inconceivable that Germany should for that reason court the slightest danger of military involvement.[18]

At this moment Lichnowsky's view of policy toward Austria was wholly congenial to the kaiser. At the outbreak of hostilities he had taken the stand that the Great Powers should not intervene in the conflict but let events take their natural course. Turkish dominion in Europe was "smashed to bits," he said. It should be "a free fight and no favor"; and he would personally not take it amiss if the Bulgarians should occupy Constantinople and Ferdinand became "Tsar of Byzantium."[19] Adopting Lichnowsky's wording in a telegram to Kiderlen on 7 November, he told the foreign secretary that a Serbian port on the Adriatic in Albanian territory constituted no clear danger for Austria.

It seems to me [he continued] that Vienna's interests are partially imaginary. Seen from the standpoint of Austrian domestic policy (that is, from a purely Austrian standpoint), they cannot be denied a certain justification, but their advocacy and their possible consequences (war etc.) are purely a matter for Austria and not for her ally.

Such far-reaching commitment does not accord with the spirit of the Triple Alliance, which a limine was intended to guarantee the existing possessions; and the vital necessities and conditions of life in the Austrian Monarchy should not require it. Certainly as a result of the war there are many changes in the Balkans that are inconvenient for Vienna and quite undesirable, but there is none so decisive that because of it we should run the danger of military involvement. That I could not justify to my conscience or my people.[20]

As the kaiser's representations were in direct conflict with the Wilhelmstrasse's decision to support Austria's proposals for limiting Serbia's territorial expansion, Bethmann took pains to answer the kaiser, and though Wilhelm on 9 November still declared that "on no account would he in a matter involving Albania and Durazzo march against Paris and Moscow," he did not prevent the Wilhelmstrasse from carrying out its proposed plan.[21]

Kiderlen probably did not know that the views expressed in the kaiser's telegram on 7 November had originated with Lichnowsky, for the prince had not favored the Foreign Ministry with a copy of the letter he sent to Wilhelm II, which obviously he regarded as a private communication. But he did send the chancellor a copy of a second letter to the kaiser which he wrote from London on 23 November. Technically this letter was well within bounds, for the kaiser, elated by his choice of ambassador, had granted Lichnowsky the privilege of direct correspondence with his sovereign—that is, the prince was not obliged to restrict his communications to dispatches and cables and *lettres particulières* addressed to the chancellor or the foreign secretary. The kaiser rarely granted this favor. He had done so when Bülow was appointed ambassador in Rome in 1893, and he had insisted upon maintaining this separate channel over the objections of Chancellor Caprivi.[22] The prospect of direct correspondence between the kaiser and Lichnowsky displeased Bethmann, who, when he heard of it, ordered the prince to confine his letters to general observations and to send copies of them to the Wilhelmstrasse.[23]

The letter of 23 November originated in Lichnowsky's continued worry over the Austro-Russian dispute. He knew that in the middle of the month both Russians and Austrians had taken military measures just short of mobilization. After the king received him, 18 November, Grey told him he feared the Russian government could not resist public pressure to defend Serbia if Austria should attack her.[24] And on 23 November, the day he wrote the kaiser, Berlin cabled him that the Russian foreign minister seemed unconcerned by the prospect of war with Austria and was still insisting that Serbia acquire an Adriatic port.[25]

In form Lichnowsky's letter was a *tour d'horizon* concerned with his cordial reception in London, with British intentions (which he considered straightforward), with his impression of Sir Edward Grey (a man "free from all duplicity"), with the limits of Anglo-German cooperation (which could be put to the proof in a colonial agreement if Germany would only stop her caviling), and only obliquely with the crisis in the Balkans, to which he devoted one short passage. "Whether in the event of a general war—which we can hardly wish upon the German people on account of Serbs and Albanians—the government here would intervene," he wrote, "is a question that is difficult to answer and depends in the last analysis on the secret agreements existing between the Entente powers. But to judge by my impressions here, I do not believe that England would decide to take active measures if the possibility somehow existed that she could remain outside the struggle."[26]

Kiderlen burst into a rage when he received the copy of this letter which Lichnowsky had sent to Bethmann.[27] His pencil cut angry slashes under the many "me's" and "my's" and under a slip in grammar in the first paragraph. "I never thought much of Lichnowsky from the beginning, and those interviews of his were no good omen," he wrote back to Bethmann.

This report gives striking evidence of Lichnowsky's mistaken view of his (?) mission. He plays up to the kaiser and thinks he's achieved something for the Reich because the king says that he will make his stay "pleasurable." Grey is friendly, but he will not give up his ententes: we don't need an ambassador to tell us things like that. It is criminal that our ambassador presumes to judge our general policy, knowing nothing of its motives, and like a beer hall politician proclaims that we will not fight at Austria's side because of trouble between Serbs and Albanians.

He said that if Lichnowsky paid no attention to the chancellor's difficulties and sought only to ingratiate himself with the kaiser he was incapable of representing German policy at such an important post as London. "If he again disregards Your Excellency's warnings (which were first necessary at the time of his incredibly tactless interviews)," he continued, "I will find myself forced to present this alternative: he or I. He is either our ambassador, in which case he must conform to our policy, or he is a garrulous blimp *(freiquatschender Fürst)*, in which case he must take his leave."[28]

Agreeing with Kiderlen's objections, Bethmann in a dispatch of 29 November ordered Lichnowsky to discontinue his correspondence with the kaiser. He wrote that the prince should know from his experience in the ministry and close association with Prince Bülow that the kaiser's excursions into foreign relations often caused the government great embarrassment. And yet the prince had presumed to give the kaiser advice that conflicted with the policy recommended by the chancellor and the state secretary. "I am thinking of your remark that we cannot wish a war upon the German people because of Serbs and Albanians," wrote Bethmann. "Further, in your letter you touch upon the colonial negotiations, on which the kaiser has received no detailed briefing. My duty," he continued, "requires me to inform you, as a friend but none the less with complete seriousness, that by reporting in such a way direct to His Majesty the kaiser you aggravate the difficulties of my position as the man responsible for policy and create dangers of the most serious nature at a critical moment when the stake is war or peace."[29]

The prince lost no time answering this rebuke. Indirectly he admitted that he hoped his report to the kaiser would influence German tactics toward Vienna. He said that experience had taught him that Austria would never take a firm stand against Serbia without the assurance of German support. "Considering the confused state of affairs in Austria and the helplessness that characteristically reigns there, I hoped that a timely suggestion would have a sobering effect upon the Vienna cabinet." But he could not have guessed that he was acting contrary to the established policy, he said. He remembered that before his departure for London the chancellor agreed with him that Germany could never put its armed might at the disposal of an ally whose policy it could not influence. He returned to his contention that the German people could not be expected to go to war "on account of Serbs and Albanians," which statement Bethmann had re-

ferred to as conflicting with German policy. Although Bethmann
had obviously balked at Lichnowsky's wording because it seemed
to belittle a serious question, the prince, for the purpose of his
argument, took Bethmann's statement at face value and said that
he could not possibly have been aware that Berlin's policy had
taken such a radical change.[30]

What had inspired Lichnowsky's letter to the kaiser was the
fear that Berlin was misjudging the other Powers' probable reactions. His letter had in fact anticipated British concern lest the
Germans be under some illusion about what would occur if
Austria attacked Serbia. Three days after he dispatched his letter,
Grey told Lichnowsky that if any of the Great Powers was drawn
into the war "it was at the moment quite impossible to judge
who might subsequently be involved in the struggle."[31] Grey may
have spoken thus at the urging of the French and the Russians
who were uneasy over the Anglo-German flirtation. In fact the
Russian ambassador, Benckendorff, informed Saint Petersburg
that it was he who had suggested Grey's démarche, and he had
done so because he thought it should be made clear that in the
event of war the Germans could not count on British neutrality.[32] According to Benckendorff, Grey had told Lichnowsky that
"Germany and England are the two powers least interested in
Balkan matters and therefore the two most interested in maintaining the peace. For if war broke out, the true reason for it
would be so much deeper than the secondary questions that
caused it that he saw no guarantee that both England and Germany would not be drawn in."[33]

There were additional warnings at the beginning of December.
These followed an address Bethmann gave in the Reichstag on
the second in which he declared that Germany would meet her
obligations under the alliance if Austria, pursuing her legitimate
interests, should be attacked by a third power, for in that event,
he said, "we should be fighting to preserve our own position in
Europe, in defense of our security and our future."[34] There is no
mistaking the effect of these strident tones upon the British.
Grey told Lichnowsky that the chancellor had "contemplated a
little prematurely the possibility of war";[35] Bethmann's speech
was a "blast on a trumpet at a moment when everyone would
have preferred to hear the tones of an organ."[36] Grey told Paul

Cambon that Bethmann's speech had ruined the possibility of a common intervention by the three disinterested Powers—Germany, France, and England.[37] Lord Haldane, secretary of war, told the prince that Britain could not condone the defeat of France, warning that if Germany were to be involved in a war through her connections with Austria, "currents would arise in England which no government could withstand and the consequences of which were quite incalculable. The theory of the balance of the two groups, he said, formed an axiom for British foreign policy and had led to the rapprochement with France and Russia."[38]

Haldane's reminder came as no surprise to Lichnowsky. In the essays he wrote in 1909 and 1912 the burden of his message was that neither France nor England could commit themselves to an alliance with Germany. While Bethmann during the discussions with Lord Haldane in Berlin in the spring of 1912 had desired a defensive agreement that would vitiate the military effect of the Triple Entente, and Tirpitz was convinced that the German fleet would force England to concede Germany's equality as a world power, Lichnowsky believed that a correct policy would permit evolution to a state of general entente. He could never have entertained hope of a diplomatic revolution that would make England an ally of Germany against France and Russia. In his private letter to the kaiser from London he had insisted that Sir Edward Grey shared "with the great majority of his country's political men an earnest desire to live with us in peace and freedom without, for that reason, wishing to give up the connection with France and Russia."[39] Although Kiderlen, when he read this passage, pretended that these facts were common knowledge,[40] the German government did not (and perhaps could not) give up the hope of destroying England's connection with Germany's prospective Continental enemies. Of course, in December, it was obvious that the goal had not been reached. A few days after Lichnowsky's dispatch arrived in Berlin, Count Lerchenfeld, the Bavarian minister in Berlin, asked what England would do if Germany and Austria were at war with France and Russia. In that case, said Kiderlen, England would support the Entente.[41]

Lichnowsky's dispatch of 3 December 1912, reporting the discusion with Haldane, completely upset the kaiser. "But that means that Marschall's work and Lichnowsky's mission are already *a limine* brought to a close," he wrote to Eisendecher. "For both had the task of securing England's neutrality for the event of a conflict with Russia-France."[42]

In his excitement the kaiser now called for a reversal of policy. He had begun to change his tune in mid-November when as a result of the Austro-Russian military preparations he could picture a great war on the horizon. He promised to accept the consequences of an Austro-Russian conflict and ordered Kiderlen to query his ambassadors about what France and England would do.[43] Now he had his answer. Convening his military advisors, but ignoring Bethmann and Kiderlen, he urged immediate preparations for war.[44] A month earlier he had repeated to Kiderlen Lichnowsky's view that Germany must restrain Austria, but now he urged the Austrian crown prince Franz Ferdinand "to strike while the iron was hot."[45] Haldane's warning drew from him the penciled remark that "the final struggle between Slavs and Germans will see the Anglo-Saxons on the side of the Slavs and the Gauls."[46] Bethmann could not himself interpret Haldane's words as a reversal of British policy. To him the important development was the shift in the balance of power resulting from Turkey's defeat and the sudden expansion of states who were a threat to Austria-Hungary. Hence on 2 December he publicly reaffirmed Germany's loyalty to Austria, and on the fourth he received the kaiser's approval to enlarge the army. At the same time he reaffirmed his plan to improve Germany's position by cooperating with England.[47]

There was no change in Germany's policy as a result of Kiderlen's death on the last day of 1912. Arthur Zimmermann was his temporary successor, and at the end of January the office of foreign secretary was filled by Gottlieb von Jagow. A more polished and benign man than Kiderlen, Jagow had once been a favorite of the "casa Bülow" and was ambassador in Rome when Kiderlen died. He was the man Lichnowsky recommended for the vacant post.[48]

German policy was put to the proof at the London Conference of Ambassadors. This unusual assembly, which convened the London representatives of Austria, France, Germany, Italy, and

Russia, began its sessions on 17 December 1912. Sir Edward Grey was chairman. The object was to discuss and reach agreement on the territorial changes that Turkey's collapse had made necessary. As Russia would not support Serbia's claim to an Adriatic harbor and it was agreed that Albania should be independent, the main tasks were to compose the differences over the borders between Albania and Serbia and to provide for Serbian access to the sea across the territory of the newly created country.[49] The Powers achieved unanimity on these questions by April 1913. The problems that remained—the status of the Aegean islands and Albania's internal constitution—were less difficult. Consultations went on until the middle of August 1913, when the ambassadors dispersed for the late summer holidays. As Harold Nicolson wrote, "They had succeeded for a while in reconstituting what was in fact a Concert of Europe."[50]

Lichnowsky's performance at the conference was very successful. He was easily the most active and flexible of the representatives, and it was he who suggested or championed the measures that eventually proved acceptable to the entire community. His proposal at the beginning of the sessions that Serbia be informed of the conference's impartiality won the approval of all the ministries, including his own.[51] In January he carried on a successful mediation between the London representatives of Bulgaria and Rumania. The latter had not participated in the campaign against Turkey but desired compensation for Bulgaria's territorial expansion.[52] In January his resistance to a proposed naval demonstration against the Turks caused the Powers to choose another means of making their wishes known.[53] Though hampered by his instructions to support Austria's proposals, his insistence upon compromise by the Triple Alliance helped to end the Russo-Austrian dispute over Albania's northern and eastern boundaries. The decision in March to cede the town of Djakovo to Serbia instead of Albania, a measure he advocated from the beginning, finally broke the deadlock. And it was he who proposed the solution that ended the crisis over Scutari. That town, though promised to Albania, had fallen to the besieging Montenegrins. King Nikita refused to budge. For a while the Austrians thought of ousting him by themselves. But Lichnowsky, fearing for the concert, proposed a naval demonstration which the

Powers all accepted. And this forced the Montenegrins to re-treat.[54]

For these successes Lichnowsky received no comparable recognition. On the contrary, he achieved them in the face of continual derogation. All through the conference Berlin cultivated and insinuated through the diplomatic corps the notion that their representative in London was naive and unreliable. Beginning with Kiderlen, the disparagement continued unabated under Zimmermann and Jagow. When in December Lichnowsky reported that he had given the Serbian representative his personal assurance of the conference's impartiality, Kiderlen (though he soon recognized the need for this assurance) noted that the prince had gone too far.[55] "Our ambassador has been gulled," he noted a few days later when Lichnowsky reported without comment Grey's statement that although he had hitherto favored the Triple Alliance he would be forced to take the other side if difficulties arose because Austria would not let Montenegro have Scutari.[56] Going beyond minutes on dispatches and confidential discussion within the ministry, which are normally unrestrained, Kiderlen and his successors all made a point of belittling their ambassador to foreign envoys who visited the Wilhelmstrasse. To Jules Cambon, Kiderlen praised the prudent and experienced diplomats gathering for the meetings in London and regretted that there was no one there representing Germany.[57] In January Zimmermann told the French and Austrians that Lichnowsky had caused the delay in delivering the collective note to the Turks because he had failed to inform Berlin of the final agreement reached at the conference. But this was untrue.[58] In June Jules Cambon queried Jagow about the prince's reference, some time earlier, to rumors of an entente plan to divide Asia Minor into spheres of influence. Jagow, who said he disbelieved the reports, told Cambon that the prince sometimes talked too much and gave little thought to what he said. But indeed Lichnowsky had raised this question in London because Berlin had instructed him to do so.[59]

Berlin's readiness to disparage Lichnowsky was out of all proportion to the actual difficulties they had experienced with the new ambassador. The problem was that at the beginning of the conference Lichnowsky did not follow his instructions to the letter. As Berlin had decided to espouse the special interests of her partners in the Triple Alliance, the representatives of this group were enjoined to consult and agree upon their proposals in advance.[60] Lichnowsky obviously did not believe that this bound him to reject automatically all contrary proposals coming from the other side. At the first session, where Mensdorff proposed that the Powers agree to draw Albania's borders along strict ethnographical lines, Lichnowsky urged the Austrian to accept the Russian proposal that Scutari be assigned to Montenegro.[61] When Lichnowsky, in partial explanation of his actions, told Kiderlen that he thought Russia's abandonment of the Serbian port and Benckendorff's conciliatory approach should be requited, the foreign secretary noted that "the ambassador has not the slightest idea of his authority. He has obviously not read his instructions. He is to support Austria and not extend favors to his cousin for the latter's conciliatory attitude."[62]

Lichnowsky had deviated from the letter of his instructions for what he thought were good and sufficient reasons of policy. It seemed clear to him that Germany's stated goals—peaceful solution of the Balkan question and continued détente with England—were better served by cooperation with London than adherence to every desire that Austria conceived. Having sponsored the idea "of toning down the differences that divide the two opposing parties by means of a personal exchange of opinion between friendly diplomats," Grey, he wrote after the first session, "was manifestly at pains during our discussions to avoid the faintest suspicion of partiality and to act as mediator whenever it became necessary."[63] In order to promote the Anglo-German understanding it was necessary to help ease tensions in Europe as a whole, and he told Berlin that he had made it his duty "to mediate between the Austrian and the Russian standpoints and to try to avoid giving the impression that Russia was to emerge from our negotiations in any way humiliated or vanquished."[64]

Berlin's impression of Lichnowsky was not only the result of their tactical and political differences but had other sources too. There can be no doubt that what Berlin thought and said of their ambassador was greatly influenced by the intelligence obtained from a penetration of the Russian embassy in London. Lichnowsky knew nothing about this operation. The source was the Russian second secretary, Benno von Siebert, a Baltic German, who had been slipping copies of the embassy's correspondence to the German military attaché since 1909.[65] Among the secret documents thus obtained by the Wilhelmstrasse there were dispatches reporting Benckendorff's conversations with Lichnowsky. It is the nature of such recordings to accentuate the cleverness and initiative of the reporter; and to the men who read the intercepted documents—Bethmann, the state secretary, Stumm, and Arthur Zimmermann—Benckendorff appeared the perfect Machiavellian taking advantage of his naive and fearful cousin.

The temptation to use this intelligence against Lichnowsky was too powerful to resist. When shortly after his arrival in London Lichnowsky reported that Benckendorff had been particularly confiding toward him, Kiderlen advised the prince to be skeptical of his cousin's remarks and to be discreet in his own favors, for the Russian ambassador, as Berlin knew from a reliable source, was a man with a forked tongue who spoke in one vein to Grey and in another to Nicolson.[66]

If Kiderlen was at the outset honestly concerned about Lichnowsky's close relations with Benckendorff, soon the pleasure of rebuking the prince dominated all other motives and distorted Berlin's judgment of the secret intelligence. When the Wilhelmstrasse learned from an intercepted report that Lichnowsky had expressed some surprise and concern over Bethmann's militant speech on 2 December, Kilderlen cabled the prince that Benckendorff was exploiting his utterances to Germany's detriment.[67] Obviously angry that the prince had presumed to pass independent judgment on the chancellor's speech and had not defended it, Kiderlen entirely misconstrued Benckendorff's information. For the Russian ambassador had reported not what Lichnowsky had said to him but what he had said to Grey, and Grey, conveying this to the Russian, had added that although Germany would defend Austria against attack by a third power she had not abandoned her policy of compromise.[68] It would seem that this was exactly the impression that Berlin should have hoped the German ambassadors were conveying.

The Siebert intelligence particularly envenomed the tone of correspondence prepared by Stumm. An example of this occurred at the end of January 1913. At that time the conference was still arguing over the Albanian borderline, and Benckendorff complained to Lichnowsky that Russian militarists were pressuring their government to be more forceful. In conveying this information to Berlin, Lichnowsky remarked that the ambassador had spoken to him privately and in family confidence. While Bethmann and Zimmermann thought this worthy of consideration, particularly since Benckendorff had impressed Grey with the same arguments (as Bethmann knew from the intercepted correspondence and so informed the Austrian ambassador),[69] Bethmann's instruction to Lichnowsky, drafted by Stumm, presented an entirely different view. Why, Stumm demanded, had the prince not responded "with the same kinsman-like frankness" and told Benckendorff that if the Russians attempted to mobilize their army the country would rise in revolt and the empire would collapse. Lichnowsky replied that even if Berlin had kept him informed of the disastrous conditions in Russia, his blood relationship would scarcely have sufficed to convince Benckendorff that the German appraisal was accurate.

But such logic was to no avail, as Stumm could draw upon and unending flow of secret information. In making report of the conversation with Lichnowsky, Benckendorff asked Saint Petersburg not to reveal the content to Count Pourtalès, the German ambassador in Russia. "I believe Lichnowsky can be useful to me," wrote Benckendorff, "but only if our conversations, if they continue to take place, remain entirely confidential. I know Berlin considers him very anti-Austrian." Thus, Stumm could write that Lichnowsky's behavior at the conference had confirmed his reputation for hostility toward Austria. And if the prince would only remember how Benckendorff had spoken in their recent conversation, he would recognize that the purpose of Benckendorff's alarms was to harness the prince to the Russian cart.[70]

By any standards of conduct, Stumm's reply was entirely unacceptable. He had changed the question at issue (whether there was danger of Russian intervention) into a question of Lichnowsky's competence, and transformed the official channels into a vehicle for polemics. His innuendo was based upon assertions which Lichnowsky, who was ignorant of their source or the exact wording, could neither refute nor explain. His argumentation distorted the facts where it did not overlook them. Lichnowsky had in fact begun to fret over the Austro-Russian differences long before his cousin raised the specter of Russian jingoism. Even if Stumm personally believed there was little danger of Russian intervention, German intelligence at that moment did not support his contention of a weakened and militarily ineffective Russia, and Pourtalès was soon sending reports about agitation of the kind Benckendorff had alleged to Lichnowsky.[71]

Benckendorff's request that Saint Petersburg withhold his reports from Pourtalès has a simple explanation. Kiderlen had sent Lichnowsky information from the intercepted Benckendorff reports which Lichnowsky, not knowing it was secret, could have mentioned to Benckendorff. In fact Benckendorff had an embarrassing confrontation with the prince because of a report that had made its way by normal channels from Saint Petersburg back to London. In his first dispatch from the conference, Benckendorff erroneously stated that the German ambassador had proposed that the Turks retain suzerainty over Macedonia. Alarmed by this proposal, Saint Petersburg had complained to Berlin, and Lichnowsky, when he was home for Christmas had to account for his behavior. Back in London Lichnowsky explained that Benckendorff had misunderstood the proposal, which Benckendorff readily admitted.[72]

Early in February there was another revealing exchange with Berlin, not connected with the intercepted correspondence. Lichnowsky had proposed to Berlin that Grey and he should together attempt to find a compromise solution. Berlin instructed him to suggest a boundary based on the Austrian proposal, which they cabled him, but to avoid the suggestion that Austria might make further concessions.[73] Although the Austrian terms proved unacceptable to Grey and Benckendorff, Grey persuaded Mensdorff to present the proposal to the conference as a whole so that the extent of the Austro-Russian differences might become clear. Thereupon Lichnowsky read the Austrian proposal in the formal session, while Mensdorff, who had agreed to the reading, explained that these were his government's final terms.[74]

Although Mensdorff reported these circumstances accurately, the Austrian foreign minister Berchtold cabled Berlin that Lichnowsky should have secured Benckendorff's consent to the proposed boundary before presenting it to the conference, for Austria could make no further concessions and the negotiations were therefore stymied.[75] Jagow repeated this complaint to Lichnowsky. The prince replied that the Russians already knew these were the final conditions and found them unacceptable, and he argued that the Russians would have no recourse if the Austrians refused any further discussion of the border question. Jagow answered that the prince could have prevented the Russians' embarrassment if he had refrained from presenting the Austrian conditions as a formal proposal.[76] Obviously wearied, and "hurt by the little rebuke" (as Mensdorff wrote Berchtold),[77] Lichnowsky could only repeat that he had acted in complete agreement with the Austrian representative and that the Austrian terms were known to everyone.[78]

It is worth noting some other reactions to Lichnowsky at this time. "An exceedingly amiable man," wrote Sir Arthur Nicolson to Goschen in March 1913, "but he does not strike any of us as having a very clear business head, and I doubt if he reports very accurately to his government."[79] Nicolson's son, who quotes this letter in his father's biography, notes that his father had been entirely wrong. Mensdorff took a patronizing view of Lichnowsky. He hoped that his excellent friend would be "an outstanding German ambassador in London," as he wrote Berchtold in May, "and he is the right man to achieve lasting successes here and inspire confidence, whereby his very defects will stand him in good stead. But in a conference he is incredibly amateurish, vague, and impatient. He invariably speaks out on every question without thinking and has made several little gaffes. With the best and sincerest intentions he is the compleat bumbler (*Konfusionsrat*)."[80] In judging this characterization two things must be borne in mind—the first is that Lichnowsky's goals during the conference were different from Mensdorff's; the second is that it was Mensdorff's way to belittle his "cousins." He found Benckendorff so nervous that it was difficult to talk to him,[81] and he reported that in London society it was said that "poor old Benckie is more absent-minded than ever and getting quite gaga."[82]

The German government was of two minds about the Conference of Ambassadors. Disputations over the allotment of Balkan towns and villages could not reverse the shift in the balance of power that had resulted from the Turkish defeat. But Austria had achieved her ends with regard to Albania, and the measures the Powers took as a result of their conference provided Germany an area of agreement and common action with England. "A pitiable affair," said Bethmann of the conference in a letter to Eisendecher, "but it has brought us quite a bit closer to England."[83]

So promising was this rapprochement that Bethmann was soon willing to subordinate Austria's immediate needs to the prospect of ever greater improvement in relations with England. He continued to hope for English neutrality in an eventual conflict between the Continental groups. In February 1913 he wrote Berchtold that England's attitude during the conference confirmed other signs that England's

Entente policy had passed its high point, and if we survive the present crisis without any conflicts we may expect a reorientation of English policy. It is of course a question of developments that are in their earliest stages and will require more time to mature. In my opinion it would be a mistake of immeasurable consequence to attempt a solution by force—even if many interests of the Austro-Hungarian Monarchy seem to require it—at a moment when we have a prospect, however remote, of facing the conflict under conditions much more favorable to ourselves.[48]

Lichnowsky's own position remained ambiguous. It was Berlin's practice to attribute his opinions and advice to defects in his character or to prejudice. To explain his criticism of Austrian conditions and his warnings against involvement on Austria's behalf it was now said that he had inherited an unreasoning hatred of Austria from his father. But Berlin could not ignore Lichnowsky's good reception in London or his accomplishments at the conference. Although Bethmann belittled Lichnowsky's enthusiasm, saying in a letter to Eisendecher that the prince was "splashing around on top of the waves, and I shan't deprive him of the belief that he created the ocean," he had to add that the prince was doing well.[85] The kaiser had a typical reaction. Although Jagow wrote Lichnowsky privately in April 1913 that Wilhelm was complaining that the conference had been forced upon him,[86] in February the kaiser had boasted to Admiral von

Müller that Lichnowsky had "excellent relations with Grey, who did nothing without consulting him."[87]

His own position in London obviously seemed promising to him. Grey told him that he had made a very auspicious debut as ambassador,[88] and wrote Goschen that Lichnowsky "comments upon his own government with a freedom which is very refreshing and quite new in my experience of German ambassadors."[89] The prince was particularly happy over this easy cooperation with Grey. The conference, he noted in a letter to Bülow, had succeeded in arriving at an agreement on all important questions, and he believed that his personal friendship with Grey had greatly contributed to that satisfactory end. "I am conscious," he wrote Bülow, "that we have achieved much more than we could have hoped for a few months ago, and if Berlin is not too impatient I hope to continue to strengthen our relations even more."[90]

Chapter V
Weltpolitik und kein Krieg

> We needed neither wars nor alliances; we needed only
> treaties that would safeguard us and others, and se-
> cure our economic development, a development that
> was without precedent in history.
>
> Lichnowsky, *My London Mission*, 1916

When Lichnowsky in April 1913 wrote Bülow of his satisfaction
with the progress made at the Conference of Ambassadors, he
had high hopes of achieving an Anglo-German entente. He knew
that England's attitude toward Germany would depend finally
upon Germany's intentions in Europe, for (as he wrote in an
early dispatch from London) "the English would not tolerate
Germany's oppressive preponderance on the Continent."[1] An indubitably peaceful European policy on Germany's part was the
sine qua non of good relations and her concerted effort at the
conference to help other powers compose their differences was a
step in the right direction. But the road to entente, as Lichnowsky and Bethmann agreed, was to settle the particular problems
at issue between Germany and England resulting from the Anglo-
German encounter in the world at large, from Germany's rise as
an overseas trading power with colonial and naval aspirations.
While the naval question was not on the agenda when Lichnowsky arrived in London, conversations were in progress "concerning
the renewal of the Portuguese colonial agreement and concerning Mesopotamia (Baghdad Railway), the unavowed object of
which was to divide the Portuguese colonies and Asia Minor
into zones of influence."[2] The negotiations on the Portuguese
colonies occupied Lichnowsky throughout his stay in London,
and once more his experience with the Wilhelmstrasse consisted
of delay, obstruction, derogation, and rebuke.

Metternich was still ambassador when the question of colonial partition arose, and the talks began in earnest in April 1912, shortly before his departure. England had taken the initiative. It was in July 1911, in the midst of the second Moroccan crisis, that Grey suggested to Metternich the possibility of colonial adjustment, and he returned to the question more explicitly that fall.[3] His purpose, most clearly, was appeasement. There were two parties he had to satisfy—the Germans and the pacifists among his own Liberals. "For a real bargain about naval expenditures," he wrote Goschen in December 1911, "in which Germany gave up the attempt to challenge our naval superiority we might agree to something substantial."[4] His domestic motivation was obvious to Lichnowsky, who wrote Berlin that Grey hoped to placate a group of parliamentarians who were accusing the Asquith government of "neglecting its relations with Germany for the sake of its friendship with France."[5] The Germans were receptive to the British proposal. Bethmann, though at first cautious, recognized an opportunity to continue the dialogue after his discussions with Haldane failed to produce the political formula he so desired.[6] At first the powers had envisaged a larger plan of colonial redistribution including the Belgian Congo. But fear of alienating the Brussels government led them instead to focus upon the possessions of Portugal.[7]

The object was to revise the Anglo-German treaty signed in 1898. Portugal in that year was on the verge of bankruptcy. As it seemed only a question of time before she would lose her overseas possessions, the two powers came to an agreement to share a loan to Portugal on the security of the colonies and to divide these should the mother country default. Portugal, however, frustrated this plan by regaining her solvency. In 1899 the British (hoping to prevent transportation of arms across Mozambique to the hostile Boers) secretly reaffirmed the ancient treaty of alliance by which they had promised "to defend and protect all conquests or colonies belonging to the Crown of Portugal."[8] Such were the unclear circumstances when negotiations were resumed in 1912. By that time the agreement of 1898 seemed clearly disadvantageous to London. For Austrialia had developed an interest in the island of Timor, which had been allotted to the German sphere of influence, and South Africa was concerned over conditions in Mozambique and coveted the Delagoa Bay.[9] And early in 1912 there was a sudden flurry of financial and commercial interest in Portugal's African possessions.[10]

The German negotiators from the start were hampered by a lack of clarity and determination. Liberal and conservative Germany accepted the need for imperialism, that is, economic, political, cultural, or territorial expansion—growth or development of one kind or another. But neither the government nor the public was agreed about where or how Germany should or must seek to expand her influence and power. In the government there were officials—Solf (who was now colonial secretary) and Rosen (who was ambassador in Lisbon), notably—who wished to concentrate on Africa where they believed it was actually possible, with the aid of England, to acquire new and economically useful territory. As they did not share the Pan-German and conservative distrust of parliamentary England, they have been called the "liberal imperialists." Their numbers included Metternich and his active and competent deputy Richard von Kühlmann, who inspired the widely read pamphlet entitled *Deutsche Weltpolitik und kein Krieg* (*Imperialism without the Danger of War*), in which the hopes for peaceful expansion in Africa achieved their best expression. Although Bethmann saw the negotiations as a means of continuing the dialogue with England and still hoped to achieve the general political agreement that had so far escaped him, he too was not blind to the economic benefits of territorial expansion. In 1913 he lent his name to a letter Solf had drawn up for the secretary of the treasury maintaining that this was the last chance to acquire control over lands that would provide markets, sources of raw materials, and space for German colonists.[11]

Lichnowsky shared these hopes. But his dispatches reveal a point of view rather different from the chancellor's. While Bethmann, in authorizing Metternich in April 1912 to go on with the negotiations, seemed to think that it was up to England to display her goodwill toward Germany,[12] Lichnowsky thought that more was to be gained if Germany could prove that she had no intention of forcing England to abandon the maxims she lived by. He had no illusions about England's motives. He saw that Grey hoped to placate his constituents and "divert our attention from the North Sea by directing what they thus assume to be our land hunger to regions which would not seem to affect Britain's power."[13] But this, in his opinion, was to German's advantage. He recommended that Germany respect the delicacy of England's position toward Portugal, her oldest ally, and not lay too much stress upon political acquisition but think in the main of economic penetration.[14] And it was he who suggested the central phrase in the preamble stating that the purpose of the treaty was to guarantee Portugal's integrity and independence and prevent international difficulties if in the future Portugal should require financial assistance.[15]

Unfortunately, Lichnowsky's optimism was not shared by Stumm and Jagow. They feared that their transaction was neither profitable nor executable, and that the German public, seeing this, would hold the Foreign Ministry up to shame.[16] The public they had in mind was the segment of nationalist writers and parliamentary orators who hated England and whose attacks on Bethmann's policy of détente had grown increasingly virulent. While in general these critics were not opposed to African expansion, for they were imperialists, they doubted the practicality of this effort, all the more so because they had no faith in England's sincerity.[17] Stumm and Jagow, plagued by these doubts, let their worries be fixed on the question whether the treaty should be secret or public. This became a stumbling block. While the British wished to publish the agreements, knowing they could not be kept secret (and because Grey was under obligation to his party to eschew all secret agreements),[18] the Wilhelmstrasse could not make up its mind to do this. Marschall, who during his brief tour in London had studied the colonial question, concluded that publication was necessary.[19] But Stumm and Jagow clung to their doubts, and the negotiations dragged on. In spite of repeated urgings by Lichnowsky, it was not until July 1913 that agreement was reached on the question of publication; Grey was willing to postpone this action until a time the Germans thought convenient, providing it was within one year of the day of signature.[20] The English draft was initialed in August 1913 and the German draft in October.[21]

Lichnowsky thought this a successful treaty. As in the earlier agreement, a loan was envisaged. In that event the customs revenues in Mozambique and Angola were to be pledged to England and Germany according to a plan that in effect described English and German spheres of influence for commercial penetration. The negotiators had experienced little difficulty in realloting the territory. The Germans gave up the Portuguese half of Timor in return for the islands of São Tomé and Príncipe in the Gulf of Guinea. The British gave up an enclave in Angola running from Rhodesia to the sea for a strip of Angolan territory along the border of Rhodesia. Angolan territory allotted to Germany included the district of the Congo, or Cabinda, an enclave lying north of the Congo River and surrounded by French and Belgian territory. The agreement on Mozambique, setting the Lukungo River as the dividing line, would leave to Germany the northern third of that colony where Germany already had substantial commercial interests. The true innovation was a set of clauses that were thought to improve the chance for political annexation of the spheres of influence. These stipulated that the two powers be permitted to intervene in the colonies in the event the Portuguese government proved incapable of protecting life and property in them, and to annex them if a political action should make them independent of the mother land.[22]

Before the signing could take place, new objections rose on both sides. At the end of October Berlin learned that Grey also intended to publish the Anglo-Portuguese treaty of 1899 reaffirming England's ancient commitment to her ally. Grey had not made this explicit to Lichnowsky, and it had come out in a discussion between Rosen and the English representative in Lisbon. Although Lichnowsky argued that this treaty contained nothing that was inconsistent with the preamble of the new Anglo-German convention, Jagow would not accept Grey's plan. He feared that the obvious incongruity of these instruments would generate in Germany a wave of indignation so strong that Bethmann could be swept from office. Lichnowsky was to impress upon Grey the thought that a new chancellor would in all probability not share Bethmann's sympathy for England.[23]

For London this revival of German hesitancy was providential. At the outset both sides had recognized the obvious difficulties involved in their plan to divide the colonies. "On every ground material and moral and even Portuguese it would be better that

Portugal should sell her colonies," Grey wrote Goschen in December 1911. "But how can we of all people put pressure on Portugal to sell: we who are bound by an alliance to protect and preserve her colonies for Portugal."[24] Heeding these sentiments, Grey would occasionally present the agreement as having a purpose other than acquisition. "Some things the ambassador said seemed to indicate that Germany hoped for more than a mere commercial development," he wrote Goschen in June 1913, as if this were new to him. "He said, in fact that the position I seemed to assume was that of medical advisor to the Portuguese colonies, while what Germany contemplated was that of being heir."[25]

Grey's plan of colonial partition had encountered considerable resistance in the Foreign Office. To the anti-German phalanx, to Nicolson, Crowe, and Bertie, the plan seemed as doubtful morally as it was impractical. Bertie had raised objections as soon as he learned that Grey had suggested it to Metternich in July 1911. He could not see "that it would be of advantage to us that a powerful Germany should stand in the shoes of a weak Belgium in the Congo State in whole or in part," he wrote Nicolson in August 1911.[26] In January 1912, misunderstanding a communication from Grey, he complimented the foreign secretary for resisting "Metternich's satanic invitation to look down on the African possessions of Portugal as a means of satisfying German land hunger." "I do not believe that we should conciliate Germany by facilitating her acquisition of territories not our property. She would attribute our good offices to fear of her and a desire to keep her away from our own possessions."[27]

While Grey had resisted these doubts, he could no longer do so at the beginning of 1914. Since 1911 the European situation had undergone a radical change. The Conference of Ambassadors, where the Great Powers had given proof of their ability to compose differences, could not prevent a rise of antagonism during 1913. France and Russia grew more nervous about England's rapprochement with Germany. The French were not in ignorance of the Anglo-German colonial discussions.[28] They did not seem to object to them. As late as October 1913 the French foreign minister told the German ambassador in Paris that an Anglo-German agreement on colonial questions could only serve to reduce the tensions in Europe.[29] But the French did not know that São Tomé and Príncipe, islands in the Gulf of Guinea, were included in the agreement, or that Germany was promised Cabinda, the Portuguese enclave north of the Congo River surrounded by Belgian and French territory. At Grey's suggestion the islands were to be allotted to Germany as compensation for the loss of Timor, which was reserved for Australia.[30]

Paul Cambon learned about São Tomé and Príncipe in a discussion with Grey in October 1913. This shed new light upon the agreement. Paris also noted that Cabinda fell under the terms of the 1911 Franco-German agreement requiring international consent to territorial changes in the Congo basin. In January 1914 the French concluded that the plan of partition would endanger their economic interests, upset the balance of power in Africa, and withal weaken the Entente; and in February Paul Cambon was instructed to inform Grey that the proposed treaty was contrary to Europe's interests and public law.[31]

Grey could not fail to heed this intervention. The Foreign Office's anti-Germans recommended a reversal of policy. "I am very much afraid," wrote Bertie, "that if and when the fresh arrangements with Germany are made public or become known there will be a great outcry in the French parliament and in the French press." Crowe, in his minute to Bertie's dispatch, wrote: "There is now a possibility of a way out of the whole difficulty: namely not to proceed with the new convention." And Nicolson agreed that it would be wise to drop the treaty.[32] Grey hence adopted a new strategy toward the Germans. Not admitting the French intervention, he pretended to accede to Berlin's wishes for secrecy. But of course now he could not sign the treaty, for he was under obligation to publish any treaty he concluded. The Russo-German press war that broke out in March facilitated his retreat; he told Lichnowsky that under the circumstances they must do nothing that would further inflame public opinion. He said that as England and Germany knew where their spheres of interest lay, the agreements need not be published.[33]

Although Lichnowsky was aware of Cambon's intervention, he thought Grey would return to the question when French fears had been allayed. "It is certainly another matter," he wrote, whether we consider it advisable to proceed to the final signature of the treaty, which has as yet of course only been initialled. . . . In my view early signature would be desirable, because it would bar the way to subsequent alterations brought in, let us say, to satisfy complaints from France. Not that I think Grey would afterwards mutilate a treaty which he had already as good as concluded. That would be entirely contrary to his otherwise honorable and straightforward nature; but you never can tell whether the Unionists may not come into power, and whether Lord Curzon or Lord Lansdowne or whoever else takes over the Foreign Office will take the same view as he. . . . I should like . . . to mention the question of signature incidentally to Grey, and in doing so to take the line that I am personally very anxious to bring our treaty to a final conclusion, so as to have a positive achievement to my credit in this special sphere.[34]

The British withdrawal was a great relief to Jagow. He did not understand what was afoot, but Grey's action helped him off the horns of a dilemma, for against his better judgment he had reluctantly come to conclusion that publication was necessary in order to protect German businessmen looking for concessions in the Portuguese colonies. At the end of March he had decided to proceed with the signature. He wished but a slight delay in publication for the Anglo-German treaty and a longer one for the Anglo-Portuguese treaty of 1899. When Grey refused to accept these conditions, saying he was under obligation to his party to eschew all secret agreements, Jagow was willing to let it stand at that. He took the position that the initialing of the agreement had created a moral obligation and felt safe in this assumption when Goschen assured him that London would consult Berlin before making agreements with other parties concerning the territory affected by their abortive treaty. Regarding the matter as temporarily closed, Jagow instructed Lichnowsky to refrain from all further initiative.[35]

It was difficult for Lichnowsky to give up an agreement so painfully achieved. He found himself discussing the treaty at a chance meeting with colonial secretary Harcourt at a dinner at the end of May. Harcourt favored the agreement, and complained to Lichnowsky that the present inconclusiveness had left British businessmen in a quandary. As no one knew where the boundaries were, the initialed treaty was no better than no agreement at all; and, what was worse, it would not be binding on a new government if the present one should be forced to resign. The alternative, said Harcourt, was to return to the old treaty or sign the new one and publish them both together with the treaty of 1899. Reporting this conversation to Berlin, Lichnowsky took the opportunity to renew his arguments in favor of signing the treaty. The agreement with Portugal that England had signed in 1899 merely reaffirmed existing commitments, he said, and the Anglo-German agreements, though they envisaged partition, could not possibly take the form of outright annexation. Of course the German nationalistic papers would condemn the treaty, as they were opposed to all diplomatic bargaining with England, but "the fear-mongering about public opinion," he suggested, "might go a little too far" since everyone knew that the Wilhelmstrasse's influence on the press was extremely powerful.[36]

This criticism was bound to infuriate Berlin. They had never been able to convince Lichnowsky that he ought to heed what they referred to as German public opinion. In an outburst to Goschen two months earlier, Jagow said that "Lichnowsky never took enough account of public opinion in Germany; he talked of British public opinion and said 'you mustn't do this and you mustn't do that because it will upset public opinion in England,' but he never seemed to trouble himself about what was thought in Germany. If he was sitting here, or if he was chancellor, which he never will be, he would soon realize the strength of German public opinion and change his tone."[37]

As a reply to the report on the discussion with Harcourt, Berlin sent Lichnowsky a severe reprimand. Although it was signed by Bethmann, it was prepared by Stumm, and could not have been more insulting in tone. It dripped with Stumm's characteristic sarcasm. In opening the colonial question with Harcourt the prince had obviously disobeyed his instructions. But what was worse was that the prince had failed to point out to the colonial secretary that the latter's view of the treaty's status was the opposite of that held by his government (which Berlin knew from discussions with Goschen). The prince had meddled in a matter that had been solved to everyone's satisfaction, and it would be embarrassing if, as a result of his meddling, London would retro-spectively adopt Harcourt's view of the treaty. If, therefore, Grey were to renew discussion of the colonial question, Lichnowsky was to tell him that the Imperial government considered the ques-tion of publication settled. He was to say that he had no further instructions on this matter, and he should request Grey to com-municate any new views or proposals to the German chancellor directly through the British ambassador in Berlin.[38]

Under the circumstances, Lichnowsky's reply to this rebuke must be considered exceptionally restrained. He informed Beth-mann that it was not he who had broached the problem of pub-lication. Having, in a casual discussion, merely touched upon the question of the treaty's validity, he thought that Harcourt's opinions on this matter would be of interest. The information Berlin had sent him would not have enabled him to demon-strate to the colonial secretary that the British government re-garded the abortive treaty as binding. He doubted whether Goschen had so reported the British view: his own impression was that although the British considered themselves bound to sign the treaty whenever the Germans were ready to accept the con-ditions—that is, the publication—they did not consider themselves bound by the terms of the treaty itself. Berlin should be pleased, the prince thought, that he had ascertained the British govern-ment's real view. In closing his reply the prince wished to point out that the instruction to refer all British initiatives on the colonial question directly to Berlin was one which he was unable to reconcile with the obligations of his office.[39]

The outcome was ironical; Bethmann's rebuke was followed within a week by another reversal of German policy. Stumm had come around to Lichnowsky's point of view. The reason for this may be that German entrepreneurs had developed promising new affairs in the Portuguese colonies. At the end of May, German interests had acquired control of the Nyassa Company, a syndi-cate exploiting the northern part of Mozambique, and a German railroad consortium had recently dispatched a surveying team to Angola. In any case, early in June Berlin decided after all that the treaties should be published. Taking stock in a letter to Jagow of his past objections, Stumm would raise no further ob-stacles, as he did not wish to be held responsible for having lost the "Eldorado." When Lichnowsky was in Berlin in June, Berlin agreed to accept the British wishes, and on 27 July Bethmann authorized Lichnowsky to proceed with the signature. The chancellor asked only that the British agree to postpone publication until the German entrepreneurs had obtained the concession for a rail line in southern Angola or promise to intervene on their behalf with the Portuguese government.[40]

All through July 1914 Jagow and Stumm took a curious position. Although they had accepted the treaty itself and the condition of publication, they brought forth new objections that amounted to an attack upon the very idea of a colonial agreement. It would seem apparent that they wished to protect themselves against the criticism they expected when the treaty was published. Commenting on a memorandum by Rosen, who urged the chancellor to sign the agreement, Stumm argued that the advantages would accrue not to Germany but to England. London had initiated the colonial discussions, he said, in order to appease the liberal left wing, which objected to the Cabinet's hostile policy toward Germany during the 1911 Moroccan crisis, and Germany had "no interest in robbing the English government of the opposition in its own camp." He still doubted whether the plan for partition could ever be effected. Jagow was equally pessimistic in his final letter to Lichnowsky on 27 July. He announced that Bethmann's authorization was on its way and washed his hands of all responsibility. He renewed all his arguments against the treaties and admitted that he considered the old one a much more favorable instrument than the new. In the draft of this letter he first suggested that the prince think it all over again. "You have got your way," he wrote, "and you will carry the full responsibility." This he changed in the final version to read, "We have given in to your wish, but because of that you now bear a special share of the responsibility."[41]

The German decision to accept full publicity, had it been communicated to London, would have thrown the British into a quandary. By July the Foreign Office had unanimously come to the conclusion that the new treaty had no validity. That is, Lichnowsky had correctly interpreted the English position while Stumm and Jagow had indulged in wishful thinking. For the sake of clarity the British now wished their relations with Germany as to spheres of interest in the Portuguese colonies to be governed by the agreement of 1898, and they were prepared to inform the German government when the occasion arose that the new agreement was invalid because the German government had refused to accept the condition of full publicity. Faced with German acceptance of this condition, they would have had to decide whether they should sign the treaty and ignore the objections of their ally. This quandary they were spared by the outbreak of the war.[42]

The Anglo-German effort to renew their agreement on the partition of the Portuguese colonies had failed because the German Foreign Ministry hesitated too long to sign the treaty and permit its publication. It was not until March 1914 that Berlin decided to accept publication of that treaty and the Anglo-Portuguese treaty of 1899. By that time Grey's interest in the object had faded. In 1911 he had felt pressed to demonstrate that he could reach an understanding with Germany while sidetracking German energies to areas outside Europe. He hoped to appease German thirsts and achieve a cutback in German naval construction. But early in 1914, when the French announced their objections, a demonstration of friendship with Germany was not his foremost concern. The international situation was murky. Russia had grown active again in Persia, and though the tsar had requested of England an agreement to coordinate their naval action in the event of war with Germany, Crowe (for one) felt that a sudden diplomatic reversal that placed Russia on Germany's side was not unthinkable.[43] England could not endanger existing arrangements for an agreement with the Germans that the Germans did not seem eager to conclude.

Lichnowsky blamed the failure of the colonial convention on Wilhelm von Stumm, and not entirely without reason. Although it is impossible to reconstruct the course of business within the German Foreign Ministry on this question, it is obvious that the treaty could have been signed and promulgated if Stumm had given the project his full support. We have noted that he seemed to doubt the treaty's intrinsic value and to fear the effect of publication on German public opinion. These were pretexts, Lichnowsky believed, and he wrote in *My London Mission* that "the treaty was dropped because it would have been a public

success for me."[44] The German stand on publication was inconsistent, as we have seen. Although Stumm and Jagow maintained that the treaties were unacceptable to the public (or an
opinionated part of it) and must therefore be kept secret, they
finally agreed to publication because they realized that this is
what public opinion would demand. (The fact that negotiations
were going on was no secret, and if the arrangements regarding
spheres of interest were to have any practical effect they would
have to be divulged to the business and financial community.)
The personal element in Stumm's motivation is hard to measure,
but that it existed is beyond doubt. We have seen examples of
the instructions Stumm sent Lichnowsky ignoring facts and in-
venting difficulties and seemingly intent upon humiliating the
recipient.

Lichnowsky regretted the slow progress on the Portuguese
colonial convention because he regarded that treaty as partner to
the agreement that Germany and England were able to reach on the
complex of problems generally known as the Baghdad Railway
question. The contention over the railway had a longer history than the negotiations on the Portuguese colonies. The problem had begun with the extension of German influence into
Mesopotamia through the construction of the German-sponsored
railroad to Baghdad. The Germans had been able to reach a satisfactory agreement on spheres of influence with the French and
Russians but not with the English, who were concerned by the
prospective continuation of the railway on to the Persian Gulf.
The Germans had made arrangements to build the railway to
Kuwait, which lay in an established British sphere of influence,
but in 1911 gave up their concession to the Turks on the condition that they be allowed to participate in any construction on
the stretch down to the gulf. It was this promise, which came up
during negotiations between the Turks and British early in 1913,
that led to detailed discussions with the Germans.[45]

Lichnowsky experienced no difficulties worthy of mention in
working with Berlin on the Baghdad Railway question. The advantages of an agreement here were obvious to all. Besides, since
Marschall died the Wilhelmstrasse knew little about the tech-
nicalities involved and relied upon proposals made by the bank-
ers Karl Helfferich and Arthur von Gwinner. Usually it was

Zimmermann who drafted the dispatches to London, where usually it was not Lichnowsky but Kühlmann, who had been involved in the negotiations for years, who carried the proposals to the British.[46] The talks were brought to a successful conclusion in June 1914. The British promised no further obstruction in the financing and running of the railway; the line was to be extended to Basra, and traffic from there to the Gulf on the Shatt-el-Arab would be controlled by an international commission. To Lichnowsky this success was entirely gratifying. As on the question of the Portuguese colonies, an area of friction was eliminated, and Germany was taking advantage of British willingness to help her find a place in the sun. "If both treaties were executed and published," he wrote in *My London Mission*, "an agreement with England would be reached which would preclude all doubts about the possibility of 'Anglo-German co-operation.' "[47]

Lichnowsky recognized that the naval question was the most delicate of all. But it never formed part of his agenda. He believed the British would become reconciled with the German fleet as it then existed, and he refused to interrupt the promising discussions on colonial matters in order to debate a question for which there seemed to be no solution but time.[48] As it happened, the German government presented no further naval bills to the Reichstag while Lichnowsky was in London. The military expenditures decided upon at the end of 1912 had left no money for increased naval construction, and the German fleet continued to grow in accordance with the plan of 1912.

The removal of the fleet from the list of open questions was welcome in Germany. Tirpitz insisted that the British had no business telling Germany what to do with her own ships, and the Wilhelmstrasse was prepared to ignore the political aspect of the fleet bills and let them be treated from a mere technical standpoint. Jagow thought that his appearance in the Reichstag during the discussions of the naval budget early in 1913 would lend to the question a highly political quality it would be better to avoid.[49]

Of course, as Lichnowsky realized, naval construction would continue to influence Anglo-German relations. As long as the building went on and the two nations were concerned about their

comparative strength, the problem was there, implicit in diplomacy. In 1913 there were two opportunities to renew the naval
discussions of 1912. The first arose in February when members of
the Reichstag budget committee asked Tirpitz whether he would
agree to an Anglo-German dreadnought ratio of 16:10 as proposed by Churchill the year before. Tirpitz said that the ratio
was acceptable but should be applied not to single ships but to
the number of squadrons of eight battleships apiece, with a total
of five German and eight British squadrons.[50] Jagow, who had
appeared at the budget committee discussions and had spoken of
the recently improved relations with England, asking that
nothing be done to disturb them, said that the Foreign Ministry
had no objections to the proposed ratio.[51] Here it was once more
apparent that German foreign policy suffered from a strategical
division. For Tirpitz's answer had amounted to a new formula
for Anglo-German relations. He had made his move on his own
account and his purpose remained obscure to the state secretary
for foreign affairs. We have the remnant of a letter to Lichnowsky at Easter 1913 in which Jagow speaks of Tirpitz. "What
Tirpitz had in mind with his 10:16 statement is still not absolutely clear to me. But he is certainly not entirely candid. . . . It is
possible that he has got the scent of rapprochement with England
and wants to turn it to his own advantage."[52]

The British authorities refused to enter into discussions on
Tirpitz's 10:16 formula. While British public opinion was on the
whole receptive, and the Foreign Policy Committee of the House
of Commons, an unofficial collection of members who opposed
Grey's allegedly antagonistic policy toward Germany, expressed
in a letter to the *Times* their gratification at Tirpitz's and
Jagow's statements in the Reichstag,[53] the cabinet itself made no
move. The Foreign Office, the diplomats, and the naval attaché
in Berlin were schooled in Tirpitz's ways and again suspected his
motives. "Tirpitz is a sly dog . . . and not the bluff sailor he posed
as being in the Budget Committee," wrote Goschen to Nicolson.[54] In his first dispatch on Tirpitz's statement, on 10 February
1913, Goschen wrote that Tirpitz "knows perfectly well that public attention is for the moment concentrated on the army and
that as regards the navy he will have to mark time for a period
of which he cannot foresee the extent. Under the circumstances

it would be perfectly natural that he would hope that Great Britain might be induced to mark time also, and abstain from taking advantage of what might appear to be the psychological moment for forging ahead.''[55] Grey determined therefore not to broach the subject with Lichnowsky and to say to him, if he brought it up, that the statements made during the proceedings of the Budget Committee would have a favorable effect upon the tone of Churchill's statement in Parliament. He instructed Goschen to say the same thing if Jagow should refer to the matter.[56]

A second opportunity for renewing naval discussions arose when Churchill in his March 1913 speech on the British naval budget proposed a complete moratorium of one year on all naval construction—a naval holiday. Churchill made a more concrete proposal in a campaign speech in October, when he suggested that during the moratorium (which he realized would have to be extended to all the powers) Germany refrain from building two dreadnoughts and England four. He presented these more specific proposals to appease the opponents of naval armament within his own party, as he now realized that the Germans would not accept his moratorium. While Bethmann in April, for the sake of his friendly policy toward England, had publicly stated that Germany would welcome concrete proposals, Churchill had encountered much skepticism from Lichnowsky as well as the naval attaché Müller. In a comment on Müller's report of a conversation with Churchill, Lichnowsky offered to let Grey know that the German government would be pleased if Churchill did not refer to the holiday again. Lichnowsky believed that the less the two countries discussed the naval question the better their relations would be. The records do not show that Lichnowsky actually made this démarche, though he was informed of the kaiser's assent to the suggestion. But the kaiser himself told the British naval attaché that he hoped there would be no further reference to the holiday, for if there were he could not vouch for the state of opinion in Germany.[57]

The effect of the German response, however well meant on the part of Bethmann and Lichnowsky, was to confirm the British cabinet's suspicion of the German leaders. Churchill, upon receiving the report of Wilhelm's statement to naval attaché Hugh

Watson, commented that the "German government cannot expect to enjoy the advantages of saying in public that they 'await proposals' and of saying confidentially that they will resent it if they are made."[58] The German government in fact never admitted its prima facie rejection of the moratorium. In February 1914 Tirpitz, once again before the budget committee of the Reichstag, said that he could not regard statements made in a campaign speech as an official proposal, but a holiday as suggested by Churchill was not feasible for Germany as it would disrupt the entire work schedule but not, in the long run, reduce the fleet. Germany would, however, receive with good will any positive proposals.[59]

Grey, now expecting Parliament to ask why the government had not made any proposals, wrote Goschen to ascertain exactly what Tirpitz meant and how British proposals would be received in Germany. Goschen concluded from Tirpitz's remarks that the German government regarded a naval holiday as impracticable, and he wrote Nicolson that Jagow had told him that "the idea is Utopian and unworkable, and because the conditions are so different here from what they are in England."[60]

Crowe's minute on Goschen's report gives an extreme but revealing British view of the difficulties of dealing with the German authorities on the naval question: "The German Government continues to speak with two tongues. I feel confident that if we make a 'definite proposal' we shall not be treated straightforwardly in the negotiation, and I regard any such negotiation with so unscrupulous an adversary as highly dangerous."[61]

Lichnowsky hoped to maintain good relations with Tirpitz and the naval attaché, Capt. Erich von Müller, who had replaced Widenmann in the summer of 1912, for no part of the naval question was to interfere with his mission in London. He agreed with Tirpitz, whom he visited before leaving Berlin, that the fleet was a political factor and that accordingly any naval agreement with England must entail mutual concessions. But he would not commit himself to support an increase in the size of the fleet. Although he told Müller that he would not be as rigid as his predecessor, the captain must turn to him should he desire to report anything of a political character concerning the navies. One-half year after Lichnowsky's arrival in London, Müller

Chateau at Grätz, Austrian Silesia, watercolor by Rudolf Alt, 1844

Chateau at Kuchelna, about 1926

Prince Lichnowsky, 1889

Wedding portrait, Prince and Princess Lichnowsky, 1904

Count Benckendorff, Russian ambassador in London and
Prince Lichnowsky's cousin, caricature by Spy

Cheers for 𝔐𝔞𝔯𝔰𝔠𝔥𝔞𝔩𝔩

"There is no end to these hostile acts on the part of Germany. Now they are even sending us their most competent diplomat" (from *Simplicissimus*, 27 May 1912). From left to right: Marschall, Grey, Lansdowne, and Haldane.

Shooting party for Kaiser Wilhelm II at Grätz, August 1913. Second from left, Mechtilde Lichnowsky; next, the kaiser; then Lichnowsky's sister, Countess Redern; Lichnowsky is third from the right.

Prince Lichnowsky, portrait by Willy Geiger, 1916

Mechtilde Lichnowsky, about 1919

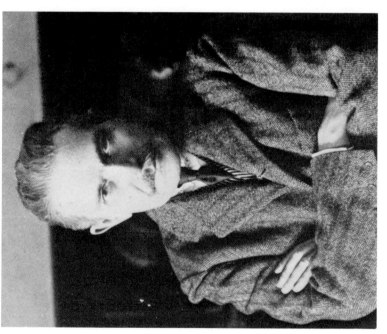

Prince Lichnowsky, April 1920

wrote Tirpitz that personally he was on the very best terms with Lichnowsky. The ambassador's squeamishness about political matters in the attachés' reports he attributed to fear of trouble with the Wilhelmstrasse, which had criticized the prince's public speeches about Anglo-German relations. The prince told him and the military attaché that the very word "politics" in their reports disturbed the Foreign Ministry. Knowing that the prince wished to avoid the naval question, Müller tried to elicit from him a written statement opposing a naval agreement. But the prince, commenting on a report by Müller, wrote that Berlin should respond to any proposal for discussions about an agreement with "cautious reserve." Müller had hoped he would say, "polite rejection."[62]

However he might try, it was not possible for Lichnowsky to avoid a clash with the navalists. Müller shared the naval prejudice against pen-and-ink diplomacy. He paid no attention to Lichnowsky's instructions about political reporting and wrote as venomously of the English as Widenmann had. In February 1914 Jagow urged Lichnowsky to try to restrain the naval attaché. "This eternal incitation and these suspicions of English policy are extremely troublesome," he wrote, "especially because they used *en haut lieu* as arguments against me."[63] Müller had no respect for the prince personally and wrote the Naval Ministry that the prince was a man who disliked detailed work but was willing to take credit for the labors of others.[64] Lichnowsky was aware of his naval attaché's opinion of him, though his official reports from 1912 to 1914 give little indication of direct and personal conflict with Müller. But in 1917 he wrote Harden that Müller "had not been a pleasant element—very Pan-German, *Tageszeitung*."[65]

Although Lichnowsky would not agree with Metternich that the naval competition would inevitably result in war, he was convinced that Germany should build no more ships than the current bill projected. While the fleet was not the primary cause of Britain's adherence to the Entente, as he wrote Bethmann, "the development of our sea power has doubtless not only fostered in England the wish to live at peace with us but also stimulated her to recognize the fact that it is in her interest to support the group opposed to us."[66] When he heard in May 1914 that Tirpitz might request authority to enlarge the existing program, he wrote Jagow that "anything provided for in the navy bill, anything in fact that does not represent some new additional item, will be accepted calmly here. We must stick to that. New demands in the form of a supplementary bill would, however, produce restiveness and bad feeling among those in authority here and would be likely to undo all that we have latterly achieved."[67]

In his views on policy toward England Lichnowsky seemed to be closer to Bethmann than to the kaiser or Tirpitz. The chancellor had a less jaundiced view of the English and a more flexible attitude toward the fleet. He agreed with Lichnowsky that the way to achieve an understanding was to negotiate solutions of individual questions, as France had done in working toward the Entente Cordiale. And their policy met with success. Between Lichnowsky's arrival in London in November 1912 and the spring of 1914, Anglo-German relations gave the appearance of distinct improvement. No fleet bills, no indiscreet outpourings by the kaiser, no encounters in Asia or Africa ruffled the smooth surface of official exchange. Agreement on division of the Portuguese colonies and on the Baghdad Railway seemed within reach. And Lichnowsky's efforts to be reasonable and friendly had greatly improved the atmosphere.

But as to the purpose of the détente Lichnowsky was separated from Bethmann by as great a gulf as he was from Tirpitz and the kaiser. Lichnowsky thought of the Anglo-German rapprochement as leading to a general European understanding that would make all alliances unnecessary. Bethmann imagined a great problem-solving reordering of power relations on the Continent to Germany's benefit. Perhaps this was possible through an arrangement with Russia; more likely, however, through an agreement with England—an alliance or a guarantee of English neutrality in a Continental war. Lichnowsky knew that Berlin continued to entertain such hopes and summarized his disappointment in a letter to Jagow on 7 March 1914:

As I have reported over and over again [he wrote], the British government is anxious to live on good terms with us no less than with France. The rapprochement with us has been greeted with lively satisfaction by most English politicians and particularly by the business world. London does not, however, desire the improvement in our relations to take place at the expense of the Entente with France. . . . For we need have no doubt that if [Grey] is faced with the choice, he will decide for France, just as we, if we had to choose between Austria and Russia, would decide for the former. The maintenance of France intact is just as much a political necessity for England as that of Austria-Hungary for us, and she would therefore, as I should like again to emphasize, under all circumstances take France under her wing in the event of a war between that country and ourselves. To my extreme regret this fact is still held in doubt despite my repeated and thorough elucidation of this important point.[68]

The differences in political conception were connected with a conflict in character. Personally Lichnowsky and Bethmann were antitheses: Bethmann was a *Grübler* who was of several minds about things but determined and immovable once his mind was made up; the prince was lively, expansive, and optimistic; and if he was, as was often said, impressionable, by the same token he was open to suggestion and accessible to argument and fact. Not since Eulenburg and Bülow were ambassadors in Vienna and Rome in the 1890s, had the German diplomatic corps known such a self-assured and personally conspicuous ambassador. Lichnowsky had his own opinion about policy, which he outlined in his dispatches; he presumed to argue with decisions made at home, he urged the gentlemen to speak up when (as on the Portuguese colonial negotiations) they moved too slowly; and, besides, the kaiser seemed deeply impressed by Lichnowsky's dazzling social position in London. For a good while Wilhelm was a buffer between Lichnowsky and the Wilhelmstrasse, and gave him (it seems) the recognition his colleagues withheld from him. When he was home on extended leave in the late summer and early fall of 1913, the kaiser had him to lunch and awarded him the Prussian order of the Red Eagle.[69]

There was talk that the kaiser would appoint Lichnowsky chancellor.[70] This seemed to have begun early in Lichnowsky's career as ambassador but reached its peak at the beginning of 1914. "They are still talking here about new chancellors: Tirpitz, Schorlemer and Lichnowsky," said Lerchenfeld in a report from the Bavarian legation in January. There was no enthusiasm for any of these, said Lerchenfeld, adding that Lichnowsky "is not a speaker and doesn't have the energy required of a prime minister."[71] In February there was an article in a provincial newspaper, the *Geraer-Zeitung*, headlined, "Fear of the Man of the Future." It was intended as a reply to the description of Lichnowsky by the *Deutsche Tageszeitung* as a "democratic unitarian." These Pan-Germans had concluded invidiously from a speech the prince had given to the assembled German community in London on the occasion of the kaiser's birthday that he would prefer to abolish the German federal system and replace it with a centralized parliamentary state. According to the *Geraer-Zeitung*, the purpose of this attack was to influence the kaiser against his ambassador. "Prince Lichnowsky," said the newspaper, "was thought by many to be the coming chancellor. He belongs to Bülow's intimate circle, and it is said that he shares the former chancellor's views on state policy."[72] There seems to have been little chance that the kaiser would force Bethmann out and appoint Lichnowsky in his place. But under the best of circumstances this talk would have complicated Lichnowsky's relationship with his chief, and all the more so if, as many leading politicians believed, Bethmann so desired to remain in office that he would subordinate public policy to that end.[73]

It is well to wonder why the prince ignored the signs of trouble and remained at his post. The key to the answer lies in his responsive and optimistic character. Was he not personally a vital force behind the steady and obvious improvement in Anglo-German relations? He thought he had achieved the peak of recognition when at Oxford University on 3 June 1914 he was dressed in the red gown and awarded an honorary doctorate. The Public Orator, who led him in and delivered a long speech in Latin, announced in ringing tones: *Totam Germaniam animo salutamus.* "For a moment one had the feeling," wrote the *Berliner Tageblatt*, "that an ambassador could really form a link between the two nations." That evening Lichnowsky addressed the German Literary Society and the Anglo-German Club. Once more he gave voice to his hope for an imperial partnership between Germany and England. "Cecil Rhodes," he said, "was of the opinion that the whole of humanity would be best served if the Teutonic peoples were brought nearer together and would join hands for the purpose of spreading their civilization to distant regions."[74]

This happy prospect outweighed the deplorable tendencies he perceived and made the personal stings seem of less consequence. How much the unfair rebukes touched him we know only from his later reflections. In *My London Mission* he wrote that the instructions he received regarding his discussion with Harcourt at the end of May 1914 showed more emotion than civility. "I now regret," he said, "that I did not immediately go to Berlin and place my post at the disposal of the monarch. That I still continued to have some faith in the possibility of arriving at an understanding with those in authority was a sinister mistake which was to take its revenge a few months later in a most tragic manner."[75]

Chapter VI

Into the Abyss

Bethmann, Jagow and Stumm, these split personalities, were compelled to show to themselves as to others
the proof of their strong will, like the neurasthenic
climbing the Matterhorn. In order to transcend the
clefts in their own natures, they pursued their goal
with methodical persistence. Is it not usually the
vacillators who, suddenly, without themselves knowing what they are doing, make the great leap, the
leap in the dark?

Theodor Wolff, *Der Krieg des Pontius Pilatus*, 1934

Lichnowsky quivering like an aspen, appreciating
only the English view, without character or dignity.

Riezler Diary, August 1914

Lichnowsky spent Christmas 1913 at home. He was back in London in January and did not return to Germany until late June
1914 when he attended the Kiel week, and where on the kaiser's
yacht *Meteor* he heard the news of Franz Ferdinand's assassination.[1] Up to that moment he had remained optimistic about the
future course of events. In his opinion France and Russia had no
warlike intentions toward Germany, and if Germany's policy remained peaceful the other Powers would follow suit. "When one
of my staff returned from leave in Vienna in the spring of 1914,
he said that Herr von Tschirschky had declared that there would
soon be war," the prince later wrote. "As I, however, was always
left in ignorance about important events, I considered this pessimism to be unfounded."[2]

Lichnowsky meant that he had not been kept informed of
Berlin's plans and calculations and could not know what dangerous moves were in the offing. But the record of early 1914
shows that he was much disturbed by the general tension in
Europe, and most particularly by the decline in relations with

Russia that set in at the conclusion of the Balkan Wars. The military increases Germany adopted at the end of 1912 induced countervailing efforts in France and Russia. In the summer of 1913 Berlin assigned General Liman von Sanders to the task of rebuilding the shattered Turkish army. "I have never seen the Russians so excited," said Grey to Lichnowsky when in December Liman and his mission appeared in Constantinople.[3]

Lichnowsky feared that the Russo-German tension would impair relations with England. In March 1914 an article in the *Kölnische Zeitung* accusing the Russians of expansionist plans evoked angry rejoinders in the Russian press to which the Germans replied in kind. "If our leading newspapers continue to write in the bullying tone they have fallen into of late," he wrote Berlin, reporting the uneasiness he had observed in London, "everything that has been achieved in the direction of an improvement in Anglo-German relations will very soon be scattered to the winds, and no personal influence of any kind whatever will then be able to prevent British statesmen from becoming closer friends than ever with France and Russia. Distrust of our foreign policy and of the sincerity of our will for peace cannot but once more lead to an alienation of the two peoples."[4]

Lichnowsky's warning was prophetic. As the tension grew, France and Russia tried to induce England to extend her military commitments. Secret talks between French and British military authorities begun in 1906 had produced plans for British aid on land, and in 1912 it was arranged that England might concentrate her naval forces in the North Sea and France hers in the Mediterranean. These agreements were so formulated as not to bind England to any definite course of action should France be involved in a war. In April 1914 Tsar Nicholas II suggested that England conclude similar naval arrangements with Russia.[5] In the past Grey's Foreign Office had resisted all temptation to enlarge the scope of their entente with a country so abhorrent to liberal opinion. In the spring of 1914, however, it seemed necessary to meet the Russians halfway. There were some who feared that Russia, if spurned by England, would turn to Germany. "If and when Austria breaks up," noted Sir Eyre Crowe, "Germany and Russia will be brought very close together, for both will prefer a peaceable division of their heritage to fighting over it, and the result may easily be a Russo-German alliance: 'Barkis is always willin'!'"[6] At the end of April, therefore, after a state visit in Paris where Grey consulted both French and Russians, the foreign secretary secretly agreed that British naval authorities should begin conversations with their Russian counterparts to prepare a plan for wartime cooperation. At the end of May the Russians presented their agenda. In addition to cooperation on technical matters, they requested the assignment of British transport vessels to carry Russian troops to the German Baltic shores.[7]

However alarming this prospect was to the Germans, it afforded Berlin an unexpected advantage. The correspondence that Siebert was smuggling out of the Russian embassy enabled Berlin to follow step by step the development of the Franco-Russian effort to entangle England in their alliance. As they watched the naval plans take shape, they devised a démarche of their own. Since the failure of the Haldane mission in 1912, Anglo-German exchanges had shifted to economic and colonial questions and avoided efforts to concoct an explicitly political formula. Now it seemed possible to force the resumption of serious political talks, to test England's commitment to France and Russia, and intensify the effort to reduce the Entente's potential.

Berlin's campaign proceeded on both public and diplomatic levels. First the Germans attempted to engage the British public in the issue. In order to publicize the secret intelligence, Stumm solicited the assistance of an impeccably pro-English and peace-loving journalist, Theodor Wolff. As a result, the 23 May issue of the *Berliner Tageblatt* carried an accurate history of the Entente's recent naval conversations. To protect Berlin's source, Wolff pretended that he had acquired his information from a friend in Paris (where he had spent thirteen years as a correspondent). His friend opined that the aim of the naval discussions was to transform the Entente into a three-power alliance so as to frustrate England's rapprochement with Germany. On 2 June Wolff published a second article appealing directly to the English liberals. He said that it was the liberals who were to be credited for the recent improvement in Anglo-German relations, and he bid them see that the proposed naval convention would destroy all they had achieved.[8]

Wolff's intervention had its expected effect. "A mischievous article," wrote Crowe on the dispatch that forwarded the clipping from Berlin. "The old theme," he said of Wolff's second article. "Germany may have allies, and make military and naval concoctions with them. England mustn't."[9] In Parliament Grey was asked whether negotiations such as those described in the press were actually going on or being planned. Taking refuge behind the careful wording of the agreements with France, which would eventually also apply to Russia, he replied: "No such negotiations are in progress, and none are likely to be entered upon so far as I can judge."[10]

The time had now come for the official démarche. On 16 June Bethmann dispatched a long summary of the international situation which Lichnowsky was to convey to the foreign secretary. Seldom had the chancellor been more pompous. He wished to remind Grey that it had fallen to their governments to work in unison to prevent European tensions from deteriorating into war. Recent developments, however, would seem to inhibit this solemn mission. In his own country it had happened that many persons whose views normally were moderate came to agree with the militarists and Pan-Germans that Russia was preparing to attack Germany—and unfortunately this was also the kaiser's opinion. Though he himself would not attribute any aggressive intentions to Saint Petersburg, he was quite convinced that in the event of another Balkan crisis the Russians would take advantage of their improved armaments to assert themselves more forcefully than on previous occasions. If the Anglo-German mission were obstructed, the most insignificant conflict of interest between Austria and Russia "could ignite the torch of war." And thus it was most gratifying that Sir Edward had categorically denied the rumors of a secret Anglo-Russian naval convention. For such an occurrence would not only stimulate French and Russian chauvinism and poison the German nation's attitude toward England but in a period of tension such as the present have consequences that one could not easily foresee.[11]

Lichnowsky transmitted this message to Grey in a discussion on 24 June. Grey politely deflected the chancellor's advance. He doubtless recognized the threat implied in Bethmann's words. But he could not admit what he had denied to Parliament nor suddenly reverse the agreement with Russia. He told Lichnowsky that he too hoped that Germany and England would continue to remain in close touch. He admitted that the Russians wished to strengthen the Entente—but only because the Triple Alliance was so well organized. And while he consulted his Entente partners on all important questions, he had concluded with them no secret agreements.[12]

The prince accepted this explanation. He could not attach the importance Bethmann did to the rumors of a naval convention. He did not know about the secret information, and he was not aware to what extent pessimism had spread through Berlin. It was enough for him to understand the motives of British policy. He was convinced that with or without a treaty British forces would go into action if the Germans threatened to annihilate France. But the British would not enter into conventions that bound them in advance to a prescribed course of action and robbed them of their freedom of decision. This fundamental point he had had to repeat once more on 10 May while answering a dispatch from Stumm, who had doubted that England must intervene in a war on the side of France.[13] As to the rumors of a naval convention, which he took note of for the first time on 10 June, the prince said that if military and naval understandings did exist, they were not binding unless accompanied by firm political agreements. Besides, the Russians needed no encouragement to go on building up their fleet, and for the moment they could offer the British no assistance of any value. He guessed that the Russians may have started the rumors in order to create the impression that something important had been accomplished during the king's visit in Paris.[14]

While Grey's denial was acceptable to Lichnowsky, it was a disappointment for Berlin. The tension between Germany and France and Russia had not abated as the spring of 1914 passed into summer. In May Chief of Staff Moltke, riding with Jagow in a railway carriage, urged the foreign secretary to prepare the diplomatic ground for a war against Russia and France. In June, the kaiser, at a private dinner, spoke to the banker Max Warburg of Russian preparations for war and wondered whether it was not better to start things now instead of waiting.[15] Vienna too was restive. Berchtold and his advisors had concluded that developments in the Balkans posed a serious threat to Austria's security.

They had intelligence that the French and the Russians were endeavoring to reconcile the Bulgarians with the Serbs and Rumanians, and supposed that this effort would succeed if Serbia were to give Bulgaria some of the land she had acquired in Macedonia. For this the Serbs would demand compensation in kind, which was possible only at the expense of Austria-Hungary. In order to thwart the Franco-Russian efforts, Vienna set about drafting a plan for a diplomatic campaign in which they hoped for German assistance.[16]

In this atmosphere the men in Berlin could not abandon the campaign they had started to take advantage of the Anglo-Russian naval talks. But it was necessary to bring Lichnowsky round to their point of view. After reading the prince's report of his conversation with Grey, Zimmermann, who was now undersecretary, commented that the prince

was completely taken in by Grey again (as was to be expected) and has reconfirmed his opinion that he is dealing with an honest, truth-loving statesman. There is nothing left to do but give Lichnowsky some indications (carefully chosen ones, of course) of the secret but absolutely reliable information from Saint Petersburg which leaves no doubts about the existence of permanent political and military arrangements between England and France and about present negotiations between England and Russia proceeding toward the same goal.[17]

It was on 27 June that Zimmerman made this notation, recommending for the first time that Berlin reveal to Lichnowsky a part of the Siebert intelligence. On 28 June the bullet of the Serb assassin cut down in the streets of Bosnian Sarajevo the Austrian crown prince Franz Ferdinand. The crisis brewing since the outbreak of the Balkan Wars now came to a boil. On 5 and 6 July a special Austrian mission met with German leaders in Berlin and presented the final draft of their plan for a diplomatic campaign to thwart Franco-Russian conspiracy in the Balkans. The Austrians also presented Wilhelm II a letter from Emperor Franz Joseph, who asserted that the work of peace was endangered so long as the "hotbed of criminal agitation in Belgrade continues unpunished."[18]

The Austrian proposals accorded perfectly with Berlin's mood. At a moment when everyone was impressed by Russia's growing strength, the assassination once more proclaimed Austria's weakness. But there was still time to redress the balance. Wilhelm and Bethmann both assured the Austrians that Germany would support any action against Serbia that Vienna considered necessary. Both chancellor and kaiser urged the Austrians to take advantage of the propitious moment and act swiftly. The kaiser said that if the Serbian involvement led to a war with Russia, Germany was prepared to meet her commitments under the alliance.[19]

It is Lichnowsky who best describes the atmosphere in which these decisions were made. On 29 June he had stopped in Berlin on his way to Silesia, and he called at the Wilhelmstrasse again on his way back to London on 5 July, which was the day the Austrians arrived with their proposals. Each time he spoke with both Bethmann and Zimmermann (who was acting for Jagow, who was on his honeymoon). The 29 June visit with Bethmann is described in an essay the prince dictated about thirty-five days later entitled "England before the War." "I explained to Herr von Bethmann," the prince stated there, "that I thought the foreign situation, as far as we were concerned, very satisfactory." Relations with England were cordial; France was governed by a pacifistic cabinet; and, he continued, "both the tsar and M. Sazonov desired peace."

The chancellor replied [Lichnowsky's report continued] that he could not share my optimistic views. The Russian armaments, concerning which the general staff had sent him a full report, were assuming proportions that could not but cause uneasiness in Germany. An increase of 900,000 men was being provided for, and in addition to this the Russians were building railways to our frontiers. Finally, he said he would tell me in confidence that, according to secret and reliable reports he had received, a naval agreement between Russia and England was being drawn up. This agreement provided that in case of war English freight steamers were to transport Russian troops to the coast of Pomerania.[20]

Later, Lichnowsky told his son that when during this visit he drew attention to the folly of Berlin's anti-Russian policy, Bethman peevishly asked him whether he wished to replace him as chancellor.[21]

Lichnowsky's conversations with Zimmermann and his Berlin visit of 5 July are described in *My London Mission*. "Zimmermann's language," the prince wrote,

betrayed unmistakable annoyance with Russia, a country which, he said, was everywhere in our way. There were also difficulties in economic policy. Of course I was not told that General von Moltke, chief of the general staff, was pressing for war; but I learned that Herr von Tschirschky had been reprimanded because he reported that he had counselled moderation in Vienna toward Serbia. On my return from Silesia to London I stopped only a few hours in Berlin, where I heard that Austria intended to take steps against Serbia in order to put an end to an impossible situation. I am sorry that at the moment I underestimated the importance of the news. I thought that nothing would come of it this time either and that matters could easily be settled, even if Russia became threatening. I now regret that I did not stay in Berlin and at once declare that I would not cooperate in a policy of this kind.[22]

Lichnowsky returned to London on 6 July, bearing new instructions from Bethmann. Having encouraged Austria to move against Serbia, Bethmann was obliged to intensify his pressure on Grey. He had already taken advantage of the reports of Anglo-Russian naval conversations to warn Grey that it was dangerous to encourage the Russians and neglect the Anglo-German mission of preserving the European peace. Now he wished to repeat these points more forcefully. Lichnowsky, upon his arrival in London, went directly to the Foreign Office. His representations to Grey were characteristically diplomatic. Within a general aperçu of the European situation he combined a gentle reference to the naval conversations with remarks on the assassination, emphasizing the possibility of acute tension between Vienna and Belgrade. "The ambassador went on to speak to me privately," wrote Grey in his report to Goschen, "but very seriously, as to the anxiety and pessimism he had found in Berlin. He explained that the murder of the archduke . . . had excited very strong anti-Serbian feeling in Austria; and he knew for a fact, though he did not know the details, that the Austrians intended to do something, and it was not impossible that they would take military action against Serbia." Berlin was concerned over Russia's military preparations and unfriendly attitude and feared that an Anglo-Russian naval agreement would inflame public opinion. Though the prince did not share the belief that Russia was ill-disposed toward Germany, Grey reported, "he was so anxious that he must speak to me immediately on his return here from Germany."[23]

Lichnowsky's anxiety was soon apparent in Berlin. Within a week of his return to London he had raised questions that forced Jagow in a series of dispatches to reveal all the fears and calculations that motivated Berlin's policy in the Austro-Serbian crisis. The exchange began with a dispatch from Jagow on 12 July. The foreign secretary told Lichnowsky that he must encourage the English press to take a strong stand against Serbia. He explained that as Austria might be forced to take drastic action against the Serbs (whose government was obviously implicated in the assassination), Germany would hope in the event of war to keep the conflict localized. When Lichnowsky replied that it was impossible to carry out his instructions because if Austria resorted to force, the British would all rally behind Serbia, Jagow attempted to make Berlin's motives absolutely clear. "This is a question of the highest political order," he wrote in a dispatch on the fifteenth,

since it is perhaps the last opportunity to attempt under relatively favorable circumstances to deal a death blow to Serbian expansionist ambitions. If Austria missed this opportunity she would forfeit her position of respect and become an even weaker element within our group. Since our policy cannot for the moment be reoriented, because of England's intimate relations with Russia, of which you are well aware, it is vitally important for us to maintain our Austrian ally's position as a world power.[24]

Lichnowsky answered this explanation without delay. In a long dispatch addressed to the chancellor on 16 July he rejected the fundamental assumption of the plan Jagow had outlined. Military chastisement of Serbia would create new problems but solve none of the old ones, he asserted. Jagow's phrase, "a death blow to Serbian expansionism," he assumed to mean that Serbia was to be conquered. That, in his opinion, would be an illusory victory. Although Serbia could conceivably be united with the Serbo-Croatian territories already under Habsburg rule to form the third autonomous region within the monarchy, the Hungarians would prevent that solution, and an attack upon Serbia would therefore have the negative result of reviving a question the Powers had just succeeded in laying to rest. Lichnowsky doubted, furthermore, that the anti-German sentiment in Russia was strong enough to force the government to make war on Germany—but he could not presume to judge how the Russians would react to an Austrian attack upon Serbia. While he recognized that the Austrian alliance was essential for Germany (if only for its sentimental value), "the real question," he maintained, "is whether it is wise for us to support our ally in this policy or to guarantee this policy, which, in my opinion, is an adventurous one since it will neither produce a radical solution of the problem nor destroy the Greater Serbia movement."[25]

Lichnowsky's initiative put Jagow in a quandary. The ambassador whose cooperation was essential to the German plan questioned it and doubted the feasibility of the tasks assigned to him. It was not easy to answer Lichnowsky's arguments, and Berlin would have to admit that it was prepared to run the risks the plan entailed. The private letter of 18 July in which Jagow answered Lichnowsky, elaborating upon his shorter statement of the fifteenth, reflects the thoughts of Bethmann Hollweg as we know them from the diary of Kurt Riezler. And it is reminiscent of the fears Holstein and Marschall expressed when Russia in 1895 seemed to threaten the Turkish Straits. Jagow admitted that Lichnowsky's remarks were, in the main, just. But the alliance with Austria, he said, was the primary and inescapable fact of life. "If your friends no longer please you, find others—if you can," said the humorist Wilhelm Busch. Austria was disintegrating, and Germany would eventually be forced to find some alternative arrangement; for the moment Germany had to sustain her ally and could not prevent her from taking advantage of an opportunity to recover her lost position. Austria must take action against Serbia, and Germany must take pains to insure that hostilities remained localized. This was possible if Germany and Austria remained firm toward Russia, for Russia was still not prepared for war. But if Russia should attack Austria nevertheless, Germany could not stand aside and let Austria be destroyed, for that would condemn Germany to isolation. Jagow asserted that Russia would soon be able to crush Germany, and (seeing the trend of his thought) added: "I do not desire a preventive war, but we dare not shirk the struggle if it comes upon us."[26]

For Lichnowsky these deliberations were much too theoretical. His reply on the twenty-third to Jagow's outline of the official position reminds one of the conclusion he reached in 1895 that Austria was a dependent power and had no choice but to follow Germany. He denied that Austria's weakness, or the old fear of Russia, or the possible hostility of the Entente (which Germany's policy had brought into being) were sufficient grounds for measures that so clearly courted the danger of war. He repeated that he accepted the special connection with Austria and desired no alliance with England or Russia. His point was that Berlin must not be misled by Austria's ambitions or illusions. Germany must be the leader and not the led—*der leitende, nicht aber der leidende Teil*. "What would you say if England or Russia were to encourage the French, in order to revive their seriously diminished prestige, to adopt an aggressive and dangerous foreign policy? France is forced to cling to England and Russia because of her relative weakness and fear of us. And the same thing is true of Austria. I should not say that Austria is a more tractable partner when she is weakened, but she certainly is when she is fearful." The prince asserted that Berlin must know that if Austria attacked Serbia it would be impossible to localize the conflict. And therefore Vienna's demands upon Belgrade must be acceptable and not be so phrased that they "must necessarily lead to war *ad majorem illustrissimi comitis de Berchtold gloriam*."[27]

There was no time for further discussion of this nature. On 28 July, when Lichnowsky's answer reached Berlin, Austria's ultimatum had been delivered in Belgrade and published in the European press. The severity of the Austrian demands came as no surprise to Lichnowsky. His Austrian colleagues in London had confirmed his fear that the Austro-German plan was to bring about a war with Serbia. When Bethmann instructed his ambassadors to deny Germany's responsibility for the ultimatum or its severity, the prince replied that Mensdorff had asserted that the ultimatum conformed to the desires of both Wilhelm II and Chancellor Bethmann. Mensdorff and his staff had maintained (as Lichnowsky testified in "England before the war") that the Austrian special mission in Berlin on 5 and 6 July had received a request for "very energetic action, and that both the kaiser and chancellor had declared that it wouldn't matter if that led to a war with Russia." On 28 July Lichnowsky reported that members of the Austrian embassy, upon hearing the news that Serbia had accepted the ultimatum, were stunned.[28]

This knowledge of the Austro-German plans placed Lichnowsky on the horns of a dilemma. For his duty was to represent Germany's interests, and Jagow had closed his letter of the eighteenth saying, "even if this exposition of our policy may not have convinced you, I know that you will nevertheless give it your support." In discussions with Grey the prince carried out his instructions faithfully, and skillfully. But he also undertook a private effort to prevent the outbreak of hostilities between Austria and Serbia. He sought out the Rumanian ambassador, Take Ionescu, an old friend, and beseeched him to have his government influence the Serbs to accept the Austrian demands without quibble. The ultimatum might be very severe indeed: but once the crisis was passed and the danger of war was over, the terms could be revised in Serbia's favor.[29] The prince also sought the assistance of his cousin Count Benckendorff. They were together at Lord Lansdowne's country home the weekend of the nineteenth. On 22 July Benckendorff wrote Saint Petersburg that his "ordinarily calm and judicious" cousin was at present in a state of great alarm. "I detest everything Austrian by family tradition" the prince said to him, "and because I know them well, that is, their faults." Lichnowsky seemed to fear that the Austrians were about to commit some grave error in Belgrade and intimated that Bethmann would not work for compromise as energetically as he had in the past. Imploring his cousin not to mention his name in his reports, Lichnowsky urged that Saint Petersburg take the initiative and offer its good offices to Vienna and Belgrade.[30]

Lichnowsky's concern was unique among the German ambassadors. He was the only German diplomat to raise objections to the chosen path or ask for clarification of instructions or to undertake any personal initiatives. Neither Schoen in Paris nor Pourtalès in Saint Petersburg saw fit to volunteer advice, and they reported only on matters that concerned the countries to which they were assigned. Such limitations were not recognized by Lich-

nowsky, who presumed that all questions bearing upon the crisis
were of concern to his office. His reports and forecast of events
beyond the Anglo-German sphere were remarkably accurate. He
informed Berlin after his discussion with Ionescu that Rumania
could not remain indifferent to the prospective disruption of the
Balkan status quo, and conveyed Ionescu's opinion that in the
event of an Austrian attack Russia would support Serbia with
military force. On 24 July he reported that the Foreign Office
believed Austria had seriously underestimated Serbia's power of
resistance and would bleed to death in a long and bitter struggle
(to which the kaiser remarked, "nonsense!"). On the twenty-
sixth the prince reported the Foreign Office's conviction that
Italy would not enter the war to help Austria (to which Zimmermann remarked: "Italy is of no concern to the ambassador!").[31]

Lichnowsky's activity stands in striking contrast to the lassitude
of Pourtalès, who bestirred himself only after the Austrians declared war. Pourtalès of course lacked the advantage of the inti-
mations Lichnowsky had received at the end of June. He received
no instructions at all until 21 July, when Bethmann prepared his
ambassadors at the Entente capitals for the Austrian ultimatum
by informing them that due to the probability of continued
provocation, Austria might find it necessary to exert strong pressure on the Serbian government or, indeed, resort to military
action. The ambassadors in their discussions with the host governments were to stress that it was a struggle between Austria and
Serbia alone and that the subversion emanating from Serbia was
a threat to the entire monarchical system. But Pourtalès had not
asked for guidance. It was not until 13 July that he sent his first
account of the Russian reaction to the assassination; on 23 July
he wrote that the strikes taking place in the Russian cities "could
cause difficulties for the government in case of external complications." Sazonov's policy he described as bluff. After the terms of
the Austrian ultimatum were published, he opined that Saint
Petersburg's wish to submit the Austro-Serbian dispute to arbitration indicated that Russia would not intervene immediately.[32]

It is doubtful whether a more penetrating analysis from Saint
Petersburg would have affected policy in Wilhelmstrasse. Berlin's
estimate of Russian intentions and capabilities was, at the least,
ambiguous. Some diplomats (Lichnowsky, for one) clung to the

traditional notion that Russia and Prussia were natural political partners because they had no natural conflicting interests; every international crisis since Bismarck's dismissal had suggested to Berlin the possibility of giving up the Austrian alliance and coming to an agreement with Russia. In the spring of 1914 such a reversal seemed quite possible to the English, who feared it and were concerned to prevent it. In the summer of 1914 a Russo-German agreement as the solution for the permanent crisis of the two blocs of powers also occurred to Bethmann. Sazonov had reportedly told the banker Robby Mendelssohn that if "Germany drops Austria, immediately afterwards I would drop France." Riezler noted in his diary on 23 July that Bethmann "seems to be reflecting upon such possibilities. It would be preferable to achieve some durable arrangement with Russia than an agreement with England."[33]

The notion of peaceful reconciliation with Russia was a fleeting thought: the prevailing view was that Russia must be forced to a showdown. This view consisted of several elements. Bethmann apparently did not trust the Russians to negotiate honestly from a position of equality; he feared that internal pressures including the revolutionary ferment would force Russia to adopt an aggressive Pan-Slavic policy; and while he accepted the military estimate of Russia's vast and growing strength, he seemed to think that Russia was not prepared for a serious military venture.[34] Thus it seems that when the Wilhelmstrasse in 1914 decided upon a showdown with Russia the expectation was that Russia would back down or, if she came to Serbia's aid, would be militarily ineffective. Stumm had written Lichnowsky in January 1913 that in the event of war the Russian Empire would collapse. If this was not the common view in the summer of 1914 (when the military men were making much of Russia's armaments), Jagow wrote Lichnowsky in his defense of the German plan to force a crisis over Serbia that Russia was not yet ready; and at the end of July Stumm reportedly boasted in public that by the next day he would have forced the Russians to their knees. When this report was published in Bülow's memoirs, Stumm denied the boastful tone (not in character, he said) but admitted that his judgment of Russia's reaction might at that moment have been optimistic.[35]

Berlin had no clear idea of what they might achieve if Russia gave in. Jagow spoke in his letter to Lichnowsky of boosting Austria's prestige. That, no doubt, would entail a corresponding weakening of the Entente and create the possibility of an arrangement with Russia on German terms including the maintenance of Austria-Hungary. This was possible, Bethmann thought, "only if Russia is not supported up to the end by the Western powers and recognizes that she must come to an agreement with us."[36] But if the terms of this possible agreement were envisaged, they were not set down and compared with the advantages of any alternative effort.

From the beginning of the crisis the Germans also reckoned with the possibility that Russia would not back down but would support Serbia with military force. In that case Germany would be at war with Russia and France, and then the crucial question for both sides was whether England would enter the war or remain neutral.

Berlin was not entirely convinced that England would enter a Russo-German war in order to support France. Denying in an article of 1928 that the German government had regarded "England's nonparticipation as probable," Jagow nevertheless admitted that "there were moments when we wavered between pessimistic fears and optimistic hopes."[37] From time to time Berlin was prepared to admit that as a general principle England must enter any war in which Germany threatened to destroy France, and in the gloomy moments after the assassination of Franz Ferdinand, while Berlin was weighing the terrible eventuality to which the crisis could lead, the pessimistic calculation was that England would not remain neutral.[38] But neither Bethmann, Jagow, nor Stumm could accept a British declaration of war as the inevitable decision when the crucial moment had come. The warning Lloyd George addressed to Berlin during the Moroccan crisis of 1911 was not convincing because his speech aroused such opposition in the ranks of the reigning Liberal party (and the Germans in their campaign against the Anglo-Russian naval conversations banked on liberal support). For years the leading German statesmen believed, or were influenced by the belief, that a show of strength or the threat of a costly armaments race would force the British to cooperate with Germany. In 1909 this was Stumm's opinion. In February 1914 Jagow also seemed to accept Tirpitz's view that England would hesitate to engage a serious naval rival; and in May 1914 Stumm, speaking for Jagow in a dispatch to Lichnowsky, preferred to believe that the English commitment to France, lacking all formality, was of no value.[39]

During July this optimism about England's intentions came to the fore repeatedly. On the twenty-third, the day Austria delivered its ultimatum to Serbia, Bethmann informed the kaiser that "it was impossible that England would enter the fray";[40] and on the twenty-eighth, the day Austria declared war on Serbia, Stumm assured Admiral von Müller, of the kaiser's naval advisory staff, that England would at first remain neutral and then, if France were endangered, bring all her influence to bear for a speedy conclusion of peace.[41]

London gave these hopes and illusions no encouragement. The Germans had tried to take advantage of the Anglo-Russian naval conversations to force Grey to admit a common Anglo-German mission to preserve the peace. They had failed. This was not Lichnowsky's fault. When he returned to London on 6 July he carried out Bethmann's instructions on this matter so competently that the British finally decided to admit that discussions were going on. On 9 July Grey told Lichnowsky that the military and naval authorities had since 1906 occasionally carried on conversations with the other members of the Entente. This was merely contingency planning; it had no aggressive purpose and left England's hands entirely free.[42] Not satisfied with this general explanation, Jagow sent shipping magnate Albert Ballin to London to explain again that the naval conversations and Berlin's growing fear of Russia could accelerate agitation for naval expansion. Grey was obviously unreceptive to this unofficial pressuring. He told Ballin that England could not refuse to discuss matters of interest to members of the grouping to which it belonged; he assumed Germany did the same within its own grouping. But he was happy to say that a naval convention (Ballin apparently spoke as if an agreement had already been concluded) did not exist and England had no intention of entering into one.[43]

To bolster their optimism the Germans resorted to ever more

pedantic interpretations. Ignoring their ambassador, all knowledge of the English constitutional system, and all other indications of English intentions, Berlin did not dismiss out of hand the erroneous renditions of a conversation on 26 July between Prince Heinrich of Prussia and King George V. The naval attaché Capt. von Müller cabled that the king had told Prince Heinrich that England would remain neutral in a Continental war, and on the twenty-eighth Heinrich himself reported that "Georgie" had said, "we shall try to keep out of this and shall remain neutral."[44] Lichnowsky, however, had reported that the king had expressed the hope that Germany and England working together with France and Italy would overcome the difficulties and preserve the peace.[45] Berlin also insisted that Grey had agreed to the program of localization. Ignoring everything Lichnowsky had said and reported from the beginning of the crisis, the Wilhelmstrasse seized upon Lichnowsky's report of 25 July that Grey made a distinction between the Austro-Serbian and the Austro-Russian disputes. Jagow replied that Grey's distinction was most apt, and Lichnowsky did not catch the implications of this approval until Bethmann, on the twenty-seventh, ignoring Lichnowsky's warnings against banking on localization, once more emphasized the distinction Grey had made between the two disputes. Lichnowsky now tried to explain that Grey had meant that he was loath to interfere in Austro-Serbian affairs as long as the dispute had not developed into an Austro-Russian conflict. That, however, is what it was now clearly threatening to do, and there was no way of eliminating the Austro-Russian dispute without dealing with the dispute between Austria and Serbia.[46] On the twenty-sixth Lichnowsky had urgently warned Berlin "against continuing to believe in the possibility of localizing the conflict. I beg," he wrote, "that our policy may be guided simply and solely by the need to spare the German people a struggle in which it has nothing to gain and everything to lose."[47]

This was the same language Lichnowsky had used in the fall of 1912, at the outbreak of the Balkan War, and at that time the kaiser had repeated his words in directives to the Foreign Ministry.

Lichnowsky attempted to persuade Berlin to give up its illusory hope for a little war and accept a solution by conference. On

24 July Grey proposed that the Austrians give Serbia more time to answer the ultimatum and that the four disinterested governments (Great Britain, Germany, France, and Italy) agree to mediate between Austria and Russia should these two become deadlocked. On the twenty-sixth Grey specified that the mediation should take the form of an ambassadorial conference, during which all military activity should be postponed. On the twenty-seventh when the extraordinarily compliant Serbian answer to the Austrian ultimatum was received, he requested Berlin to urge Vienna to accept the reply or treat it as the basis for further negotiations.[48] Lichnowsky supported Grey's initiatives. After Grey on the twenty-seventh urged Berlin to intervene with Vienna to accept the Serbian reply, he wrote Berlin as follows:

I should like to emphasize the fact that our entire future relations with England depend upon the success of this step of Sir Edward Grey's. If at this significant moment, a moment in which, despite all internal differences, the whole British nation undoubtedly stands behind the Minister, he should succeed in preventing the situation from becoming still more acute, I guarantee that our relations with Great Britain will for many a day to come bear the same confidential and intimate character that has distinguished them for the past eighteen months.

The British government, no matter whether Liberal or Conservative, sees in the maintanance of European peace on the basis of the balance of power between the two groups its most vital interest. The British government is convinced that it lies entirely with us whether Austria shall jeopardize European peace by stubbornly pursuing a policy of prestige. Any signs of compliance on the part of Austria would therefore be interpreted by Great Britain as a proof of our sincere wish to unite with her in preventing a European war and would be looked upon as consolidating our friendship with England and our desire for peace. Should we, on the other hand, regard our sympathies for Austria and the exact observance of our treaty obligations as being of so much importance that all other considerations have to yield to them, and that we subordinate even the most important point in our foreign policy—our relations with England—to the special interests of our ally, I believe that it will never again be possible to reknit the ties which of late have bound us together.

The impression is gaining ground here, as I clearly perceived in my interview with Sir Edward Grey, that the whole Serbian question is fast developing into a trial of strength between the Triple Alliance and the Triple Entente. Should therefore Austria's intention to make use of the present opportunity to 'crush Serbia,' as Sir Edward Grey put it, become more and more apparent, England will—of this I am convinced—place herself unconditionally on the side of France and Russia, in order to show that she is not willing to permit a moral and still less a military defeat of her group. If under these circumstances it should come to war, we shall have England against us.[49]

But Bethmann was not to be moved. He rejected Grey's proposal for Great Power mediation unless the Austro-Serbian dispute was excluded,[50] and held it against Lichnowsky that he had not attempted to prevent Grey from making his suggestion.[51] The chancellor clung doggedly to the plan of localization even though he recognized, on 27 July, that all signs pointed to war. Riezler noted in his diary on that day that Bethmann had perceived that France and England seemed prepared to support Russia because they were afraid to antagonize her.[52] The British were also aware that affairs had reached a crucial point. A decision of immeasurable consequences was being forced upon them. "So far as this country is concerned," Prime Minister Asquith noted after the cabinet meeting of 27 July, "the position may be thus described. Germany says to us, 'If you will say at St. Petersburg that in no conditions will you come in and help, Russia will draw back and there will be no war.' On the other hand, Russia says to us, 'If you won't say you are ready to side with us now, your friendship is valueless, and we shall act on that assumption in the future.' "[53]

On 27 July Bethmann had also recognized that Berlin's obstinacy had created a very bad impression. He now forwarded to the German ambassador in Vienna Grey's suggestion that Austria accept the Serbian reply as sufficient in itself or as the basis for further discussion. If the Germans "rejected every suggestion of mediation," he wrote, "the whole world would make them responsible for the conflagration and make them out to be the true war mongers."[54] But he did not urge the Austrians to accept Grey's proposal (which is what Grey had wished Berlin to do),[55] and when the Austrians rejected the Serbian reply and on 28 July declared war, Bethmann once more insisted that Grey had accepted the program of localization. Grey had abandoned that position, he cabled Lichnowsky, and he instructed the prince to continue to press the view that Austria could brook no interference in its right of self-defense against Serbian subversion.[56]

On 29 July both Grey and Bethmann decided the time had come to clarify the question of British intervention. On that day Austria had opened hostilities by bombarding Belgrade, and Russia had answered Austria's declaration of war on Serbia by ordering a partial mobilization. In the afternoon Grey took Lichnowsky aside. "The minister was quite calm but very grave," Lichnowsky reported. Grey hoped that "our cordial personal relations and intimate exchange of ideas on all political questions should [not] lead me astray, as he did not wish later to be reproached with insincerity."

The British government [Lichnowsky's report continued] desired now as heretofore to foster the friendship that had hitherto prevailed between the two countries, and as long as the conflict was confined to Austria and Russia, it could stand aside, but if we and France were drawn in, the situation would at once be altered and it was possible that the British government would then be forced to make up its mind quickly. In such an event it would not be practicable to stand aside and wait for any length of time. 'If war breaks out, it will be the greatest catastrophe that the world has ever seen.' It was far from his thoughts, he said, to wish to express any kind of threat, he only wanted to save me disappointments and himself the reproach of insincerity, and had therefore chosen the form of a private communication.[57]

Grey prepared a record of this conversation for Goschen, saying that Lichnowsky "took no exception to what I had said; indeed, he told me that it accorded with what he had already given in Berlin as his view of the situation."[58]

At about 10:30 that evening, before Lichnowsky's report of his conversation with Grey had arrived in Berlin, Bethmann received Sir Edward Goschen and told him plainly he hoped the British would remain neutral if Germany were at war with France. Bethmann knew England would not allow France to be crushed—and that was not Germany's intention. If England remained neutral, Germany, if victorious, would seek no territorial aggrandizement at France's expense. He could not guarantee the French colonies, however, and though he vouchsafed the integrity of Holland, he could make no such promises for Belgium. "Finally," wrote Goschen, "His Excellency said that he trusted that these assurances might form a basis of a further understanding with England which, as you well know, had been the object of his policy ever since he had been chancellor."[59]

Shortly after Goschen left Bethmann, Lichnowsky's report on his conversation with Grey arrived in Berlin. The next day Jagow told Goschen that if Lichnowsky's report had arrived earlier, the chancellor would not have made such an offer[60] (which the British in due course rejected). Bethmann told Bavarian representative Lerchenfeld on 30 July that in case of war England would join the Entente.[61] Stumm's reaction to Lichnowsky's report was characteristically exaggerated. He told British journalists who visited the Wilhelmstrasse on the thirtieth that they would have to leave Germany.[62] The kaiser, having been assured by Bethmann that England would remain neutral, was deeply shaken by the news of Grey's warning. When he first learned of it from the report of the naval attaché received on the morning of the thirtieth he preserved outward calm,[63] but when subsequently he received a copy of Lichnowsky's report, and which contained no comment by Bethmann or Jagow, he gave his bitterness full rein: "Common pack of peddlers!" he wrote in the margin. "Common scoundrels! The sole responsibility for war or peace is England's not ours any longer!"[64]

The kaiser might have found less bitter expressions if he had been reading the full text of the reports Lichnowsky had dispatched that month. But the Wilhelmstrasse had eliminated the discouraging passages from the copies sent to the palace.[65] Lichnowsky somehow sensed this. According to Kühlmann, he once said he could not suppress the feeling that the kaiser was not being told the truth, and he was convinced that Berlin would have followed a different course if he could have spoken to the kaiser face to face.[66] Although the Wilhelmstrasse could not refute the prince's arguments, or, as yet, doubt the accuracy of his factual reporting, and Jagow had thought it necessary to reply at length to Lichnowsky's protest of 16 July, the old habit of treating Lichnowsky as naive and impressionable made it easy to ignore his counsel now. To make matters worse, the penetration of the Russian embassy in London gave Berlin immediate intelli-

gence of Lichnowsky's alarm, and his intimation to Benckendorff that Berlin was now less inclined to work for a peaceful
solution in the Balkans. Riezler noted in his diary on 27 July
after a talk with Bethmann that the prince "had completely
lost his composure."[67] "Ach, Lichnowsky," said Stumm, when
Theodor Wolff on 30 July asked what the prince was reporting
from London. "Naturally he's filling his pants, after telling us all
this time that England wished to be reconciled with us."[68]

Grey still hoped to find some way to avert the catastrophe. After
the bombardment of Belgrade on 29 July, he hit upon the idea
of limited military engagement. He proposed to Berlin that the
Austrians should discontinue their advance into Serbia after oc-
cupying Belgrade and submit their differences with the Russians
to mediation by the Powers,[69] hoping that the Russians would
then consent to suspend their military preparations. "It is a
slender chance of preserving peace," he wrote the British ambassador in Saint Petersburg, "but the only one I can suggest if
Russian Minister of Foreign Affairs can come to no agreement at
Berlin."[70] Grey's efforts seemed to be on the verge of success.
The Germans accepted his proposal and urged the Austrians to
do so too.[71] And on the thirty-first the Austro-Russian conversations, broken off when Austria declared war on Serbia, were
resumed.

It was the cabinet's indecisiveness, if nothing else, that forced
Grey in his search for peace to consider ever more desperate
means. As the war between Germany and Russia drew closer, the
cabinet's divisions became clearer. The pacifist majority still opposed intervention in a European war, and Lord Morley argued
that a Russian victory over the Central Powers spelled disaster
for Western civilization.[72] Although the British fleet remained
mobilized after maneuvers, the cabinet was not prepared to permit the military authorities to honor their agreements with
France. Lichnowsky was aware of this indecision. On the thirty-
first he reported that "today for the first time I have the impression that the improved relations with Germany of late years
and perhaps also some friendly feeling in the cabinet make it
appear possible that in case of war England may adopt a waiting
attitude."[73]

On the thirty-first it appeared that France would soon be facing Germany alone. That afternoon the Germans had responded to the full mobilization in Russia by proclaiming the state of imminent danger of war. The next step was mobilization, and mobilization was tantamount to hostilities. Russia and Germany would be at war, and the terms of alliance required France to come to Russia's aid immediately. From Paris, London was receiving reports of German military preparations on the French frontier. That evening Nicolson wrote Grey that it was "useless to shut our eyes to the fact that possibly within the next twenty-four hours Germany will be moving across the French frontier—and if public opinion, at present so bewildered and partially informed, is ready in event of German invasion of France to stand by the latter, if we are not mobilized our aid would be too late."[74] At midnight on 31 July the German embassy passed to the Foreign Office a summary Berlin had prepared of the German efforts to prevent hostilities. The Germans stated that if the Russians would not stop their warlike measures within twelve hours, Berlin would mobilize too, "and that would mean war." "We asked France," the German note continued, "whether in a Russo-German war she would remain neutral."[75]

Out of this situation there arose on 1 August a series of exchanges between the British and the Germans that left both contemporaries and historians baffled. The true history of this affair, known for a long time erroneously as "Lichnowsky's misunderstanding," is here reconstructed in its proper details.[76] In spite of the Austrian declaration of war, Grey on 31 July had not yet given up his hope that it might be possible to limit or postpone hostilities. On 1 August, after the German declaration of imminent danger of war, this means of preserving the peace was possible only if the military standoff could be extended to Germany, Russia, and France. Grey made an attempt to do this. Early in the morning of 1 August he sent Sir William Tyrrell to the German embassy. At 11:14 Lichnowsky cabled Berlin that Tyrrell had just informed him that Grey hoped that afternoon to make a statement that might help avert the catastrophe, and this seemed to mean that if Germany would not attack France, Britain would remain neutral and guarantee France's passivity.

The prince had given the assurance, when Grey called him on the telephone a few moments later, that "in the event of France's remaining neutral in a war between Russia and Germany we should not attack France." Tyrrell also asked Lichnowsky to use his influence to prevent violations of the French border by German troops.[77]

Shortly after this cable was dispatched, Lichnowsky and Grey somehow learned that in their morning discussions they had not reached perfect agreement. They differed in their understanding of which powers were to be included in the *arrêt militaire*. Lichnowsky in the informal essay entitled "England before the War," which he dictated some ten days after the outbreak of hostilities, said that he had understood Grey to mean that Germany should not attack France. This Lichnowsky felt he could guarantee. "But [Grey] had meant that we should hold back vis-à-vis Russia as well—an error which I had Tyrrell correct soon thereafter."[78] By this Lichnowsky meant that he could not guarantee German forbearance toward Russia. Grey, who was not aware of Lichnowsky's testimony, gave a similar explanation of their misunderstanding in the House of Commons on 28 August 1914. Although he distorted the incident and attributed the initiative to Lichnowsky, which the record shows is not correct, he likewise alleged a misunderstanding with regard to Russia. He thought the standoff was to include both Russia and France, while Lichnowsky had thought of it as extending only to the latter.[79]

It is apparent from the situation in the cabinet that Grey must have hoped that warlike activities could be postponed on all fronts. He knew that if Russia and Germany were at war there would soon be war between Germany and France. This he intended to avoid. But he felt that a formal declaration of war did not necessarily mean that the armies would be plunged into battle. In spite of the state of war the Serbian and Austrian troops were still not engaged. After Lichnowsky informed him that Germany would not postpone hostilities against Russia, he still had to hope that the war in the west could be postponed. It was crucial to win time until the cabinet could reach a decision and permit the Expeditionary Force to come to France's

aid. As Lichnowsky was willing to guarantee German forbearance toward France if England were to remain neutral, Grey
could continue to hope for a military standoff even if war had
been formally declared. That is why Lichnowsky at 2:10 P.M.
cabled Berlin that Tyrrell had been to see him and informed him
that Grey "wants this afternoon to make proposals for England's
neutrality in the event of our being at war with France as well
as with Russia. I shall be seeing Sir Edward Grey at 3:30 and
shall report at once."[80]

Lichnowsky's first cable arrived in Berlin just twenty-three
minutes after the kaiser had signed the order of mobilization.
The march on Belgium and France began. Berlin's reaction was
an equal mixture of surprise and gratification. Not waiting for
the details but acting as if the prospect were the proposal itself,
the Germans set about drafting an acceptance. But the decision
was reached after an emotional debate between the civil leaders
and General Moltke.[81] Wilhelm was elated and wished to turn
the bulk of his armies eastward toward Russia, and his civilian
leaders, though suspicious, were gratified; it was just what they
wanted to hear. England's remaining neutral in a Continental
war was a diplomatic success that totally justified the risk Bethmann, Jagow, and Stumm had chosen to run. In his argument
with Moltke, Bethmann had the support of Tirpitz, who likewise could regard England's hesitations as his doing. When the
second cable arrived, while the answer to the first was being
drafted, he exulted, "The risk theory works!"[82] Of course Bethmann and Tirpitz argued that even if it were an English trick,
for appearances' sake Germany would have to give a positive reply.
But their motives were personal gratification and, doubtless, the
hope of being rescued at the last minute from the great war they
had invited.

As Moltke complained that the reversal of his armies would
reduce them to confused masses of men, the civilian leaders
agreed to continue the normal deployment while postponing the
seizure of Luxembourg. Ignoring the second cable, they completed their answer to the first, saying that they would accept the
proposal "if England would guarantee with its entire armed
strength the unconditional neutrality of France in a German-

Russian conflict."[83] While the mobilization would go on, no troops would cross the French border until 7:00 A.M. on 3 August. The kaiser repeated this acceptance in a cable to King George, adding that he hoped "France will not become nervous. The troops on my frontier are in the act of being stopped by telegraph and telephone from crossing into France."[84]

The proposal to which the Germans had given their conditional advance consent was never forthcoming. Before Grey met Lichnowsky at the Foreign Office that afternoon British attention had shifted to Belgium. Grey had brought up the matter of Britain's commitment to that country after the Austrians attacked Serbia, but, according to Lord Morley, "it was thrown back day after day as less urgent than France."[85] By 1 August this situation was reversed. On 31 July Grey had asked Paris and Berlin for pledges to respect Belgian neutrality. While the French readily gave the desired assurance, the Germans refused to answer at all, pleading that any reply would give away the German military plan.[86] Although Grey may not have had this answer in hand when he first spoke to Lichnowsky on the morning of 1 August, he was obviously apprised of it when the full cabinet met at noon. "Grey very properly asked leave," wrote Lord Morley, "to warn the German ambassador that, unless Germany was prepared to give us a reply in the sense of the reply we had from France, it would be hard to restrain English feeling on any violation of Belgian neutrality by either combatant. This leave of course we gave him."[87]

The Belgian problem pushed aside the quest for a Franco-German standoff—at least in the exchanges between Grey and Lichnowsky. When Lichnowsky visited Whitehall for his afternoon meeting he found himself the recipient not of a proposal by which Britain's neutrality could be guaranteed but of a statement of conditions under which the British might intervene. The prince took this calmly. His response was to ask whether the foreign secretary could give him a definite assurance of Britain's neutrality if Germany did agree to respect Belgian territory. This clever question, consistent with the search for a means to assure military passivity in the West, caught Grey unawares. The foreign secretary simply said that he could not give this assurance. In

Lichnowsky's report of this conversation, which he dispatched at 5:47 P.M. on 1 August, the question of a Franco-German military standoff assumed a subordinate, almost incidental, status:

[Grey] had also been wondering [wrote Lichnowsky] whether it would not be possible for us and France in the event of a Russian war to remain facing each other without either side attacking. I asked him whether he was in a position to give me an assurance that France would agree to a pact of that sort. Since we intended neither to destroy France nor to annex parts of her territory, I could imagine that we might enter on an agreement of that sort since it would assure us of Great Britain's neutrality. The minister said that he would enquire, but was not blind to the difficulties of restraining the two armies and keeping them in a state of inactivity.[88]

Here Lichnowsky made no explicit reference to his earlier cables that day, which had announced the agenda of the afternoon meeting, and failed to explain what now remained of the expectations those cables would have aroused or what he next intended to do. Of course, as yet he had no inkling of Berlin's response. Grey had not yet abandoned his thought of a military standoff. As it was no longer a pressing matter to formulate a proposal to the Germans, he could continue a theoretical discussion with the French. After meeting Lichnowsky, Grey received Paul Cambon.[89] Grey did not tell Cambon what he had told Lichnowsky about a military standoff or Britian's concern about Belgium but said that the position now was that "Germany would agree not to attack France if France remained neutral in the event of war between Russia and Germany. If France could not take advantage of this position, it was because she was bound by an alliance to which we were not parties, and of which we did not know the terms."[90] But in reporting this discussion to Ambassador Bertie in Paris, Grey made the enquiry he promised Lichnowsky in the afternoon. He wrote as follows:

German ambassador here seemed to think it not impossible, when I suggested it, that after mobilization on western frontier French and German armies should remain, neither crossing the frontier as long as the other did not do so. I cannot say whether this would be consistent with French obligations under her alliance. If it were so consistent, I suppose French Government would not object to our engaging to be neutral as long as German army remained on frontier on the defensive.[91]

Bertie's response to this halfhearted suggestion contained the criticism that Grey might have received had he or Tyrrell broached this question seriously with other officials at Whitehall.

Do you desire me to state to the French Government [wrote Bertie] that after mobilization of French and German troops on Franco-German frontier we propose to remain neutral so long as German troops remain on the defensive and do not cross French frontier, and French abstain from crossing German frontier? I cannot imagine that in the event of Russia being at war with Austria and being attacked by Germany it would be consistent with French obligations toward Russia for French to remain quiescent. If French undertook to remain so, the Germans would first attack Russians, and, if they defeated them, they would turn round on the French.[92]

To this Grey on the morning of the second replied: "No action required."[93]

Grey had in fact been in full retreat from the quest of an *arrêt militaire* hours before Bertie sent his incredulous cable and had dubbed it all a misunderstanding. The crucial moment occurred when he was called to Buckingham Palace to answer the kaiser's cable to King George, which arrived in London around 8:00 P.M. on 1 August. Grey was forced to draw his thoughts together. Some time between eight and ten o'clock, using a pencil on a scrap of notepaper,[94] he drafted the king's reply, saying that "there must be some misunderstanding as to a suggestion that passed in friendly conversation between Prince Lichnowsky and Sir Edward Grey this afternoon when they were discussing how actual fighting between German and French armies might be avoided while there is still a chance of some agreement between Austria and Russia."[95] Apparently it did not occur to Grey that Berlin would not have had time to respond to a report on the afternoon conversation and therefore must have been reacting to some earlier communication.

Berlin's reaction to Lichnowsky's afternoon cable and the king's response is remarkably sluggish. There is no record of any immediate reaction to the prince's report on the face-to-face meeting with Grey, which arrived in Berlin at 10:02 P.M. on 1 August,[96] and apparently it was not until after 11:00 P.M., when Berlin received the king's report alleging a misunderstanding, that Moltke was ordered to resume the march on Luxembourg. The machinery set in motion by the morning cable creaked on. Until close to midnight the Wilhelmstrasse sent out instructions as if a positive proposal existed or was soon forthcoming. At 11:30 P.M. Bethmann cabled Lichnowsky that as a result of the French mobilization the Germans would not cross the French frontier until the morning of the third (as promised in the cables accepting London's proposals) only if the French respected the German border.[97] And at 11:55 P.M. Berlin informed their embassies in Rome and Vienna of "the prospect of a British proposal to guarantee French neutrality" and the hope that the German conditions for this would prove acceptable.[98] This was the only telegram from Berlin on 1 August that, alleging a "prospect" of neutrality, accurately reflected the meaning of the Grey-Tyrrell-Lichnowsky discussions. But by 11:55 the prospect no longer existed. Finally, fifty minutes after midnight, on the morning of 2 August, Bethmann cabled the ambassadors that "Prince Lichnowsky's report [is] based on misunderstanding."[99]

While Grey had held to the hope of a military standoff until after 8:00 on the evening of the first and Berlin did not catch up with the cancellation until toward midnight, Lichnowsky seems to have thought that the prospect had dissolved with his 3:30 conversation with Grey. Thus, when he received the ministry's cable of acceptance about the time the king received the kaiser's cable, he replied immediately that his morning cable had been canceled by the cable reporting the afternoon conversation with Grey. "Since there is no positive British proposal at all, your telegram inoperative. Therefore have taken no further steps."[100] The continuing flow of correspondence drew from him several additional cables. At 5:00 on 2 August he cabled *en clair:* "As follows from my last telegrams, the matter referred to again in your telegram [repeating the promise not to violate the French border] is completely terminated and no longer limits our freedom of action."[101] At 6:28 A.M. he cabled in cipher that Grey had spoken without consulting the French and in ignorance of the French mobilization and in the meantime had given up his suggestions as completely hopeless.[102]

On the morning of 2 August Prince Lichnowsky visited Prime Minister Asquith at breakfast. The prince was very agitated and wept. He had come to make a final plea for British neutrality before the cabinet met in its 11:00 session. He implored Asquith to recognize that it was not France but Germany who was threatened with annihilation. "I told him," wrote the prime minister, "that we had no desire to intervene, and that it rested largely with Germany to make intervention impossible if she would (1) not invade Belgium and (2) not send her fleet into the Channel to attack the unprotected north coast of France."[103]

Lichnowsky had already informed Berlin that these would be the British conditions for neutrality. He continued to hope that the British would adopt a waiting attitude because he truly believed that they had no desire to intervene in the war. He knew that there were strong antiwar forces in the nation at large, and he was aware of the struggle going on within the cabinet. This had first given him the hope, on 31 July, that the British government might choose to watch the development of events on the continent before making its decision. But he also knew that the British attitude would depend partly upon Germany's willingness to make concessions. On 31 July he thought the necessary concession to be the cessation of Austrian hostilities against Serbia; on 1 August it was German respect for Belgian neutrality. He made the point repeatedly that the British could remain neutral if the Germans would not do the things that were certain to make them intervene. On the morning of 2 August he had cabled that since the British fully expected Germany to invade Belgium, it was not impossible that they would take a stand against Germany in the very near future.[104] He would not phrase this warning more definitely; he did not want Berlin to throw everything over and concentrate on making war. Both despair and hope spoke from his dispatches and were manifest in his behavior. He was aware of the dangers from the very beginning of the crisis, and he gave physical signs of his excitement earlier than his colleagues. On 31 July Mensdorff noted in his diary that the prince was "tearing out his hair and wants us to give in at the last hour."[105]

While Lichnowsky's urgings could not prevent Berlin from going ahead with the attack on Belgium, his dispatches did encourage the Wilhelmstrasse to try to dispel the distrust of German motives that Lichnowsky said prevailed in London. On 3 August Lichnowsky held out the prospect that the British would delay their final decision as long as possible. He could do this because on that morning Grey had evaded giving him a straight answer about the cabinet's decision concerning a German invasion of Belgium, and partly because he misinterpreted the reports of the speech Grey gave in Parliament that afternoon. On the evening of 2 August the cabinet had decided that it would consider the violation of Belgian borders as reason for going to war with Germany. Grey hid this from Lichnowsky the following morning when the prince spoke to him about Belgium and urged him not to make Belgian neutrality the condition of British neutrality. He said that Germany had no territorial ambitions in Belgium, and promised that Germany would refrain from attacking the north coast of France. As Grey gave him no definite answer to these representations, he cabled Berlin that the British still hoped to remain neutral.[106]

From a report that Lerchenfeld sent Munich on the third one must assume that someone in the Wilhelmstrasse was informing interested parties that Lichnowsky, as Lerchenfeld said, was still maintaining that England would remain neutral after all.[107] This is not what Lichnowsky meant. He was saying correctly that the British wished to keep out of it and had not made a final decision and that they might still remain neutral if Germany would make the concession that made neutrality possible—and that concession was to keep hands off Belgium. What Lichnowsky reported to Berlin reflects exactly how Asquith viewed England's position. "Happily I am quite clear in my mind," the prime minister recorded on 2 August,

as to what is right and wrong. (1) We have no obligation of any kind to France or Russia to give them military or naval help. (2) The dispatch of the Expeditionary Force to help France at this moment is out of the question and would serve no object. (3) We must not forget the ties created by our long-standing and intimate friendship with France. (4) It is against British interests that France should be wiped out as a Great Power. (5) We cannot allow Germany to use the channel as a hostile base. (6) We have obligations to Belgium to prevent it being utilized and absorbed by Germany.[108]

In answer to the prince's cable on this talk with Grey in the morning, Bethmann on the evening of the third cabled for Grey an explanation of the German actions, stating that the Russian mobilization and French armaments threatened to overwhelm Germany. Self-defense dictated the German violation of Belgian neutrality, "which was the act of a man fighting for his life."[109] Late that evening the German naval authorities repeated an order given first on 2 August prohibiting all activity that might lead to clashes with British naval forces.[110] On the morning of the fourth, Jagow, at Moltke's insistence, cabled Lichnowsky *en clair* in English to "dispel any mistrust that may subsist on the part of the British Government with regard to our intentions, by repeating most positively formal assurance that, even in the case of armed conflict with Belgium, Germany will, under no pretense whatever, annex Belgian territory."[111] And at five minutes after four o'clock that afternoon Jagow cabled Lichnowsky again *en clair* an English summary of Bethmann's declarations to the Reichstag. The chancellor once more promised to respect Belgian territorial integrity and independence and not to attack the northern coast of France or French commercial navigation as long as the English remained neutral.[112]

Berlin took no action, however, on Lichnowsky's rather encouraging but mistaken report on Grey's speech to Parliament on the afternoon of the third. This speech was later seen as Grey's announcement of Britain's intention to go to war against Germany. But it was clothed in the same diplomatic, safety-valve language that he had employed all through the crisis. Paul Cambon, reporting the speech that afternoon and noting that the Parliament was now adhering to the government, was not yet prepared to say that the British had decided to intervene in the struggle.[113] While Grey made much of England's long-standing obligations toward Belgium and the military arrangements with France, informing Parliament that England had just engaged to protect the French northern coast, and contended that England would suffer terribly in this war even if she remained outside, he was careful to avoid the impression that the cabinet had already committed the country irrevocably to military intervention. From the parliamentary report of this speech, which was the only rendition available that evening, Lichnowsky concluded that "Germany could be satisfied with the speech." Since the British widely believed that Germany for unknown reasons desired this war and had forced it upon its neighbors and were aghast at Germany's disregard for treaty obligations, Berlin could consider it a great success that England had not immediately joined her Entente partners. He thought that the British hoped yet to remain neutral, which might be possible if Germany retreated from Belgium territory without engaging in any large battles. But the attitude of Parliament and public opinion would tell.[114]

At 10:02 on the morning of the fourth Lichnowsky corrected his impression of Grey's speech. He had now received the full wording, and he reported that Germany could not count on Britain's neutrality much longer. "I do not know what form British intervention will assume or whether it will follow immediately. But I cannot see how the government here, after said speech, which was known to me yesterday only in excerpts, can turn back if we are not in the position to evacuate Belgian territory in the shortest possible time."[115] Early that afternoon, when reports of serious fighting in Belgium had reached London, Lichnowsky cabled that a break between Germany and England was imminent. "Maybe he'll finally accept it," wrote the kaiser in the margin. "Poor Lichnowsky!"[116]

In the afternoon of the fourth Goschen notified Jagow that the British would do all in their power to uphold the neutrality of Belgium unless by midnight the Germans agreed to halt their operations. As Jagow replied that Germany must go on into Belgium, Goschen asked for his passports, as he had been instructed to do. At 12:00 midnight (Berlin time) on 4 August Great Britain and Germany were at war. In the evening the British sent Lichnowsky his passports accompanied with a written explanation of their action. The British had to come back to Lichnowsky a second time with a corrected version of their explanation. The original statement had read that the German Empire had declared war on Britain, an error due to misinterpretations of warnings sent to German ships which the Admiralty had intercepted.[117] When the Foreign Office discovered the error, they dispatched Harold Nicolson to replace the statement with the one they had intended to send in the first place, which read:

The result of the communication made at Berlin having been that His Majesty's Ambassador has had to ask for his passports, I have the honor to inform your Excellency that in accordance with the terms of the notification made to the German government today His Majesty's Government consider that a state of war exists between the two countries as from today at 11 o'clock P.M.[118]

Nicolson has described his visit to the German embassy as follows:

It was by then some five minutes after eleven. After much ringing a footman appeared. He stated that Prince Lichnowsky had gone to bed. The bearer of the missive insisted on seeing His Excellency and advised the footman to summon the butler. The latter appeared and stated that His Highness had given instructions that he was in no circumstances to be disturbed. The Foreign Office clerk stated that he was the bearer of a communication of the utmost importance from Sir Edward Grey. The butler, at that, opened the door and left young Nicolson in the basement. He was absent for five minutes. On his return he asked Sir Edward Grey's emissary to follow him and walked majestically towards the lift. They rose silently together to the third floor and then proceeded along a pile-carpeted passage. The butler knocked at a door. There was a screen behind the door and behind the screen a brass bedstead on which the Ambassador was reclining in pyjamas. The Foreign Office clerk stated that there had been a slight error in the document previously delivered and that he had come to substitute for it another, and more correct, version. Prince Lichnowsky indicated the writing table in the window. "You will find it there," he said. The envelope had been but half-opened, and the passports protruded. It did not appear that the Ambassador had read the communication or opened the letter in which the passports had been enclosed. He must have guessed its significance from the feel of the passports and have cast it on his table in despair. A receipt had to be demanded and signed. The blotting pad was brought across to the bed, and the pen dipped in the ink. While the ambassador was signing, the sound of shouting came up from the Mall below, and the strains of the Marseillaise. The crowds were streaming back from Buckingham Palace. Prince Lichnowsky turned out the pink lamp beside his bed, and then feeling he had perhaps been uncivil, he again lighted it. "Give my best regards," he said, "to your father. I shall not in all probability see him before my departure."[119]

On the morning of 5 August Lichnowsky had his last conversation with Grey, which the prince reported as follows:

Sir Edward was visibly moved when he received me. He said that the decision that he had had to make was the most difficult in his entire life. . . . The decisive consideration here was that the damage that England would suffer from the war would be no smaller if she remained passive than if she were a combatant power and that as a participant England's word would carry greater weight than as a neutral since she could always threaten to withdraw from the struggle. The disregard of internationally recognized treaties . . . made it impossible for him to stand aside any longer, and he also thought that it was impossible to accept a deal with us like the one proposed by the chancellor setting the conditions for British neutrality.[120]
The foreign secretary went on to say that he wished to make the following confidential communication that might be of importance in the future. If events should not take the course that our military party seemed to hope they will, or if we should sincerely desire, in the not too distant future, for whatever reasons, to put a quick end to this war which was disastrous for all Europe, he would always stand ready, should he still be in office, to assume the role of mediator and to help us. He had no intention of crushing Germany. The only thing he desired was to reestablish peace as soon as possible on acceptable terms and to limit as much as possible the unspeakable misfortune that had befallen the entire civilized world.[121]

Lichnowsky spent one more night in Carlton House Terrace. He went back to the embassy after his departing conversation with Grey in the morning. The king could not see him but sent Sir Arthur Ponsonby to express his regrets at the ambassador's departure.[122] In the afternoon Walter Hines Page, the American ambassador, arrived at the embassy to take charge of German interests. Lichnowsky came down to greet him in pyjamas. Page was deeply moved and thought Lichnowsky "might literally go mad."[123] The prince had been building up to this crisis longer than all his colleagues, and the calamity seemed to strike him hardest of all. Mensdorff, who remained behind vainly hoping that the British would not find it necessary to declare war on Austria, wrote in his diary on the ninth that "Prince Lichnowsky had exerted himself so yeomanly and had been completely frustrated. He of course spoke ill of the military influences in Berlin and of us as well—particularly that we were not more conciliatory and didn't accept the responsibility of discussing the Serbian reply with the Powers. That was of course scarcely possible—but now, the *pity of it*."[124] Each in his way felt helpless before the stubborn opposition of national policies. Bethmann exclaimed against the scrap of paper—the guarantee of Belgian neutrality— for which all Europe would be plunged in bitter war. Goschen had broken into tears, and so had Asquith. "I hate it, I hate it," said Grey to Mensdorff, and told him that this war "is the greatest step towards socialism that could possibly have been made."[125]

On 6 August the Lichnowskys and the entire German embassy, accompanied by members of the German colony, left London by special train for Harwich where they embarked upon a British steamer for Holland. A guard of honor was drawn up for the prince in Harwich. "I was treated like a departing sovereign," he wrote in *My London Mission*.[126] Before their departure Princess Lichnowsky wrote Paul Cambon: "I am leaving London in fifteen minutes and must say a word to you before I go. . . . Though everything grieves me, there is a feeling of hatred in me that I cannot describe against the authors of this crime. I would like to see and tell you so many things."[127] After the Germans had left and their affairs were turned over to the Americans, the Irish writer Shane Leslie, who knew the Lichnowskys from London society, visited Carlton House Terrace in the company of the American chargé d'affaires. He found everything in pathetic confusion—"rosary lying in the bedroom, toys, letters, and a *Marcus Aurelius* from Margot Asquith to Prince Lichnowsky dated 'the day of war' but forgotten in the rush. It was inscribed 'To the most true and honorable of men,' which I believe he is."[128]

Crossing the Channel Prince Lichnowsky sat alone in the prow of the steamer wrapped in a greatcoat.[129] In Germany when his train was sidetracked to let a troop train, decorated with flowers, pass, he burst into tears at the sight of innocent young men going to their deaths, singing war songs and overflowing with enthusiasm.[130]

Chapter VII

Contentions, 1914–1918

> As soon as I arrived in Berlin I saw that I was to be
> made the scapegoat for the catastrophe for which,
> despite my advice and warnings, our government had
> made itself responsible.
>
> Karl Max Lichnowsky, *My London Mission*

When Lichnowsky's train arrived in Berlin on 7 August, German troops were streaming over the Belgian border and the French were advancing into Alsace. He went immediately to the Wilhelmstrasse, where, it is fair to assume, his interview with Bethmann was tempestuous.[1] The kaiser, who normally summoned every returning ambassador, did not see him. As the prince was not prepared to resign, he remained in Berlin until the end of August when he was transferred to the army. In the middle of the month he requested assignment to a new post abroad, which was immediately refused him.[2] We can scarcely doubt that he hoped in a neutral capital to reknit his ties with the British, for Grey had intimated in their parting conversation that England would cooperate in bringing the war to a quick close. On the nineteenth he dictated and deposited in the Wilhelmstrasse an account of his dealings with Grey during the last month before the outbreak of hostilities which he entitled "England before the War." The passages on his conversations in Berlin at the beginning of the crisis we have already quoted. Here he also wrote: "My dispatches and the tenor of my repeated urgent warnings shield me from the reproach that I had not foreseen and predicted the development of events."[3]

Lichnowsky had foreseen the outcome of Austro-Serbian hostilities even before he left Berlin for London in the fall of 1912. For two years he had warned against the very policy that Berlin chose to adopt in the summer of 1914. When the war broke out as predicted, he found, upon his return home, that it was believed on all sides that he had misled his government and was at fault for the catastrophe. Such was the bitter fruit of the mésalliance with Bethmann. Since 1909 the main task of German diplomacy was to secure England's neutrality for the event of a Continental war. Although in 1914 Germany had manifestly not achieved this goal, the German leaders were so bedazzled by the prospect of English neutrality that when London decided to go to war in defense of Belgium, they were sorely disappointed. Navalists and others who imagined the English as hypocritical and perfidious would now maintain that the outbreak of hostilities invalidated Bethmann's policy of the pleasant word and friendly gesture. But the onus fell primarily upon the man who could not defend himself. It was a common view which Wilhelm II repeated in his memoirs that Lichnowsky had mistaken hospitality for political friendship.[4] And military and civilian officials who saw the diplomatic correspondence had seeming proof that Lichnowsky on 1 August had falsely reported a British offer of neutrality and that even after Grey's speech to Parliament on 3 August he was still reporting that the British would try to stay out of it.

The true nemesis of German diplomacy was Admiral Tirpitz. He washed his hands of all responsibility for a war that matched Germany against the world's three most powerful nations. "A government unaccustomed to thinking in global terms," he wrote in his memoirs, "took the plunge in a moment of weakness when the odds could not conceivably have been more unfavorable."[5] The outbreak of hostilities had not, however, put an end to the inter-departmental conflict over strategy toward England. For Bethmann still believed he could come to terms with the enemy power and split the Entente in two. Convinced that the English had entered the war reluctantly and against their best interests and would withdraw from it if they could do so with honor, he wished to prevent unnecessary bitterness between the warring powers and argued that the German navy should avoid serious encounters with the British in the North Sea.[6] Tirpitz would not hear of this. His projection had been no better than Bethmann's. The house of cards he had patiently constructed came tumbling down when in spite of the German fleet England decided to risk hostilities. Were the German ships now to remain bottled up in the harbors, the naval program would be forever discredited. To prevent this, Tirpitz launched an attack upon the chancellor's program in the columns of the navalist press.[7]

The campaign against Bethmann coincided with attacks already underway against Lichnowsky. They began the day Lichnowsky arrived in Berlin. The author was Count Reventlow, a former naval officer who was foreign affairs editor of the Pan-German *Deutsche Tageszeitung*. He had been the chief critic of Lichnowsky's diplomacy in London, and the British Blue Book on the war's origins, which contained a selection of diplomatic correspondence, provided him with new ammunition.

His attack on 7 August took off from Grey's report to Goschen of the conversation he had with Lichnowsky on 29 July. On this day Grey first ventured to warn Berlin explicitly that in the event of a European war England would not be able to stand aside, and he had told Lichnowsky he hoped the prince was not misled by the friendly tone of their conversation. Although Grey spoke thus in order to dispel any illusions that might exist in Berlin, Reventlow preferred to interpret the dispatch as meaning that Lichnowsky was unable to penetrate the friendly tone and that Grey therefore chose to use the British ambassador for all serious communications. The next day Reventlow informed his readers that Lichnowsky had simply swallowed everything the British fed him and constantly reassured his government that England was under no special obligation to France.[8]

The anti-Bethmann element appeared in the article of 12 August. Not mentioning the chancellor by name, Reventlow ridiculed the notion that through "mutual forbearance on the main fields of battle the Anglo-German conflict might develop into a 'war without losses.'" Rejoicing that a British cruiser had been sunk in the Thames estuary, he asserted that "German mines will not be treated as if they were mere pawns of British diplomacy, and neither will they be misled by the 'friendly tone of the conversation.'"[9]

Lichnowsky was not prepared to let these attacks go unanswered. After all, he had foreseen and warned against the outcome that was now charged to his account. The first step in his defense was to petition the support of his sovereign. On 11 August he wrote Wilhelm requesting the audience which had been withheld him. Recalling that a few short months ago the kaiser had praised his accomplishments in London, the prince stated that he had never concealed his conviction that England could not be completely separated from the Entente and that in case of war she would support France. "It was invariably in this sense that I reported," the prince wrote, "and though I exerted myself to the utmost during the recent crisis, it was to be predicted that I could not succeed in keeping the British neutral." "I therefore consider it an undeserved slight that Your Majesty has suddenly withdrawn the favor you have shown me for so many years without giving me the opportunity of an audience to clear up possible misunderstandings."[10] The kaiser thereupon summoned his ambassador to the palace:[11] but if he gave him any satisfaction (there is no record of the conversation), it was not apparent in the attitude of the imperial authorities when the prince at about the same time also petitioned their support.

Although the letter Lichnowsky then wrote to Jagow has been lost, it is apparent from the reply Jagow made on 15 August that he had requested an official rebuttal of Reventlow's attacks. Jagow was perfectly aware when he replied to Lichnowsky that Reventlow had intended his censure for the entire diplomatic establishment. He knew as well that Bethmann's policy and performance were difficult to justify from a military standpoint, for at the end of August he proposed an official Foreign Ministry study of the war's origins for the purpose of "strengthening the position of the diplomacy vis-à-vis public opinion and the military."[12] He must have realized that to rebut Reventlow's attacks would undermine the diplomatic position even more, for had Lichnowsky not warned that Russia would defend Serbia and England would join her Continental partners? Jagow's response to the prince's request for official support was therefore belittling. He said that Reventlow seemed upset mainly about the speeches the prince had made in London, which (the prince would surely recall) many observers had found rather out of place. "We wrote you about that often, but you would not believe us," said Jagow. "After all, Reventlow was right—truly or seemingly—in being so distrustful of the British, and it is no wonder that he makes a great deal of it now." Jagow was prepared to enquire whether any official action might be possible, but he personally could not engage in a polemic of such general nature, and he left it to the prince to decide whether to make a reply himself.[13]

Lichnowsky now turned to the public press. In a short article published anonymously in the *Vossische Zeitung* on 19 August he took issue with Reventlow's interpretation of Grey's 29 July dispatch to Goschen. Grey's reference to the friendly tone of the conversation, said the article, was meant for Berlin's ears, not the prince's. Reventlow had ignored Grey's rendition of Lichnowsky's answer, which was that Grey's warning "accorded with what he had already given in Berlin as his view of the situation." Besides,

Prince Lichnowsky needed no express warning to know that the British would come to France's defense just as we would defend Austria. Even so, the course of history and the Prince's own experience had shown him that under Bismarck and even in later times we had succeeded in spite of our intimate relations with Austria in coming to an agreement with Russia. The Prince was convinced that in spite of Franco-British amity, we could likewise achieve a friendly relationship with England—if we continued in peace.[14]

Two days later Lichnowsky was once more compelled to make a public response. On 20 August the Foreign Ministry began to publish the documents on the "misunderstanding" of 1 August. They did this at the behest of the kaiser, who believed that his offer to spare France would prove that Germany had no aggressive intentions toward her neighbor.[15] The selection consisted of Lichnowsky's report of Grey's offer of British neutrality, the kaiser's acceptance of it, the British reply that Lichnowsky had misunderstood his conversation with Grey, and Lichnowsky's explanation sent on the morning of 2 August, that is, an apparently belated correction of his error.[16]

As this skimpy collection left the impression of great negligence on his part, Lichnowsky decided to seek public rectification. In an article in the *Berliner Tageblatt* on 21 September, Theodor Wolff, Lichnowsky's friend, informed his readers that the official disclosures contained no reference to Lichnowsky's morning conversation with Tyrrell, who was the first to suggest the possibility of British neutrality, or to his afternoon meeting with Grey, when the foreign secretary told the prince, who was expecting clarification of the morning's proposal, that the British were deeply concerned over the German threat to Belgium. While Grey had then suggested a Franco-German military stand-off, this he soon gave up as impracticable, and it was to this inconclusive discussion that the final cable in the *Norddeutsche*'s selection had reference.[17]

Bethmann lost no time countering Lichnowsky's move. On the day Wolff's article appeared in the *Berliner Tageblatt*, he telegraphed Lichnowsky that any publicizing of his differences with the Wilhelmstrasse was incompatible with his official position. When Lichnowsky replied that these articles were not meant as criticism of the government's policy and insisted upon the right to defend himself against outrageous charges, Bethmann notified the ministry that he intended to place Lichnowsky on half-pay status and inquired whether the prince could be arraigned under administrative procedure for revealing classified information. But as Reventlow's attacks (which had resumed when the 1 August documents were published) had ceased, and the prince promised to refrain from all further publicity, no action seemed necessary. Bethmann ignored the prince's offer to resign and approved his transfer to military duty.[18]

The prince's military service was brief. He was assigned first to General Headquarters in Luxembourg and then to von Kluck's army in northern France. Military life afforded him no escape from galling thoughts. "Here I am completely withdrawn, ignored," he wrote to his wife.

I don't know what's going on elsewhere in the world; and I can't do a thing to counter the attacks against me. I have nothing to do. Every day I go out and observe a position where there is fighting. . . . Can't you visit Frau Solf and listen to what her husband says? . . . Go to Brockdorff and then to T. W. [Theodor Wolff] and then to the crown princess. It would be well to clarify the situation for them, to explain that I sent back urgent warnings and that I considered world war inevitable if we placed ourselves . . . in the service of Austria's policy in the Balkans.[19]

When he reported for duty at headquarters he had an interview with the kaiser where he was sharply reprimanded and dismissed because (as the kaiser recalled in 1918) he had intimated that

the German government was responsible for the war.[20] Lichnowsky later told his wife that although Wilhelm had shouted at
him, at a later tetê-à-tête he admitted: "you are quite right:
Bethmann is an ass."[21]

The prince was in uniform just a few days when the government
resumed its campaign against the British on the "Misunderstanding of 1 August." In reply to the first series of documents published
in the *Norddeutsche*, the British Foreign Office had arranged for
a parliamentary interpellation whether the German publication
was complete and accurate. Grey explained that it was not. "It was
reported to me," he told Parliament,

that the German ambassador had suggested that Germany might remain neutral in a war between Russia and Austria and also engage
not to attack France if we would remain neutral and secure the neutrality of France. I said at once that if the German government
thought such an arrangement possible I was sure we could secure it.
It appeared however that what the ambassador meant was that we
should secure the neutrality of France if Germany went to war with
Russia. This was quite a different proposal and as I supposed it in
all probability to be incompatible with the terms of the Franco-
Russian alliance it was not in my power to promise to secure it. Subsequently the ambassador sent for my private secretary and told him
that as soon as the misunderstanding was cleared up he had sent a
telegram to Berlin to cancel the impression produced by the first
telegram he had sent on the subject. This telegram does not seem
to have been published.[22]

The Wilhelmstrasse now published on 6 September the full
correspondence with only minor deletions. The editor made no
attempt to unravel the complexities but in a short commentary
pointed out that, contrary to what Grey had said, Lichnowsky had
not informed Berlin that there had been a misunderstanding.[23]
This left the reader three possibilities: that it was all a British
trick which Lichnowsky had not penetrated, or that Lichnowsky
had misunderstood Grey and Tyrrell throughout but did not
know that he had, or that when he perceived the misunderstanding he neglected to report it. This was not the last of revelations
damaging to Lichnowsky. On 16 October the government published a selection of correspondence concerning Britain's secret
naval discussions with France and Russia. The selection con-

tained Lichnowsky's dispatch reporting Grey's denial that England had entered into such discussions with Russia. There the prince had added that anyone who knew Grey could not for a minute assume that he was trying to conceal the truth.[24]

These revelations, which he could not answer or explain, intensified Lichnowsky's bitterness against the government. He was determined not to let the false impression of his service that was forming in the public mind go unchallenged. He aired his grievances to everyone. His constant criticism of Berlin's policy, which allegedly made him unpopular with other officers,[25] reached the ears of Bethmann, who at the end of October obtained the kaiser's personal order to the prince to cease and desist from all public discussion of the events preceding the outbreak of war.[26] He may have complied with this order, but with great reluctance. "I have obviously been chosen to play the role of Dreyfuss," he wrote Jagow on 1 November, "and I have every right to defend myself against that fate."[27] Finally, in mid-November he was released from duty and permitted to go home.[28]

Until the end of 1914 the prince did his best to influence military strategy toward England. He was convinced that Germany could never win a long war against the British Empire, but like Bethmann he also believed that England had no intention of crushing Germany and had entered the fray with the greatest reluctance. If therefore Germany conducted the war against England with restraint, a satisfactory settlement was entirely possible. Bethmann had abandoned his hopes of a separate peace with England early in September, when the Allies swore to fight on to the end as a unit;[29] but Lichnowsky clung to his for the remainder of the year. His goal was not to split the Entente but to bring about a general peace. The channel he chose to convey these ideas was Admiral Tirpitz. "I ask you to say nothing about [my proposals] to the three leading 'statesmen,' " he wrote Tirpitz in December, "as they ipso facto oppose anything that comes from me." He was convinced that although Germany could not defeat England, the English would reply in kind to gestures of goodwill. Above all, he warned that attacks upon the civilian population would only intensify Britain's resolve.[30] (How correct this prognosis was, we know from a report on the effect of the air attacks on London which Bethmann received from a Danish intermediary in 1917.)[31] But Lichnowsky's appeal to Tirpitz, as he may have expected, was in vain.

When the prince left military service in November 1914 he withdrew once more, as ten years earlier, into a state of retirement. Technically he was still a member of the service with the rank of ambassador and subject to the chancellor's orders. But in fact he lived as a private citizen, residing alternately in Silesia and Berlin. The effective end of his public service disrupted the flow of his political life. In London he had served his sovereign as an individual champion; general principles of diplomacy and statecraft had guided his conduct; he had represented only himself, not a definable political tendency or even an organized party; and now Free Conservatism was dead. His father's party (and his) had not only supported Bismarck's domestic compromise but his practical and unromantic approach to foreign policy. Now it had shed its liberal accretions and succumbed to the infatuations of Pan-Germanism. Lichnowsky had no political matrix to which he could return for strength and comfort.

In the public mind the prince was now reduced by events to the opposite of what he personally and socially represented. The antithesis of the aristocrat, writes Otto Brunner in his study of nobility and the European spirit, is the character of the fool, "who cannot control his impulses and sustains vices rather than virtues."[32] The prince's wartime scribe, the late novelist August Scholtis, has recalled the attitudes toward Lichnowsky among the villagers and the employees on the prince's estate. A peasant woman, seeing the pennant fluttering over the chateau at Kuchelna denoting that the prince was in residence, remarked that Lichnowsky had betrayed Germany and was to blame for the war. This she had gleaned from newspapers her husband brought back from the Rhineland.[33] Stable boys of the most brutish sort mocked the prince's speech. "What an ass," said Lichnowsky's general manager, Paul Püschel, one day in August 1914, after the prince had said, "Germany, my dear Püschel, has already lost this war." "Why don't we simply confiscate his property," said Püschel.[34]

The prince intended to be a loyal subject. In October 1914 he wrote Prince Heinrich zu Schönaich-Carolath (a supporter of the

National Liberals and therefore known as the "Red Prince") that "so long as the war continues it is necessary to be silent. But afterwards I will under no circumstances acquiesce in the charge that I let Grey deceive me."[35] In May 1915 he wrote Eduard Bernstein that "in the interest of the common cause all the political parties are obliged above everything else to support the government and not to undermine the public's trust in it."[36] The prince refrained from further publications touching directly upon the 1914 crisis. And by subscribing heavily to the war loans he put his profits from the flax factory into paper his political judgment must have warned him would in a few years be worthless.[37]

But it was not possible for him to maintain perfect silence. He could not mask his feelings, which were alternately depressed and aggressive, or keep his views entirely to himself. "To talk to poor Lichnowsky last night was really sad," Daisy of Pless noted in her diary in 1916. "He is frightfully depressed, feeling that the emperor and others blame him for the war."[38] Baroness Rothschild, wife of the member of that famous family who owned lands to the south of the Lichnowsky estates, reported in Vienna that the prince was uttering extreme criticisms of Germany even before the servants.[39] Mensdorff, who visited Lichnowsky in July 1915, noted that "he is still bitter, full of spleen toward sovereign, chancellor etc."[40] In time the prince's views became widely known. He made no secret of his feelings when political matters were discussed in his own home or when he visited friends or acquaintances. A Swedish journalist recalled his attendance at a gathering in Lichnowsky's home in May 1916. The guests included a newspaper editor, German officers, and many foreigners, and numbered about fifty. Before this large audience the prince poured forth his criticism of the government's policy in 1914.[41]

The prince had a brief flirtation with the *Bund Neues Vaterland*. Founded shortly after the outbreak of hostilities, this organization at first presented a program of pacifism and diplomatic and political reform similar to that of the British Union of Democratic Control. At the beginning of 1915 the *Bund* distributed a short analysis of Germany's prewar policy taking note of the opportunity for peaceful expansion overseas and condemning the decision to support Austria's attack on Serbia,

which the authors of the pamphlet described as morally inde-
fensible and politically stupid. Reading this, Lichnowsky hastened to the *Bund's* offices. He introduced himself to the head of
the organization, expatiated upon his experiences, and praised the
pamphlet to its chief author, a twenty-five year old leftwing Socialist named Ernst Reuter.[42] (After World War II Reuter was to
become famous as the anticommunist mayor of West Berlin.) In
the spring of 1915 the *Bund* was banned, whereupon it went
underground and became progressively more radical.

On the question of diplomatic reform the prince could not
fully share the views of the *Bund* or the Union of Democratic
Control. In the essay entitled "Diplomacy and Democracy" published in the *Berliner Tageblatt* in the summer of 1917 he asserted
that foreign policy would have to be subject to parliamentary
control and the foreign service democratized. But he rejected the
notion that diplomacy had failed because the diplomatic corps
was dominated by aristocrats. " 'Give the man of ability a chance
to come to the front' is doubtless an excellent principle," he
wrote, "but it has no more value than the mottoes on coats-of-
arms which everyone interprets to his own taste." Nor could he
have agreed with English criticism of Sir Edward Grey and the
British system of conducting diplomacy. He noted that while in
England all important questions of foreign policy came before the
cabinet, in Germany the nation's destiny lay in the hands of a
single official. That was no longer to be tolerated: "The bureau-
cratic state . . . has passed away, never to return; the days when
nations were kept in a state of tutelage are as obsolete as those
of theocracy, and it will no longer satisfy a people merely to have
the right to say 'Yes' and to cry 'Hurrah' when faced with accomplished fact."[43]

As these words indicated, the prince in the course of the war
had come to accept democracy. That this might entail destruction
of the monarchy caused him no regret. The traditions of a Catholic aristocracy had not prevented his cool and objective appraisal
of the Habsburg monarchy, and he would not now indulge sentiments about the Hohenzollerns or the lesser ruling houses. He
saw that true parliamentary government was incompatible with
the Reich's confederal organization. Parliamentary government
"means the unitary state," he wrote Maximilian Harden, "and

that in turn means. . . ." Though he left the implication blank, he added: "We cannot abolish all dynasties and leave but one standing."[44] A few months after war's end he was to write that a republican Germany "must come out resolutely for the unitary state and turn its back on that system of petty states which has for so many centuries burdened monarchical Germany."[45]

Lichnowsky had made Harden's acquaintance in the fall of 1914. The editor of the personal and individualistic weekly magazine *Die Zukunft* had been Germany's leading critic and political commentator for over twenty years. Lichnowsky was not the first statesman to invite Harden's confidence. Some twenty years earlier Bismarck had summoned the young journalist to his estate and divulged to him his concern about Wilhelm II. In 1906 Holstein, having left office with accounts unfinished, unburdened himself to Harden, his erstwhile critic.[46] Lichnowsky and Harden developed an easy relationship. "I know," he wrote Harden in 1916, "that I am in accord with you more than with anyone else."[47] By this time they were indeed in close agreement on the two burning questions: who or what was responsible for the outbreak of the war; and how was the war to be brought to a satisfactory conclusion. The prince had preceded Harden in rejecting all annexations, and Harden had anticipated the prince in concluding that Bethmann's diplomacy in 1914 provided the classic example of a policy of preventive war.[48]

Lichnowsky's search for an answer to the question of responsibility was long and dolorous. His agony began in 1914 when he had to defend the plan of localization to Sir Edward Grey. All through the critical month it is obvious that he suspected Berlin hoped the attack upon Serbia would result in a general war. In the imploring dispatch he sent Jagow on 23 July he argued against the illusions of a prophylactic war; and in "England before the War," the account he dictated from memory shortly after his return from London, he submitted that Germany had ignored every opportunity to turn the crisis into a diplomatic success and instead had pursued a policy that had no possible issue but military conflict. His feeling reached a peak of intensity in December, for it was now that German propaganda began to shift the blame from Russia to England. The picture of a provocative Russia mobilizing with full knowledge of the consequences gave way to the sinister figure of an England moving with malevolent purpose to destroy the hated rival.

"The responsibility for this greatest of all wars is plain," Bethmann told the Reichstag on 2 December. "The external responsibility is borne by those men in Russia who agitated for and carried through the general mobilization of the Russian army. The internal responsibility is borne by the government of Great Britain. The London cabinet could have made the war impossible if it had told Saint Petersburg unequivocally that England had no intention of permitting a Continental war of the great powers to grow out of the Austro-Serbian conflict." "The only conclusion left," the chancellor said further, "is that the London cabinet permitted this world war, this terrible world war, to come because it appeared to be an opportunity to destroy, with the help of England's political entente allies, the vital nerve center of her greatest European competitor in the markets of the world."[49]

Lichnowsky took issue with this interpretation in a long letter to his friend Wilhelm Solf on 24 December.

You can scarcely imagine my mood [he wrote]. Unfortunately everything occurred as I foresaw it would. . . . Who caused the war—the one who made repeated attempts at compromise, or the one who rejected everything? . . . The main question is not: Could Grey have prevented it? but why did we not prevent it? They blame Grey because he did not employ a tone of command in St. Petersburg and did not prevent the mobilization (which he first heard of from me) while we declared that we had to reject all pressure on Vienna in a matter that because of contractual commitments put the very existence of the whole nation at stake. Only he who knows the truly fabulous incompetence of our leading statesmen will understand that such a policy was indeed possible *without* their desiring war! Or did they want war? I still cannot say which.[50]

It was in this spirit, induced by the attacks upon Grey, that Lichnowsky pondered the question of responsibility in a second essay, completed in January 1915, which he entitled "Wahn oder Wille?" (delusion or design). For many years this essay was known to us in the revised form included in his collected papers of 1927 under the title "Wahn, nicht Wille" (delusion, not design), and the original version is available to us now only because he sent copies of it to various friends whose papers were not later destroyed.[51] It was Lichnowsky's purpose to give the question of responsibility its proper formulation. He attempted to refute the proposition that English policy was calculated to produce a war —a proposition which implied that he had misconstrued the policy it was his duty to follow and interpret. But it was not at all a question of England's intentions but of Germany's. "What on earth made the German people plunge into a world war to fight against the South Slav movement for national unity?" he asked. His answer was not to provide the deeper causes for this action but to note the existence of attitudes and an atmosphere that favored it. As in many of his wartime writings, here too he noted that the Bismarckian tradition of *Realpolitik* had given way increasingly to sentiment and romance. A policy that placed 5 million German soldiers at the disposal of Emperor Franz Joseph to avenge the murder of his nephew reminded him of wars in bygone ages "sparked by personal differences between princely families."

His questioning of German policy grew sharper as he tried to explain why England entered the war. His guiding principle as German representative in London had been that England would cooperate with Germany as long as Germany's policy remained unequivocally peaceful.

But we quitted this path [he wrote] when we allowed Count Berchtold to strike at Serbia, and indeed urged him to do so. Such a policy was bound to lead to a world war and to the collapse of all my efforts to bring about an understanding. For it was not to be expected, from reasons already explained, that the conflict could be localized.

We either wanted this war for purposes of prophylaxis—and indeed the chancellor reportedly spoke in this vein to the Austrians— or we seriously deceived ourselves as to the consequences of our policy when we put our armed forces entirely at the disposal of Count Berchtold for bickering with Serbia.

I ask: Is it a peaceful policy to urge war when it is probable, if not more than probable, that this war means a world conflagration? It is said that we wanted peace—but only on the condition that Russia give her blessing to the annihilation of Serbia in the name of the monarchical principle.

We imagined that by taking up a stand-to-attention, drill-book attitude we could win a diplomatic success and thus rejuvenate Austria-Hungary. That was our fatal and terrible mistake.

On our side absolutely nothing was done to preserve the peace, and when we finally decided to do what I had advocated from the beginning, it was too late. For as a result of the brusque attitude that we and Count Berchtold had assumed, Russia lost all faith and mobilized.

Our policy reminds me of the Anglo-Saxon king, who sitting at the water's edge commanded the tide to stop before his feet. It was not his fault that his feet got wet, but that of the tide. The tide should have stopped!

Such a policy is intelligible only if the aim was war, but not otherwise.

The men who exercised authority in the foreign ministry told me repeatedly that Russia would be "ready" in 1916 and that we dare not stand back and let that happen. Our relations with Russia had rapidly deteriorated. But instead of working for an improvement by transferring personnel, by greater reserve in supporting Austrian wishes, and respect for Russian sensitivity on other matters, we took to arms. Who will undertake to prove that we truly would have to fight in 1916? For what purpose would Russia have attacked us? England and France were unconditionally peaceful and would have remained so; they would never have supported a Russian attack.

The crucial question is not: Did Grey want war? Why did he not prevent it? What did he do or what did he fail to do to prevent it? The question is rather: Did we want war? Why did we not prevent it? What did we do or fail to do to prevent it?[52]

But Lichnowsky would not answer these questions explicitly: he would not decide whether *Wahn* or *Wille* had prevailed that summer.

It was not until the end of 1916 that Lichnowsky seemed to have found his answer to the question. When the historian and publicist Hans Delbrück asked him in November 1916 to join an organization formed to combat Pan-German influence, he answered that "unfortunately, in July 1914 our government took its stand on the platform of the Pan-German party, whose apostles for years had been preaching the preventive war."[53] In December Lichnowsky wrote to Solf: "What I think about this war is known to you. The mistake of preventive wars is that they have no positive goal, but a negative one, and that it is impossible to discover retroactively a purpose that will justify the sacrifices that have been made."[54]

As he was pessimistic about all attempts at retroactive justification, he opposed the propagation of war aims envisaging territorial occupation or Europe's economic restructuring. He condemned the popular plan for closer economic union with Austria-Hungary and the extension of German influence in Turkey. Still believing in the beneficence of peaceful colonial expansion, he wrote in *My London Mission* that "the policy of the Triple Alliance is a return to the past, a turning aside from the future, from imperialism and a world-policy. The idea of an all-powerful 'Middle Europe' belongs to the Middle Ages, Berlin-Baghdad is a blind alley and not the way into the open country, to unlimited possibilities, to the world mission of the German nation."[55] He rejected the *Mitteleuropa* program because it would seal Germany's marriage with the problems of her partner and, as German trade before the war had been carried on primarily with the enemy countries, ignored Germany's true economic interests.[56]

His reasons for opposing annexation are given in a letter he wrote Bülow in 1915. Bülow had taken serious notice of Lichnowsky's views on the war.[57] As to the origins, Bülow's conclusion was that Berlin wanted a war with Serbia but not with Russia, as he remarked on his copy of "Wahn oder Wille?"[58] On the question of annexation he was in thorough disagreement with Lichnowsky. He thought that Germany must take advantage of her victories to improve her strategic position.[59] In the margins of "Wahn oder Wille?" he noted that Germany should control "the North Sea coast from Antwerp to Calais, or at least to Dunquerque, [and] the fortresses along the Maas, Brey and Belfort."[60] What he wanted was "guarantees of a substantial nature." When he conveyed these ideas to Lichnowsky in July 1915, the prince replied that Germany did indeed seem strong enough to keep the enemy away from her borders, as Bülow had said.

But [Lichnowsky continued] it is quite another question whether we shall win such decisive victories that our enemies will be forced to abandon all further resistance. I do not believe this is possible, and I have met no one who puts faith in such a turn of fortune. But even in the most favorable circumstances not even you, I think, could show any advantages that would in any way correspond to the losses we have suffered. How do you imagine these guarantees of substantial nature? That could only mean the erection of a military dictatorship in Belgium and Poland à la Napoleon. How long would such a situation last, and what would come after it? All that might be possible in Bokhara, in Turkestan, or Mongolia, and in a pinch, in Persia, but even in India this system can be maintained only through the antagonisms among the different communities and the attraction exerted by British civilization—which has resulted in every Maharadja apparently knowing no greater satisfaction than to be taken for a British gentleman even when he is in opposition to the government. But I cannot imagine that the desire to imitate a Prussian lieutenant or bureaucrat will work in our favor in Belgium or Poland, nor that a system based entirely on force can have lasting success among civilized Europeans. For we must wish to create *lasting* and not temporary conditions—not such that will lead inevitably to new complications. The fault of the policy that led to this war is that, unlike 1870, it is impossible to justify this war by its results and that there are no absolute guarantees at all without world dominion. That alone can put us in a position to impose our will at any time on all other peoples. But history teaches that every effort to wrest dominion of the world has collapsed—and must collapse. The mistake of this war cannot be mended. Let us therefore not worsen the situation by creating conditions that are clearly untenable and by purposelessly prolonging the war; that will only increase the disparity between input and output. In spite of the animosity that, as you say, prevails among our opponents, they will see the need, just as we will, to enter into relations with us after the conclusion of peace, for we need one another in this society of peoples.[61]

Lichnowsky feared that in the end it would be Germany who would have to give up territory. He wrote Harden in the fall of 1916 that from the beginning he had known that the war would go on "until we were forced to give up; and then all the nonsensical projects would collapse of their own weight."[62] The next year he wrote Bernstorff that Germany's one hope was to make concessions to the war-weary Russians on the Serbian and Polish questions[63]—and this is one reason he opposed the Central Powers' plan to reestablish an independent Poland.[64] The prince made one effort to present his views to the government. In December

1916, when President Wilson had requested the warring powers to state their goals, Lichnowsky wrote Solf that Germany would probably be forced to give up her colonies; in any case, she should avoid everything that could conceivably give the impression that she desired to prolong the war. He added that Solf might show this letter to Zimmermann, who had just succeeded Jagow as foreign secretary.[65]

By 1917 Lichnowsky could hope no longer for a moderate peace. The novelist Heinrich Mann recalls an encounter in the spring of that year at a political soirée in the home of the banker Richard Witting, who was Maximilian Harden's brother. Lichnowsky had been speaking in a controlled manner, stating many more or less ominous truths, when Witting asked if he remembered a conversation they had the previous spring. "You said, if we offered Alsace-Lorraine and the kaiser abdicated, we could get out with our skins whole. Is that still your opinion?" Lichnowsky, after some hesitation, while holding his head and eyes completely still, answered: "No."[66]

In the summer of 1916 Lichnowsky wrote a third wartime essay entitled *My London Mission, 1912–1914*.[67] He could not know that this was the form in which his thoughts on the origins of the war and Germany's wartime policy would be broadcast throughout the world. This essay was the fruit of an angry exchange with Bethmann arising in a dispute between Theodor Wolff and Count Reventlow.[68] Reventlow had authored a nationalistic history of German foreign policy. In a new edition just off the press he stated that the Anglo-German agreement on the Portuguese colonies was to remain secret at the insistence of the English. When Wolff in the *Berliner Tageblatt* found this improbable, Lichnowsky cabled him that indeed it was the Germans who had insisted upon secrecy and thereby obstructed the progress.[69]

Apprised of this telegram by the censors, Bethmann once more bestirred himself to face Lichnowsky's challenge. Threatening to arraign the prince before an administrative court, he said that in giving this incomplete and misleading account of the treaty negotiations, the prince had again disregarded his official and personal responsibilities. Lichnowsky replied that this was not the case. For he had told Wolff nothing that was not already known to the public, and in general he had conducted himself with unusual forbearance toward an agency that (as he knew from reliable information) had encouraged the public to believe that he had held to an illusion and was responsible for the catastrophe. Bethmann denied this charge. Not only had the press chief once been instructed to show journalists a dispatch in which the prince had expounded his view of England's commitment toward France, but the Wilhelmstrasse in publishing the correspondence of 1 August 1914 had taken care to hide the fact that the prince had been guilty of a misunderstanding and then had failed to report his misunderstanding though the consequences of delay might well have been fatal. While the Wilhelmstrasse had taken Lichnowsky under its shield, he could not vouch for the military and naval authorities: they too were aware that up to the very last the prince had continued to report that England was hoping to remain neutral.[70]

Less than three weeks after the last letter from Bethmann, on 1 August 1916, Lichnowsky put his signature on the manuscript of *My London Mission*. This was an account of his ambassadorship beginning with the history of his appointment. The content and wording were similar to "England before the War" and "Delusion or Design?" His mission as ambassador in London had been to eliminate the tension between the two countries which had arisen from the naval rivalry and pave the way for a general understanding. This goal was within reach "when the outbreak of the war destroyed everything I had achieved." Two years of fighting showed that Germany could not hope for victory. The opportunity to found a colonial empire had vanished for ever. While Germany remained tied to Austria-Hungary, the rest of the world would fall to the Anglo-Saxons, the Russians, and the Japanese.

Why did his mission fail? Not because he was given to illusions or misunderstandings—for his estimate of British intentions had been absolutely correct. Not because the Foreign Office hated Germany—for it was Grey's plan "to bring the two groups together." Relations had improved under his care, and goodwill had prevailed to the very end. The arrangements for his departure were dignified and calm, and he was treated like a departing sovereign.

"Such was the end of my London mission. It was wrecked, not by the wiles (*Tücken*) of the British policy but by the defects (*Lücken*) of our own."

From Bismarck on, German foreign policy had moved inexorably toward the conflict with Russia and England. "Our enigmatic Morocco policy had repeatedly shaken confidence in our pacific intentions and, at the very least, had given rise to the suspicion that we did not quite know what we wanted, or that it was our object to keep Europe in a constant state of alarm and now and again to humiliate France." The desire for a dominating position on the Bosphorus forced Russia, "by nature our friend and excellent neighbor, into the arms of France and England and away from its policy of Asiatic expansion." "In Russia they began to think that the road to Constantinople and the Mediterranean lay via Berlin." Germany's alliances only intensified differences with Russia and were otherwise worthless since, as everyone knew, Italy would fail her allies in case of war and Austria was condemned by the nature of things to be Germany's vassal. "We needed *neither wars nor alliances;* we needed only treaties that would safeguard us and others, and secure our economic development, a development that was without precedent in history."

"The ultimatum to Serbia was the culminating point of the policy of the Berlin Congress [1878], the Bosnian crisis [1908–1909], and the Conference of London [1913]." But if Bismarck was the father of the "miserable Triple Alliance," he had never intended it to be a political life-and-death union. That transformation had occurred more recently. The Vienna statesmen, bent on securing revision of the Treaty of Bucharest, which had confirmed the territorial gains made by the Balkan powers in 1913, were confident of German support. "In fact, Berlin was pressing for 'rehabilitation of Austria.' " "Needless to say, a mere hint from Berlin would have decided Count Berchtold to content himself with a diplomatic success, and to accept the Serbian reply. This hint was not given; on the contrary they urged in the direction of war. It would have been such a splendid success."

Berlin had clearly perceived the likelihood of a war with Russia. At his conferences in Berlin at the end of June and early in July 1914, both Zimmermann and Bethmann expressed distrust of Russia. "Of course I was not told that General von Moltke, chief of the general staff, was pressing for war." "Subsequently," he noted, "I ascertained that, at the decisive conference at Potsdam on 5 July, the Vienna enquiry received the unqualified assent of all the leading people, and with the rider that no harm would be done if a war with Russia should result." Upon his return to Berlin he was told that in any case the war would have come about in 1916. "Then Russia would have been ready; therefore it was better now."

The German statesmen persisted in this dangerous policy because they could not bring themselves to accept the advice of Prince Lichnowsky. Their motives were personal, he implied. Bethmann feared he was aspiring to become chancellor; Stumm wanted the London post for himself. "Nothing can describe the rage of certain gentlemen at my achievements in London and the position that I had managed to make for myself in a short time," he wrote. Berlin had obstructed and finally dropped the treaty on the Portuguese colonies "because it would have been a public success for me." During the crisis his efforts were directed "towards obtaining as conciliatory a reply from Serbia as was possible, since the attitude of the Russian government left no doubt as to the gravity of the situation." Then he supported the British proposal for mediation between Austria and Serbia. "But Berlin insisted that Serbia must be chastised. The more I pressed, the less they were inclined to come round, if only that I in conjunction with Sir Edward Grey might not have the success of averting war."

The prince pondered his own role in these affairs. He mentioned the impudent dispatch Stumm had sent him in May 1914 ordering him to stop interfering in the matter of the Portuguese colonies. "Looking back after two years, I come to the conclusion that I realized too late that there was no room for me in a system that for years had lived on routine and traditions alone, and that only tolerated representatives who reported what their superiors wished to read." "I had given up my opposition to the insane Triple Alliance policy, as I realized that such opposition was useless, and that my warnings were attributed to 'Austrophobia,' to my *idée fixe*." "I had to support in London a policy the heresy of which I recognized. That brought down vengeance on me, because it was a sin against the Holy Ghost."

On the question of responsibility for the war *My London Mission* was not entirely explicit. Apparently the prince had not yet achieved the certainty with which he spoke of a preventive war a few months later. While in one passage he wrote that from Mensdorff's record of the 5 July discussions he had learned Berlin did not fear war with Russia—even welcomed it—in another passage he wrote that only Berlin and Vienna had failed to recognize that the Austrian ultimatum to Serbia actually meant world war. It was to the British and not to himself that he attributed the impression that Germany wanted war at all costs, and even here it was not clear whether he meant an Austro-Serbian or a German-Russian conflict.[71] Toward the end of the memoir he came directly to the question of responsibility. Summarizing the contents of the official publications, he showed that Germany had encouraged Austria to attack Serbia, that she had rejected the proposals for mediation, and declared war on Russia merely because of the Russian mobilization. "In view of [these] undeniable facts," he concluded, "it is no wonder that the whole of the civilized world outside Germany places the entire responsibility for the world war upon our shoulders."[72]

When the draft was completed, Lichnowsky sent it to his office to be typed. Obviously he intended to distribute this memoir to friends and acquaintances as he had "England before the War" and "Delusion or Design?" Eight copies were prepared, according to August Scholtis.[73] By the end of the year Lichnowsky had distributed one each to his brother-in-law Count Arco, Theodor Wolff, Maximilian Harden, Albert Ballin, Geheimrat von Gontard (a manufacturer), and Richard Witting.[74] Scholtis recalls that all recipients (he remembers sending some copies by common mail) were enjoined to the strictest secrecy.[75] Witting later said that he had first learned of this new essay when Lichnowsky mentioned it to him during a conversation in the fall of 1916. Although the prince was reluctant to part with a copy, when he finally did so, he failed to request that it be returned to him.[76] And thus *My London Mission* was started on its way to worldwide fame.

Witting, president of the Nationalbank für Deutschland, had lost a son on the battlefields in 1914. He became a pacifist and opened his villa in Berlin's Tiergarten section to gatherings of men of all political hues who shared his opposition to the war.[77] If there was any leader of an interparty peace movement, it was Witting. One evening in June or July 1917, after a meeting in his home, he lent his copy of *My London Mission* to Hans Georg von Beerfelde, an army captain attached to the intelligence section of the general staff in Berlin.

Theodor Wolff remembers Beerfelde calling on him once near midnight: "tall and dignified, in uniform, with bushy bristling eyebrows and the fixed, accusing stare of an evangelist."[78] Before the war Beerfelde was a follower of Rudolf Steiner's Theosophism. In 1914 he was at the front and was wounded and decorated. As the war went on he progressed to more radical views, and in the 1920s he was to be the advocate of a "general strike of the soul" that was to precede the great social revolution.[79] He had made Witting's acquaintance through the *Bund Neues Vaterland*, which he joined after returning from the front. When Witting told him about the prince's essay that evening in the summer of 1917, he begged permission to read it, promising to bring it back the next day. Although he kept his promise, he did not tell Witting that he had made fifty copies of the memoir.[80] These (as he then wrote Lichnowsky, a stranger to him) he sent to prominent officers and civilians such as the editor of the Socialist *Vorwärts*, National-Liberal leader Gustav Stresemann, the industrialist Walther Rathenau (who had become the wartime raw materials administrator), General Ludendorff, and the crown prince.[81]

A copy reached the press chief at the Foreign Ministry on 6 August 1917. Fearing that it was an Allied forgery that would soon be distributed among the neutrals, he hurried his copy along to Chancellor Michaelis. (Bethmann had resigned in July.) The press chief noted that the memoir referred to a crown council on 5 July 1914, that fictional event (so the press chief thought) which Allied propagandists had invented and were now exploiting so successfully.[82]

The government was determined to reduce the impact of the memoir. When a check with Lichnowsky proved it to be authentic, Michaelis ordered the prince to recall all the copies he had personally distributed.[83] The Bavarian legation wrote to Munich that Kühlmann (now foreign secretary) believed the prince had not recovered from his collapse in London; he was suffering from monomania. It was also reported that the chancellor had demanded an accounting from Lichnowsky, hoping this would lead to a complete mental breakdown and commitment to a sanatorium, which would destroy the prince's credibility.[84]

The suggestion of mental breakdown had a precedent in the strange case of Baron von Eckardstein who had been councillor of embassy in London from 1899 to 1902. Admitted to the service without examination because of excellent social connections in London (his wife was the daughter of a prominent Englishman), he had during his incumbency through inaccurate reporting encouraged on both sides the hope of an alliance and quit the service in a pique when the embassy was entrusted to Metternich (who, he said, was the "sworn enemy of every form of initiative").[85] To the professional diplomats Eckardstein was anathema. Having taken his files with him when he left the service, he repeatedly revealed his secrets to the press. In 1908 his documents enabled Theodor Wolff to say that at the turn of the century England and Germany had been engaged (so it seemed) in discussions concerning an alliance; and in 1912 Eckardstein leaked the story of the 1898 negotiations on the Portuguese colonies.[86] Although the German government in 1913 learned that he had sold his filched documents to a publisher, it was not until November 1914 that the federal attorney took action against him. By that time the charge of misappropriation of documents was enlarged by the suspicion of espionage. In June 1915 he fell sick and was hospitalized. Soon he was transferred to the psychiatric ward; and although the legal authorities had him released in January 1916, the military authorities, fearing he would take revenge with further publicity, had him restricted to a sanatorium.[87]

In Lichnowsky's case there was no need for such drastic action. He had not sought this publicity and he was more than willing to help the authorities in preventing *My London Mission* from circulating. Only briefly did the Wilhelmstrasse deliberate whether the prince was subject to administrative punishment or to trial under the criminal code. A representative of the Foreign Ministry interrogated him on 27 August and then took testimony from Witting and Beerfelde. Lichnowsky deposed that he had written the memorandum as a record of his ambassadorship and solely for his personal use. Although he had drawn heavily on classified information, he had in the main set down personal impressions that could make no claim to historical objectivity. The prince admitted that on certain points, which he did not specify, he was misinformed. After gathering all the evidence and considering the legal alternatives, the government agreed that litigation would create a publicity it would be best for them to avoid.[88]

The Foreign Ministry, the military authorities (who had the responsibility for censorship), and the secret police worked hard to limit circulation. Although Stresemann and the Social Democrat Ledebour made brief reference to *My London Mission* in a session of the Reichstag budget committee in August, the subject was declared confidential and no news of the discussion reached the public.[89] In the *Vorwärts* building the police discovered and confiscated two thousand copies of the memoir, but it appeared that the Majority Socialists who controlled the newspaper had no intention of distributing them. Lichnowsky himself intervened with Eduard Bernstein to prevent distribution of an apparently different set of two thousand copies that had come into the hands of a certain Minority Socialist.[90] These efforts were successful, and at New Year 1918 there had still been no mention of Lichnowsky's memoir in the press.

But suddenly in January 1918 *My London Mission* was available in printed form. It was a pamplet of thirty-one pages bearing the imprint of a fictional publisher. Although the text was complete and unaltered, the cover bore the title, *Die Schuld der deutschen Regierung am Kriege* (The German government's responsibility for the war). According to Beerfelde, the printing had been arranged by the *Bund Neues Vaterland.*[91] A postscript by an unidentified editor asserted that although the prince had failed to perceive the deeper causes of the war and the ramifications of imperialism, he had rendered his people a great service by tearing through "the web of lies in which the German people had been ensnared since the beginning of the war."[92]

As the German press still took no notice of *My London Mission*, the dissidents proposed to smuggle copies abroad. (Those destined for Switzerland were discovered by the secret police.)[93]

In the search for a northern channel, they turned to Hans Peter Hanssen, Reichstag representative of the Danish minority in northern Slesvig. He was receptive to their approach, and, as he noted in his diary, "after urgent requests on the part of a large group of malcontents of all parties," he agreed to smuggle copies of the memorandum across the border. It was arranged that on 30 January Beerfelde would transfer the copies to him at his hotel. But at the appointed hour Beerfelde arrived empty-handed. He had left his package at the fashionable Kempinski restaurant where he had stopped on his way to the rendezvous. He hurried back to Kempinski's and was relieved to find that the waiter had set the package aside against his return.[94] Years later Hanssen reported that while he was engaged in his mission across the Danish border, other dissidents whose names were unknown to him were simultaneously smuggling the memorandum into Sweden.[95]

On 6 March 1918 the Stockholm left-socialist newspaper *Politiken* began to serialize "Prince Lichnowsky's remarkable memorandum" under the headline, "Clarification of Germany's Military Imperialism." The *Politiken* spread the memorandum over six issues, completing publication on 6 April. Although the editors never explained how they acquired their manuscript, in the issue of 26 March, noting the worldwide reverberations, they expressly absolved Prince Lichnowsky from all complicity.[96]

This was an unexpected boon for the Allies. The appearance of Lichnowsky's confessions could not have been more timely. The German spring offensive had broken through the defenses in the West; the Bolsheviks had stopped fighting and were publishing the agreements by which the Allied governments had approved one another's plans for conquest and domination of foreign lands. To counter this the Allies could now point to the admission of a high German official that the Entente had pursued a policy of peace and Germany had brought about the war of her own free will.

The Allies hastened to obtain an authentic text. The London *Times* and Crewe House, center of wartime intelligence, combined their resources in Stockholm. The *Politiken* was prepared to give up the German original for twenty-five thousand Swedish Crowns.[97] Although the files do not show whether this amount was actually paid, it is apparent that the English had acquired the German text by the end of March. The *Times* published an English translation on the 28th and the National War Aims Committee soon issued an abridged edition under the title *Guilty! Prince Lichnowsky's Disclosures.*[98]

There was no end of the copies of *My London Mission* that now rolled off the Allied presses. In England two complete editions appeared in pamphlet form. By May four million free copies had been distributed, mainly among the industrial workers of the north.[99] Versions supported by the British appeared in Chinese, Serbian, Danish, Polish, Lettish, Portuguese, Afrikaans, and Swedish. During 1918 six different editions of the *Mission* appeared in Switzerland, five in France, four in the United States, and three in Italy. For German-Americans the American Committee on Public Information prepared an edition of over six hundred thousand.[100] A Spanish version was prepared for distribution in Mexico. George Creel, head of the committee, wrote that travelers to Mexico "constantly brought us word of having seen in remote places copies of the more popular pamphlets, President Wilson's Fourteen Points . . . and Prince Lichnowsky's pillorying of his government for precipitating the war."[101]

The British were responsible for the first complete and separate publication of the *Mission* in German. It is the edition published by Orell Füssli in Zurich in April 1918. This edition corresponds word for word with the original text except where the British editors chose, for reasons of delicacy, to eliminate Lichnowsky's parenthetical remark that Grey was not really married to the woman thought to be his wife.[102] Though this small deletion suggested to the historian Friedrich Thimme that the prince himself had had a hand in the Füssli edition,[103] the British records confirm that the publication was in all respects the work of British propaganda. It was Sir Horace Rumbold, British ambassador in Bern and former councillor in Berlin, who suggested the publication and recommended the addition of three appendices. (These contained an abbreviated version of Grey's speech of 3 August 1914, the text of Berlin's instruction to von Schoen demanding permission to occupy Toul and Verdun for the duration of Germany's war with Russia [which the French had deciphered], and the recently published account of Germany's financial preparations for war by Dr. Johann Muehlon, a former executive of the Krupp organization.)[104] London suggested the introduction be written by Prof. Ottfried Nippold, a German pacifist living in Switzerland who was active in the *Bund Neues Vaterland*.[105] The British paid Nippold's honorarium and bore the costs of advertisement.[106]

In the meanwhile the Germans themselves went to work on the *Mission*. They were determined to frustrate the Allied campaign. The Wilhelmstrasse hoped that some Dutch author would lend his name to a summary and refutation of the *Mission* which they hastily put together and (not finding a willing collaborator in Holland) finally published in Sweden under the pseudonym "Spartakus," who was said to be a retired diplomat. The Germans hoped that this shorter version would reduce interest in the full text which the Allies had now made available in Sweden in pamphlet form.[107] In Switzerland German agents set about buying up the Füssli edition while a "group of peace-lovers" who published the complete memorandum rearranged the paragraphing, inserted lurid or sarcastic headings, and added a mock impartial commentary intended to prove that the prince's assertions really amounted to an indictment, not of Germany, but of Britain.[108] The prince supported his government's efforts. Through legal action he forced the Danish and Dutch authorities to seize the pirated editions on sale in Copenhagen and Rotterdam.[109] And at his behest Eduard Bernstein had tried, in vain, to persuade the Swedish Socialists to halt the publication in *Politiken*.[110]

The propaganda war over *My London Mission* spread to the fighting lines. French military propagandists early in the war had concluded that they could undermine the morale of the German army only if they could prove that Germany had started the war.[111] Prince Lichnowsky's memorandum eminently met their requirements. They prepared a small-format edition of the *Mission* which their planes scattered over the German trenches.[112] The German military authorities were slow to react. General Ludendorff had little faith in wordy propaganda and argued that morale would improve as soon as Lichnowsky was arrested and punished.[113] But the German Fourth Army, holding down the sector facing the Belgians and British, after vainly requesting a reply to the *Mission*, itself issued a rebuttal entitled, "Prince

Lichnowsky and the Truth."[114] And, at the end of August, the military propaganda service engaged the Social-Democratic functionary Dr. Alwin Saenger[115] to prepare a countermemorandum. Appropriating the title of the underground version of the *Mission* published by the *Bund Neues Vaterland,* he too struck socialist tones, asserting that the mistakes of the German government were as nought compared with the wicked imperialism so praised by Lichnowsky. He predicted that the British and their lackeys would "bite the dust before the invincible fighting front of the German working class."[116]

The German authorities began to prepare for the reverberations at home even before the *Politiken* series began. In spite of all precautions, knowledge of the memorandum had gradually spread. From several quarters there was pressure to make public response to the prince's allegations. In January 1918 National Liberal deputy Gustav Stresemann inquired as to the government's intentions toward Lichnowsky.[117] He noted that the prince had recently written in the *Berliner Tageblatt* that the war had come about because Berchtold was determined to alter the power relations established by the Balkan Wars. In February, Count Pourtalès requested of the chancellor a public and official denial of Lichnowsky's charge that he had reported Russia would not move under any circumstances. The prince, when queried, had told him that without further examination of the documents he would not retract his charges.[118] But the Austrian government, when consulted in February, encouraged Berlin to resist these pressures.[119] "It was a dangerous, a very slippery terrain," the Austrian diplomat Mérey told foreign minister Czernin. "Either we turn out to be the whipping boy, as being solely responsible for the war, or the blind instruments of the German imperialistic policy. These are both equally dangerous and false."[120]

The *Politiken* series forced Berlin to bring *My London Mission* into the open. The censors relaxed their ban on publication; the full text was first published in the *Berliner Börsen-Kurier* on 21 March. In a statement read at an open session of the Reichstag budget committee on 16 March, Vice-Chancellor von Payer attempted to refute Lichnowsky's allegations. He pointed to the errors of fact (though they were few), to the prince's apparent vanity (which impressed many readers), to the naiveté toward the English statesmen (who, as all Germans knew, were perfidious). Von Payer's tactic, obviously, was to show the piece to be of little importance. He also read a statement by Lichnowsky in which the prince said that *My London Mission* consisted primarily of "subjective observations of our foreign policy since the Congress of Berlin." The roots of the war, he said, led back to Germany's estrangement from Russia and the extension of the alliance with Austria to Balkan matters. He had written *My London Mission* for his own justification, wishing to record the details of his experiences before they faded from his memory. After reading this explanation, the vice-chancellor announced that the prince had resigned his office, and that the government, recognizing that the prince's actions, though careless, were not malicious, considered the matter closed.[121]

It was obvious that the government had not made a very good case. Von Payer's statement was much too meager and lifeless for a matter of such notoriety. And the rebuttal by Jagow published in the *Norddeutsche Allgemeine Zeitung* on 23 March was even less successful. The former state secretary had acquired a copy of the *Mission* in the fall of 1917 when it was still under wraps and had thereupon composed a reply from memory.[122] He reviewed his manuscript before it was published. He made a few changes. In the original version he had written the following: "But if the war had become inevitable, the present moment was more favorable than a later one; that was also General von Moltke's view." He excised that sentence and wrote in its place that in spite of Russian armaments "the thought of a preventive war was far from our minds."[123] But these excisions did not improve his message. Although he too discovered Lichnowsky's errors and exaggerations, he could not deny that in 1914 Germany had chosen a path that was dangerous in the extreme.

Indeed, in this piece as in the private letter he wrote Lichnowsky on 18 July 1914, he could not avoid the admission that in general Lichnowsky was right.[124] The alliance with Austria, he conceded, was not the ideal arrangement. But (as he had said in his 1914 letter) there was no substitute for it, for the approach to England had not yielded the desired fruits. And of what use was the alliance if the partners could not contemplate the eventuality for which it was concluded—namely, military action against a threatening enemy. In 1914 Austria's existence was at stake; Russia was armed against Germany; and the Russian mobilization forced Germany in self-defense to declare war. Britain's proposal for a new conference of ambassadors to solve the Austro-Serbian dispute was not acceptable because it would have produced a crushing defeat for Austria and Germany. "Our position, in Europe and in the world at large, would not have survived another loss of prestige," he said.[125]

Both sides recognized that this was a self-incriminating statement. British propagandists wished to add it to their Swiss edition of *My London Mission*,[126] while the Americans coupled it with the Putnam and Sons edition of K. M. Lichnowsky, *The Guilt of Germany or the War of German Aggression*. Stumm warned Jagow that the German press might well conclude from his statement that his reason for favoring closer relations with England was that he was opposed to the alliance with Austria.[127] Other rebuttals were planned. In July 1918 the Foreign Ministry prepared one of forty-six pages for which Stumm asked Jagow to write the introduction and make textual changes as he thought necessary; in August Stumm urged the press chief to prepare a new "White Book" on the war's origins designed to refute Lichnowsky's memorandum.[128] But these projects were not completed.

The government's failure to rebut Lichnowsky's charges did nothing to improve his reputation. The attacks upon German diplomacy were renewed, and once more he was made to symbolize its failure. This criticism found conservatives and liberals on common ground. Before the war it was the National Liberals who had repeatedly attacked the foreign service as the preserve of noblemen and a refuge for incompetents, and during the war this egalitarianism merged with a general resentment of diplomacy itself. "The world is becoming ever more democratic," Stresemann told the Reichstag in 1916, "and forms and methods of diplomacy must accordingly change." He suggested that Germany should choose her diplomats from among her splendid navy men.[129] In August 1917 in a closed session of the budget committee he asserted that Lichnowsky's memorandum was a typical product of the undisciplined Old Diplomacy.[130] And in June 1918, when he attacked Lichnowsky once more, blaming him for prolonging the war, his remarks met with applause and "Hear, Hear" from the Conservatives.[131]

From the right to the left opinion was solidly against Lichnowsky. The Majority Socialist leader Scheidemann held the prince up to contempt. He told the Reichstag that Lichnowsky's brochure might impress mere pacifists, but not socialists, who saw the war as a product of the whole imperialistic system. And it was nothing short of ridiculous, he said, to see Germany's statesmen as fools one and all and the foreigners as such sterling characters.[132] In the liberal *Vossische Zeitung* Georg Bernhard attacked the prince and the government equally. He recalled that George Bernard Shaw had thought Lichnowsky silly to trust his Englishmen while the British lion was crouching for a final lunge at the German rival; he doubted whether the law would have been applied so leniently if the culprit had been a common citizen and not Prince Lichnowsky.[123]

Although von Payer had told the Reichstag that the case was closed, the government did, however, make an attempt to bring Lichnowsky to trial. It did this with the greatest reluctance, for the laws and ordinances concerning treason and the misuse of official documents did not seem applicable to him. But the kaiser and the military authorities insisted that he be punished. Wilhelm would not sign the resignation, presented to him in anguished haste on the eve of the interpellation, until the prince had been arraigned under administrative procedure. The kaiser thought this necessary because the military intended to press a suit against Beerfelde.[134] When the Foreign Ministry explained that administrative action was impossible because the vice-chancellor had already announced that Lichnowsky had resigned, the kaiser agreed to sign the release on the condition that the prince be tried under the criminal code. The ministry gave in, and also accepted the High Command's proposal that he be forbidden to engage in political activity.[135] But the government found it impossible to draw up a bill of particulars, and at the end of August gave up its attempt at criminal prosecution.[136]

In the meantime the prince was under trial in the *Herrenhaus*. In May a committee had been appointed to inquire whether he should be deprived of his hereditary seat. Had he behaved in a manner in keeping with the dignity of the High House? The evidence included the prince's wartime correspondence with Bethmann and several commentaries on *My London Mission* prepared in the Foreign Ministry.[137] Lichnowsky's defense followed the tactical line he had adopted the previous summer when his memoir came to light and Michaelis demanded an accounting from him. Since then he had tried to prove his message was innocuous. In his deposition for the *Herrenhaus* he repeated Harden's argument that the selection of diplomatic documents in the government's "White Book" was more incriminating than *My London Mission*. "Whilst I, for my part, argue that we did not believe that Russia would intervene, in other words, that we did not actually will the war, the German White Book declares that we steered deliberately into the world war, fully realizing what might be the result of our attitude."[138]

Lichnowsky's goal was a technical or legal excuse. He knew that it was much too soon to expect historical vindication. From the letters he wrote to Maximilian Harden it is plain that he was, for the moment, resigned to obloquy. Almost alone among the publicists, the editor of the *Zukunft* had risen to Lichnowsky's defense. His long excursions into the political and legal questions surrounding the disclosures lifted the prince's spirits without blinding him to the difficulties of his position.[139] On the day von Payer and the party leaders rose in the Reichstag to ridicule his behavior or his opinions, he wrote Harden that he was "taking comfort from the fellowship of others who had suffered his fate."[140] At Easter he swore to avoid all political controversy for the duration of the war. (It would not last too much longer, he thought, in view of the German advances on the western front.) [141] In June the two men gave up a project they had briefly considered to publish a selection of their essays and articles knowing that they would only succeed in reviving the attacks.[142] "The whole thing will be attributed to personal bitterness," he wrote Harden. "But in time it will be seen that I was right and that Theobald's policy was to blame for the catastrophe."[143]

The *Herrenhaus* reached its decision on 12 July. During the five-hour debate, which was conducted in secret, the prince was once more subjected to severe castigation. But according to Bülow a reading of selected passages in the *Mission* caused many to conclude that Lichnowsky was not a serious or dangerous critic and hence to cast a white ball. And so it was by a narrow margin that the *Herrenhaus* declared his membership to be forfeit.[144] Lichnowsky's peers chose to abolish his inherited privilege in the week when it was apparent that the military initiative had passed to the enemy. Four months later, the prince once remarked to his daughter, they were all thrown out.[145]

Chapter VIII

𝔓illoried, 1918-1928

> When he returned from London a broken man, they ridiculed him. And this is the attitude the authorities have maintained to this day. It has penetrated as far as the official collection of documents, and as late as 1927 it inspired the pedantic archivist Thimme to his superfluous and essentially untruthful polemic. The Republic had no use for the author of the historic memoir. . . . it snubbed him, boycotted him, like all the others who stood with the opposition during the war.   Carl von Ossietzky, "Carmer und Lichnowsky"
> *Die Weltbühne,* 6 March 1928

In November 1918, when Wilhelm II stepped into his motorcar and drove away to exile in Holland, Prince Lichnowsky was in his fifty-ninth year. The kaiser had ceased to be his friend, and soon after the war began Lichnowsky saw he had to accept a republican Germany. There are indications that it was his intention to resume his public career. Mensdorff after visiting Kuchelna in 1915 remarked that Lichnowsky "seemed not without certain ambitions for the future,"[1] and Theodor Wolff later recalled discussions—they must have occurred during the war—in which the prince intimated that full parliamentary government on the English model was the condition under which he would consent to become prime minister.[2] In October 1918, after the German authorities had sued for an armistice, he indicated in a letter to Harden that he was waiting for the right moment to put in an appearance.[3]

In the meantime, the crumbling empire had thrown other men to the surface. His friend Solf became the last imperial foreign secretary, and his friend Bernstorff head of the *Paxkonferenz* (which was preparing studies to be used at the coming peace talks). After the kaiser fled, Lichnowsky wrote Harden that though he would accept appointment to Bern or The Hague, he would not actively seek these posts nor volunteer for the delegation Germany would be sending to the peace conference.[4] His daughter recalls that once after the war (it was perhaps 1920 or 1921) she asked her father whether he would accept some public post. "I told them," he replied, referring apparently to the time of confusion at the end of war, when the political parties were forming anew, "either everything or nothing!"[5] Nothing was his likely expectation. Imperial appointees still manned the Foreign Ministry, and the Socialists who controlled the provisional government emerged from the national elections of January 1919 as the dominant party. Although Harden now proposed that Lichnowsky was the perfect choice for the republican presidency,[6] in a state dominated by Social Democrats and Catholic Centrists this distinction was as improbable as the chancellorship had been under Wilhelm II.

It was as a private citizen, therefore, that Lichnowsky, in the months following the collapse, was engaged in a national political effort. Banking upon his name and reputation, he embarked upon a campaign to improve the terms of peace. The armistice with its harsh demands had intensified the uneasiness he felt in October when Berlin was negotiating with President Wilson. Wilson, he wrote Harden, was an ideologue "who apparently was convinced that the brotherhood of peoples will dawn and all antagonisms will cease when justice is victorious and national borders are drawn democratically. He forgets, however, that sometimes national claims are justified on both sides even if they are mutually exclusive and that therein lies the tragedy of history."[7] Once the government did seek his assistance. In mid-November the Ministry of War requested Lichnowsky and the Socialists Bernstein and Ledebour to lecture a group of British prisoners, who would soon be going home, on the advantages of a democratic, or nonvengeful, peace. Although Lichnowsky agreed to do this, he withdrew his consent because he had already attempted to influence British opinion, and he thought a second effort would weaken the effect of the first.[8] In an "Appeal to the British Nation" published in the *Vorwärts* he had implored his friends in England in the interest of future peace and reconciliation to revise the terms of the armistice.[9]

As Lichnowsky's appeal to the enemy failed (for Asquith replied that the Germans had brought it all upon themselves),[10] he tried to influence his own government to reject the peace treaty if it should be unreasonable. He was convinced that the Allies would give in to a show of resistance. "If we play our cards with care," he wrote Bernstorff, "it is they who will be in a quandary, and we can make our conditions for a speedy restoration of peace."[11] When the Treaty of Versailles was completed in May, Lichnowsky called upon President Ebert and urged him to reject it.[12] Although Ebert agreed with him and thought the cabinet would remain firm, Lichnowsky knew that the two most influential ministers, Scheidemann and the Catholic Centrist Erzberger, favored signature, and he therefore appealed to Bülow to try to convince Erzberger that "our only hope lies in rejection. For in that case," he said, "public opinion in England and America would turn in our favor and protest the use of force. No one can of course predict [the reaction] with absolute certainty, but we dare not empty the poisoned cup until every hope has been destroyed."[13]

The prince now withdrew from active political life. For a brief period at war's end he was a member of the German Democratic party (DDP). The number of aristocrats who gave up their prewar allegiances and accepted republican institutions was very small. His adherence to the left wing of German liberalism, the party led by Theodor Wolff, was the natural culmination of his political development. He was long estranged from conservatism, and he had no sympathies for the right-wing liberals now gathered in the People's party headed by the wartime annexationist Gustav Stresemann, who had been his critic. He was a conscientious member of the DDP until he felt he could no longer condone the personal attacks upon Wilhelm II. He was aware of the kaiser's failings, and he appreciated the descriptions of Wilhelm's eccentricities that now filled all the remembrances. "If you had known the kaiser as I knew him," he once said, shaking his head over a memoir by someone from the court, "you would know how true this all is."[14] But the kaiser had been his benefactor and, up to a point, his friend, and he rose to his defense whenever he was criticized in his presence. When Theodor Wolff told him he could do nothing about these attacks, the prince had no choice but to turn in his resignation.[15]

During the last ten years of his life Prince Lichnowsky lived in reduced circumstances. As a result of the peace treaties his lands came under the control of three different authorities. By the Treaty of Versailles the Hultschiner Ländchen was transferred to Czechoslovakia, and the Council of the League of Nations in 1921 awarded that part of Upper Silesia lying south of Ratibor and east of the Oder to Poland. Since 1748 the Lichnowsky possessions had lain on the territory of two Germanic sovereigns. Now five-sixths of their property lay in Czechoslovakia and Poland. Only a small strip of land along the west bank of the Oder around Kreuzenort remained under the German flag.

These lands all became subject to expropriation. Both Czechoslovakia and Poland adopted laws authorizing confiscation and partition of the large estates. The Polish law, when applied, left the Lichnowskys only their forest lands and the fishery at Grabovka. In Germany the local officials attempted to thwart Polish propaganda promising land and a cow to all if during the plebiscite Upper Silesia elected to go to Poland and urged German landowners to give up some of their property. In this more or less voluntary reform the Lichnowskys lost something less than a third of the lands that eventually remained on the German side of the border, including the best beet fields at Kreuzenort. Because the Lichnowskys could therefore no longer fulfill their delivery quota to the Ratibor sugar refinery, the other members of the cooperative voted to confiscate their shares.[16]

The critical losses were suffered in Czechoslovakia. The Czechs intended to confiscate primarily the large estates based on the lands taken from the Czech nobility at the time of the Thirty Years War. Although the Lichnowskys were natives of the region and had acquired their property by purchase and inheritance, the law was applied against them with utmost severity. The authorities confiscated all the agricultural lands at Grätz, and at Kuchelna left them but a remainder of one hundred eighty hectares around the chateau. This vigorous application of the law in the Hultschiner Ländchen was doubtless intended to win the gratitude of the inhabitants, who had greeted the Czech occupiers in 1920 with a hail of stones. The Prague authorities also permitted the municipality of Troppau, largely German though it was, to take over a strip of the Lichnowsky forest, though because of the glut in lumber such land was not frequently expropriated (the Lichnowskys retained something over five thousand hectares). The greatest financial loss involved the flax factory. Being on the Czech side of the border, it had lost its German raw material sources and markets. The Czech authorities had begged Lichnowsky to continue operating his factory because it provided employment for so many inhabitants of the Ländchen. They promised to remember his favor when applying the land reform law. But the result for Lichnowsky was an enormous deficit. To cover the necessary loans the prince had to sell the most valuable paintings from the gallery at Grätz. Finally, in 1927 he decided to sell his house on the Buchenstrasse in Berlin.[17]

The prince suffered this reduction without resentment. In 1918 Silesian partition seemed to him to be an abysmal prospect. "To deliver us up to Polish administration would be to destroy us," he wrote Harden.[18] At the end of the war he had also argued against the popular proposals to break up the large estates, for although reform was in itself a worthwhile goal, he admitted, it should not be undertaken precipitously and thought should be given to the problem of capitalization.[19] But when the treaties went into effect and the land reform laws were applied he would not ignore stubborn facts. Emil Ludwig recalled how indifferent he was when a Polish border guard stopped him on his own property and searched his car for contraband.[20] On his own expropriated estates he solved the problem of capitalization himself by lending teams of horses to cart the building materials from his own stores to the new dwellings his former laborers were now erecting.[21] And still the prince and his family lived in the style that was natural to them. Golo Mann recalls a visit in Kuchelna at Christmas 1923. There was a "kind of representation that was meant only for itself. No guests came, except a schoolmaster from Troppau, who appeared twice a week to play chess with the prince. A melancholy loneliness lay over the whole, and the master of the house was probably without any hope."[22]

Lichnowsky had also retired from the public discussion on the causes of the war. This is a question that obsessed his mind no less than that of any other participant. But while Bethmann and Jagow and countless others wrote remembrances and explanations of the war's advent, he added nothing to what he had already set down during four years of fighting. Even at war's end, when documentary evidence was published and public enquiries begun, his contribution to the accumulating record was meager. To the committee that was editing the Foreign Ministry documents on the prewar crisis he sent the letters he had received from Jagow in July 1914.[23] But when the committee of the National Constituent Assembly established to inquire into the causes of the war asked him for a statement, he referred them to the new edition of *My London Mission*.[24] In 1919 he had allowed the *Bund Neues Vaterland* to publish the "authentic" version of that memoir achieved by deleting "confidential and personal remarks of an unpolitical character."[25]

It was not that he had lost any certainty about the major premises. There was no shaking his belief that "Theobald's policy" was to blame for the catastrophe, as he had earlier written to Harden. Although he was also critical of the provocatory actions that Bülow had taken after 1904, he told his son Michael many times that Bülow would never have made the mistake of going to war in 1914. Bethmann, he believed, wished to emulate Bülow's success in 1909, when the Powers acquiesced in Austria's annexation of Bosnia and Herzegovina. The chancellor thought he could out-Bülow the consummate master of intrigues by playing the same game for higher stakes. The prince's son recalls that while Bülow had a good laugh about this, his father "was too sad about the results of Bethmann Hollweg's criminal idiocies to enjoy them like Bülow, but many times he said to me, 'That would never have happened under Bülow.' " Now as before he would give no credence to the view that the war was caused by the Anglo-German naval rivalry. He expressed this opinion with such emphasis in conversations with Metternich, who quite as stubbornly took the opposite view, that the two men had no choice but to stop seeing one another.[26]

If anything, his certainty as to Germany's guilt intensified. New evidence had come to his attention. Once while on a holiday in Meran, in the summer of 1926, he saw Count Berchtold approaching on the promenade and averted his gaze. "I know you might not want to speak to me," said the erstwhile Austrian foreign secretary, coming up to him, "but I have something important to tell you." Berchtold said that he would not have adopted such a rigid stand toward Serbia if Berlin had not urged him on, under the threat of terminating the alliance.[27] At the end of 1926 he wrote Prof. Fritz Kern, who had asked him to read his account of the Potsdam meetings of 5 July 1914, that Berlin had toyed with the idea of going to war long before the Austrian delegate Count Hoyos arrived with the request for support against Serbia.[28] To some it seemed that the prince thought of nothing else but the circumstances of 1914. It was his custom when in the capital to take solitary walks through the city parks, and on these walks, wrote Herbert von Hindenburg, his former assistant in the ministry, who sometimes joined him, "there would burst forth a deep-seated hatred of the men in Berlin who were conducting our policy at the outbreak of the war. To him they were nothing but criminals."[29] But what Lichnowsky said to individuals he did not repeat to the general public.

This reticence was due to his respect for the national interest. The Allies had justified the reparations and other burdens imposed upon the fledgling republic on the grounds that it was Germany alone who bore responsibility for the war. He wished to be a loyal citizen of the new Germany, and he would do nothing to support the Allied contentions. He tried to avoid temptations to do so. When Princess Lichnowsky returned to London for a visit in 1924, the prince told his daughter that he would never be able to go himself, for "as an honest man I must tell the truth, as a patriot I cannot. And therefore I cannot visit England."[30]

In Germany's effort to throw off the burdens imposed by the treaty of peace historical research was an important weapon. The government was determined through scholarship to destroy the Allied thesis of Germany's sole guilt. To deal with this question there was established in the Foreign Ministry a separate office known as the *Schuldreferat*. It supported private research on matters connected with the outbreak of the war and produced in record time the justly famous forty-volume collection of diplomatic documents known as the *Grosse Politik*.[31] A flyleaf advertising this publication asserted that "the German people dare not rest until the admission of guilt in the Treaty of Versailles is annulled."[32] Chief editor of the *GP* was the capable historian

Friedrich Thimme. His conviction that Germany had not desired the war and was not alone responsible for it amounted to
a passion.

Thimme conceived of his duty as an official of the Foreign
Ministry as defending Bethmann and his collaborators against
Lichnowsky—and Tirpitz. He let the *GP* serve this purpose, and
when that collection was completed he continued to struggle
with other means. In 1927 he asked Stumm for information that
would help him to rap the knuckles of the "one-sided pacifists
and the equally one-sided naval exponents of power politics."[33]
Tirpitz had published his memoirs in 1919 and had later added
a series of documents and letters from his private papers defending his conception of *Weltpolitik*. He painted a picture of diplomatic and strategic incompetence on the part of the civilian leaders and implied that they had made the choices that caused the
war. But the most damaging testimony on Germany's intentions
in 1914 was still *My London Mission*. The Report of the Allied
Commission on the Responsibility of the Authors of the War and
on Enforcement of Penalties, drawn up to justify reparations,
quoted repeatedly from Lichnowsky's memoir to prove that the
war was the premeditated act of the Central Powers.[34]

It was not difficult to discredit Lichnowsky's testimony. The
diplomatic record as it became available would seem to show that
he was indeed a vain, resentful, and incompetent diplomat who
had once supported the policies and tendencies he later criticized.
A reader of the small selection from his Vienna dispatches might
conclude that he had been a Pan-German, or from the one piece
he wrote on Morocco that he had even anticipated the flamboyant
incursions into that area in 1905 and 1911. The record contained
his eulogies of the perfidious Grey, his misunderstanding of
Grey's proposal for neutrality on 1 August 1914 (a notion
Thimme continued to publicize even after he recognized that
there had been no misunderstanding),[35] the prince's misjudg-
ment of Grey's speech on 3 August, and his continued vain hopes
for British forbearance. Few professional readers of the evidence
in the 1920s would have agreed with Richard Kirchner's view
presented in the *Frankfurter Zeitung* in 1920 that Lichnowsky's
dispatches were the remarkable record of a man who took his

responsibility to heart.[36] Johannes Victor Bredt, one researcher who agreed with Kirchner, wrote in 1928 that "to represent the prince's work in a favorable light was an act of daring."[37]

Lichnowsky remained silent until the end of 1926, when he took a step in his own defense. He decided to make a formal protest against the editorial license in the *GP*. This was after the appearance of volume 37 (which contained the correspondence on the Portuguese colonies) and volume 39 (which contained the dispatches on the Anglo-Russian naval conversations). In a footnote in volume 39 Thimme attempted to refute Lichnowsky's statement in *My London Mission* that he had been left in ignorance of the naval arrangements or discussions between the British and the French and Russians. Quoting Zimmermann's remark that Lichnowsky would have to be given some hint of the secret information because he had again been taken in by Grey, Thimme said that on 29 June Bethmann had in fact informed Lichnowsky of the main outlines *(in grossen Zügen)* of the Anglo-Russian naval conversations. Thimme added that naval attaché Müller had informed Lichnowsky of the Grey-Cambon exchange of letters in February 1914, not at the end of July, as Lichnowsky had said.[38]

On 21 December 1926 Lichnowsky wrote the editors of the *GP* requesting that they include in the next volume a statement by him as follows:

1. During my official sojourn in London I learned nothing whatever either of the arrangements between the English and French Naval and General Staffs or of the correspondence between Grey and Cambon. On the contrary, the German Foreign Office had intentionally withheld from me all information concerning the material collected by its secrets agents, published in the *Norddeutsche Allgemeine Zeitung* on October 16th, 1914, some time after the outbreak of the war.

2. It was not through information given me by my chiefs that I received the first hint of an Anglo-French Naval Agreement, but through a jeering remark made during the latter part of my stay by Herr von Müller, our naval attaché, who had been informed of it by the General Admiralty.

3. If the Foreign Office was of the opinion that I was letting myself be "taken in" by Grey, and if statesmen in Berlin had grounds for

supposing that Sir Edward Grey was not an "honest and truth-loving statesman," it was the duty of the Chancellor and of the Foreign Ministry to inform me and to warn me by laying the necessary material before me.

4. This was not done either on the occasion of my visit to the chancellor on the 29th of June or when I called upon Herr Zimmermann, the under-secretary of state, or at any other time. Herr von Bethmann Hollweg merely complained of the Russian armaments and pointed out the painful impression caused by certain things that had come out with regard to Anglo-Russian agreements.

5. Your contention that I had been informed of the correspondence between Sazonov and Benckendorff or of that between Grey and Cambon is therefore incorrect. Neither the chancellor or anyone else ever told me about it.

6. You refer to a statement made by Herr von Jagow to the effect that I hadn't been left in ignorance concerning the most "important things," so far as they had a bearing upon my mission. The statement in question is an untruth. Herr von Jagow must know perfectly well that "important things" of which I should undoubtedly have been informed, things that were of the greatest importance for my mission, were withheld from me purposely in order if possible to lead me astray and to make me appear a fool. The conduct of our foreign policy lay at that time almost entirely in the hands of Herr Wilhelm von Stumm, the worthy successor of Herr Fritz von Holstein. Herr von Stumm was guided by the notion that he might become my successor in London. He therefore endeavored with the willing support of Herr von Jagow to paralyze and thwart my efforts with all the means at his disposal. Among other things, he proposed with this end in view to wreck the colonial treaty that had been drafted some time before. Does Herr von Jagow perhaps not reckon the Grey-Cambon correspondence and the Anglo-French naval agreements among the "important matters" he refers to? Does he really consider that Ballin's mission to Grey and Haldane in July 1914 undertaken apparently with the object of undermining my position in London, an incident of which I remained in ignorance until 1915, was merely another of the "unimportant things" that had no "bearing" on my mission?

As witnesses to the truth of the above statements, I might, if need be, name the secretaries of state who have now retired, Dr. Zimmermann and Herr von Kühlmann, my councillor of embassy in London.[39]

Thimme refused to publish this statement. His letter is missing; but it is apparent from Lichnowsky's reply that Thimme maintained Bethmann had informed Lichnowsky of the Grey-Cambon correspondence during their discussion on 29 June. Lichnowsky denied this, replying that the exchange of letters had nothing to do with the Anglo-Russian naval agreement. It was true that Bethmann may have given him some general hints about these conversations, but the real question, he insisted, was "not whether he touched upon the Anglo-Russian agreements already published in the press or not, but whether he brought to my notice, as it was his duty to do, the secret facts of which the Foreign Office had a precise knowledge, that is to say, the Anglo-French naval agreement, the Sazonov-Benckendorff correspondence, the Grey-Cambon correspondence, and other similar matters."[40] Thimme's reply was totally disingenuous. He said that Berlin hadn't known the full text of the Anglo-French naval agreement, and that Zimmermann, when consulted, had said that on 29 June he too had given the prince clearly to understand that the reports of an Anglo-Russian naval agreement were correct. It was to protect the source of this most secret information that Zimmermann had not shown Lichnowsky the correspondence itself. The prince's view of Berlin's objections to publishing the Portuguese colonial agreement, Zimmermann said, was incorrect.[41]

Having rejected Lichnowsky's long statement, the Foreign Ministry by April 1927 was willing to replace it with some shorter declaration that would not be offensive to the authorities of 1914. Thimme was willing to state that the prince wished it to be known that he had not been informed of the Benckendorff-Sazonov or the Grey-Cambon correspondences. But as the prince wished to state that he had been informed of neither the Anglo-Russian naval agreements nor Ballin's mission, Thimme proposed to add that Bethmann, Jagow, and Zimmermann all agreed that at end of June 1914 the prince had been informed in the main outlines (*in grossen Zügen*). This was the very phrase to which Lichnowsky had objected, and Thimme (perhaps inadvertently) had now extended it to more questions than in the original footnote. State Secretary Schubert suggested a much shorter statement incorporating the points Lichnowsky agreed to and adding that the Foreign Ministry had learned the text of the Anglo-French naval agreements only after the war was over.[42]

This put an end to the exchange. The prince rejected the compromise wording as nonsensical. His naval attaché, he said, had been informed of the Franco-British naval agreements; and, besides, the formula contained nothing at all about his contention as to the failure of the agreement on the Portuguese colonies. Angered by Thimme's suggestion that if the formula were unacceptable the prince should publish his objections in a newspaper, giving Thimme the opportunity to reply to them, Lichnowsky wrote him that he had no need to seek public rectification "since I would thereby lend to your attacks, based as they are on a deficient knowledge of the personalities and circumstances of that time, a weight they do not possess."[43] Thereupon Thimme refused once and for all to make any remark about his footnotes in volume 39 concerning the prince.[44] Lichnowsky now wrote Schubert that since Schubert had been unable to convince Thimme of the impropriety of the footnotes, he, the prince, reserved the right to demonstrate at some later time how an official publication had been put to improper use.[45]

The exchange with Thimme and Schubert led directly to the publication in the fall of 1927 of the prince's reminiscences and collected papers, *Auf dem Wege zum Abgrund* (The road to the abyss). The work was underway at the publisher's, Carl Reissner Verlag, by the end of July.[46] Explaining his purpose in the foreword, he wrote that

the official records now published are, by their sheer voluminousness, rendered inaccessible to all but a few. I have therefore resolved to publish a special edition of the weightiest of my London dispatches, written between 1912 and 1914, and have appended to them a number of other correlated documents. In taking this course I have not been actuated by any desire for personal justification. Events themselves have shown only too completely that I was right. Unluckily, among our diplomats mine was the only voice raised in protest to predict what has since come to pass. I am anxious that the reasons that led England to enter the war may be made evident through my dispatches.[47]

Lichnowsky soon had serious misgivings about his undertaking, and the owner of the publishing house, Harry Schuhmann, had to persuade him to go on. A letter from Schuhmann to the prince, of which we have only a fragment, indicates that Lichnowsky agreed to publication on the condition that it be approved by Stresemann, who was now the republican foreign minister. At Lichnowsky's request, Schuhmann at the end of July had asked Stresemann whether he had any objections to the project. He apparently had none, for in September Schuhmann wrote Lichnowsky that although he would write the foreign minister once more (Lichnowsky seems to have asked him to do this), he could not agree to the suggestion that he submit the proofs to Stresemann. Schuhmann argued that there was no better judge of the political effect of the publication than the prince himself. More important to Schuhmann, it seemed, was his business relation with the foreign minister. Stresemann was contractually bound to publish all his writings in the Reissner Verlag if Reissner would meet the financial terms offered by any other publisher. While Schuhmann considered this an advantageous agreement, he was afraid that submitting to Stresemann the manuscript of another author would create an undesirable precedent.[48]

As Lichnowsky obviously bowed to these arguments, the work went ahead. On questions of format and editing the publisher seems to have acted with considerable freedom—he rejected Lichnowsky's suggestion that the subtitle be "Londoner Berichte und politische Schriften" (Dispatches from London and political writings), and it was at his suggestion that all French and English quotations in the original documents were translated into German.[49] The galley proofs were ready in October, and in November there issued two attractively bound volumes. The title was *Auf dem Wege zum Abgrund: Londoner Berichte, Erinnerungen und sonstige Schriften* (The road to the abyss: dispatches from London, memoirs, and other writings). The first volume contained political aphorisms the prince had written (but not published) after the German collapse in 1918, "England before the War" and "Delusion, not Design" (both published for the first time), "My London Mission," "Diplomacy and Democracy," "The Roots of the Catastrophe," various private letters (including some of his exchanges with Thimme), and a selection of his dispatches from London. The second volume contained additional dispatches up to the outbreak of the war, some other diplomatic correspondence, and an appendix, entitled "After the

Flood," with the essays he had published in the newspapers in 1918 and 1919.

This book that showed how Germany had taken the road to the abyss and plunged into it provided no answer to the question of who was really responsible for the war. The once clear and specific indications of his thoughts and experiences the prince had now turned into a general complaint:

I have never on any occasion maintained that our so-called statesmen in July 1914 wanted the world war, so far as they had any clear idea of what they actually did want. I have tried to show that the world war was the ultimate consequence of an entirely mistaken policy and that if you stumble from one crisis into another, the moment is bound to come when things will go wrong, whether you want it or not. In my memorandum [*My London Mission*] which, to my deep regret, was divulged during the war and which though much discussed since, has, as I have often enough perceived, been more condemned than read, I have reproached our "statesmen" of that time not with their will for war but with their hasty decisions, their infatuation and their incompetence.[50]

Looking for the deeper roots of the catastrophe, he now located the personal element in the failings of Bismarck and Holstein. The fatal event was the estrangement from Russia, which was due to the hatred Bismarck had conceived for the Russian foreign minister Gorchakov. Had Wilhelm I stood his ground in opposing the alliance with Austria, "had he but let the Great Man go, the most terrible catastrophe in the world's history would have become impossible and Germany today would be the first nation on the whole Continent."[51] It was Bismarck's successors who developed the master's errors into a system. Holstein "guided our foreign policy with an ascendancy that knew practically no limits." "His chief aim was personal power and influence. Both of these he possessed during his life and even after his death." Holstein's policy "was fantastic and whimsical and full of contradictions." "He quite lost touch with realities and lived in a world of illusions." "As a rule Holstein protected only mediocrities or diplomats who were content to be as putty in his hands." "It thus very often came about that men who were mere nonentities attained to most important posts. He was, in short, a national misfortune and the real begetter of the world war."[52]

If Lichnowsky's purpose had been clear, his book would still have been a failure on other accounts. Emil Ludwig reports that for many years Lichnowsky's friends had urged him to write his memoirs;[53] what he had produced in the aftermath of the exchange with Thimme was something of a different order. The autobiographical aspect was limited; the work was a collection of published and unpublished writings, a selection of private correspondence, and an edition of official documents. The form was inadequate for this multiple character. There was no table of contents and no index. There was no statement of the criteria or purposes that had governed the choice of documents and essays. The reminiscences promised by the title were limited to *My London Mission*, which had already been published, and to a few personal remarks in the foreword and in the short and facetious gloss of his appointment to London. There was no information on how the prince had come to write the essays or where they had first appeared or whether they were original or edited versions. Worst of all, there was no indication that he had made some changes not only in his own writings but in the documents he had taken from the *GP*.

In the War Guilt Section of the Foreign Ministry Friedrich Thimme soon discovered these defects. He compared every essay and document with the originals in the Foreign Ministry files.[54] He noted that the prince had excluded the essays in which he had supported Germany's naval expansion and overlooked more than twenty dispatches essential to the history of the July crisis. Among these were his dispatch of 31 July 1914 reporting that for the first time he had the impression that England would maintain a waiting attitude, and his optimistic telegram on Grey's speech of 3 August. Thimme discovered that Lichnowsky had made changes in five dispatches, of which three were substantial. In a dispatch of 4 December 1912 he deleted the paragraph reporting that he had told Grey that during the crisis in the Balkans Austria had displayed considerable moderation. In the dispatch on the discussion with Grey concerning rumors of an Anglo-Russian naval agreement the prince had simply eliminated the final paragraph reporting Tyrrell's statement that the British did not have and would not in the future conclude a naval convention with the Russians. In the report on his discussion with Grey on 3 August 1914, before Grey's historic speech in the House, he deleted: "I repeat today they are hoping to remain neutral and count upon our support to achieve that end."[55]

Thimme presented his findings in a harsh review in the *Kölnische Zeitung*, and, after the prince had replied, in a much longer article, "Fürst Lichnowskys 'Memoirenwerk,' " published in the *Archiv für Politik und Geschichte*.[56] In the latter Thimme was concerned primarily with the changes the prince had made in his wartime essays. Not having a copy of the original version of "Wahn oder Wille?" (delusion or design?), he could not catch the significance of the new title: "Wahn, nicht Wille" (delusion, not design). He thought the concerns of this piece proclaimed it a work, not of 1915, as the prince said, but of a much later time. But he was mistaken. In Bülow's papers there is a typescript of this essay under its original title, dated January 1915 with marginal notes by Bülow made in June of that year. In "Wahn oder Wille?" there are echoes of the letters of Solf and Bülow in which the prince discussed not only Berlin's policy in July 1914 but the bleak prospects for a victorious peace.[57] Discovery of the original title would have made the author's intentions more evident.[58]

For *My London Mission*, Thimme would not shy from the word "falsification," and tried to show that this had begun when the prince permitted the *Bund Neues Vaterland* to publish a new edition in 1919. Here the prince had attempted, as he said in the foreword of the edition, to eliminate nonpolitical remarks of a personal character. Indeed, the prince also deleted passages containing obvious mistakes and struck the sentence, "soon [after the decisive conference at Potsdam on July 5] Herr von Jagow was in Vienna to consult Count Berchtold about all these matters," and the first five words of the sentence, "Till the very last minute I had hoped that England would adopt a waiting attitude." In the version presented in the collected papers he made further deletions. Passages suggesting vanity or resentment disappeared. From the paragraph on the discussion of 5 July he now eliminated the statement that the German leaders had intimated that "no harm would be done if a war with Russia should result."

And to the sentence in which he had originally said that the German government was responsible for the war he added, "even if they did not want it."

Thimme was even more excited by the extensive changes in "England before the War." To illustrate the prince's duplicity, Thimme published the original version of this essay side by side with the version published in *Abyss*. Lichnowsky had added several passages, afterthoughts and factual elaborations. More important were the deletions and rewordings. Although he had originally written that some of the ideas Grey hit upon in his search for a means to avoid war had had little practical value, he now said that a conference of ambassadors, which was the form of mediation Grey finally proposed, "appeared to me an opportune means of avoiding the threatening catastrophe." As in the new version of *My London Mission*, here too he eliminated all reference to Berlin's willingness to run the risk of war with Russia.

The prince attempted to defend himself, evoking heavier attacks from Thimme. He denied that he had made the alterations for the purpose of this publication. At first he said that he had made the corrections in "England before the War" in the fall of 1914,[59] and then, when Thimme pointed out that he had been at the front at that time, he found the stenographer who had typed a revised version of this essay in the late summer of 1916.[60] (In the family archives there is an undated copy of a version that differs from the original and is similar, though not identical, to the one published in the collected papers.) For the rest, the prince fell back on the argument that an author has an inalienable right to change what he has written and for a while attempted to dispute the significance of the alterations. But, upon Theodor Wolff's advice, he soon let Thimme's attack go unanswered.[61]

The prince was once more impaled on the horns of a dilemma. He knew that his essays possessed a deep truth and that his dispatches were clear and accurate; and he wished the public to know them. But since 1918 tactical considerations and a feeling of responsibility toward his country had forced him to disown his knowledge and experience. For the purpose of the collected papers he had obviously compared the wartime essays to make them compatible in expression and to support the thesis presented in the foreword that Germany "blundered into the war by mistake."

Although Thimme was aware of the shift in emphasis, he was not concerned to understand or explain it. "Even though his memorandum was universally regarded as evidence of Germany's responsibility for the war," he said, "the Prince now pretends that its sole purpose is to show that the German statesmen did not desire the war but in their efforts to avoid it had not found the means that assured success." To Thimme it was all too obvious that the prince had modified his views in order to promote his own rehabilitation. "But we fear," Thimme concluded, "that posterity, or, in any case, the German people, which Prince Lichnowsky has so dreadfully wronged, will judge that of all the German statesmen of 1914, he—as a publicist, statesman, and patriot—is the one who has failed most completely."[62]

Chapter IX
Redeemed

Lichnowsky's life is a political novella written by German reality.

Carl von Ossietzsky, *Die Weltbühne*, 6 March 1928

Lichnowsky attempted to repair the faults in his collected papers in an English edition which was translated and annotated by Sefton Delmer and given the title *Heading for the Abyss*. In an introductory letter the prince said that his aim was "to investigate the deeper causes of the catastrophe, and to do this if possible without touching on the so-called war-guilt question and without attributing the whole burden of responsibility to this or that individual in Germany or elsewhere." "I have attempted to show that it was mainly the fatal system of groups and alliances inaugurated by Bismarck that led to the world war, and that the Great Powers were thereby drawn into conflicts which were quite alien to their real interests."[1]

The translator undertook to "forestall further bickering on the matter of alterations" by reinserting in brackets all the deletions in *My London Mission* and by indicating the passages added to the original version of "England before the War" and printing separately the most important deletions from that document.[2] The prince did not supply the original version of "Wahn oder Wille?" which therefore appeared in its recast form translated as "Delusions." Delmer also added twenty-four items of diplomatic correspondence comprising all those Thimme thought essential for a full picture and three of his own choosing, and he retained the kaiser's marginalia which Reissner had not printed.

Lichnowsky had agreed to the numerous alterations and had asked to see the proofs when they were ready.[3] These proofs he never saw. A physician he had consulted for a regular check-up some ten or twelve months earlier had told him, "You are one of those persons about whom it is impossible to say from what you will eventually die." His health was good throughout his sixty-eighth year. But the attacks on his book had, it was generally agreed, put him under a severe strain. Late in February he had an apoplectic stroke and took to bed, but symptoms were so slight that he and his family did not believe in any serious danger. He planned to travel to Meran soon for a rest cure. On 27 February 1928 he suffered a second attack from which he died peacefully and painlessly.[4] Prince Lichnowsky was laid to rest in the family vault at Kuchelna. Three local priests officiated and a choir from Troppau sang the requiem. His immediate family, a number of relatives, and an endless procession of friends, neighbors, members of the household, tenants, farmers, and laborers followed the casket to the grave. Huge crowds from the whole of the surrounding district lined the road. But there was no representative from the Wilhelmstrasse.[5]

The news of Lichnowsky's death was widely reported in German and English newspapers. The commentaries reflected the interest aroused by the bitter attacks on his book. Friend and foe alike described an essentially naive man who was not up to the task he had assumed when he accepted the appointment to London. His enemies found in him nothing at all that was commendable. "As ambassador in London he was completely under the influence of Sir Edward Grey, who knew how to indulge his vanities," stated the Nazis' *Völkischer Beobachter*.[6] Theodor Wolff wrote that while the prince's comprehension of the larger questions was superior to Berlin's, his popularity in London had impaired his judgment of the British statesmen, who were craftier than he knew, and of the situation, which was more dangerous than he realized.[7] In England there was a similar response. The obituaries described a good-natured and sensible diplomat who was the unfortunate victim of a trick perpetrated by perfidious Teutons. The *Times* wrote that "the Wilhelmstrasse sent us an ambassador who himself believed that their policy was a policy of peace, and they kept him in the dark as to their real intentions either because they knew that he would not support those intentions or because they thought that a representative who is duped himself is the most likely to dupe others."[8]

This is the picture of Lichnowsky that was common at his death. That revision has proved difficult is due in no small measure to the testimony, soon available, of the man who knew Lichnowsky better than anyone else—Prince Bülow. Bülow died in 1929. He had labored over his papers all through the 1920s, and the four heavy volumes of his *Denkwürdigkeiten* appeared in 1930–1931. The references to Lichnowsky are surprisingly meager, and they are not the work of a friend. Although Bülow admitted that as a person Lichnowsky was high-minded, kind, and good, he was professionally of little consequence, being a "neurasthenic," a "dilettante," and a "cliché-monger rather than a political thinker." Bülow repeated what he had heard others say about his friend. Count Lerchenfeld, whose opinion was the most acceptable, had said that Lichnowsky was no captain for stormy weather, though he would do well "when the sky is clear and the sea is calm." Holstein had once said that "good old Lichnowsky thinks that talking about something is the same as doing it," and Kiderlen that intellectually Lichnowsky was a mere "infant."[9]

Bülow's spitefulness reaches its peak in the section on 1914. It must be remembered that although Bülow and Lichnowsky agreed that Berlin could have avoided war, they were opposed on the question of war aims and the prince had written an eloquent refutation of Bülow's proposal for "guarantees of a substantial nature." In his memoirs Bülow blamed the war on Bethmann, Stumm, and Jagow. These men had stumbled blindly onward not revealing their intentions to anyone and refusing to seek or take advice. There were experienced diplomats who could have told Bethmann what was wrong with his policy, but Bülow, listing these, did not include his friend among them. Quoting the dispatch of 18 July 1914 in which Jagow had attempted to explain Berlin's rationale, Bülow failed to note that Jagow had had to write this dispatch because of the unanswerable objections raised by Prince Lichnowsky. Only once in the section on the war did Bülow mention Lichnowsky's name, and then only to paraphrase a letter the prince wrote him shortly after hostilities began. At that time Lichnowsky still hoped that Germany could reknit the broken ties with England. "In the midsummer of 1914," wrote Bülow, "our London ambassador entertained equally foolish illusions [as Bethmann and colleagues], even after war had been declared."[10]

Bülow's publication shocked the war-guilt historians. There were cries of outrage on many counts; Lichnowsky was not the only contemporary Bülow had slyly or openly defamed. What offended most was the implication that Bethmann and his subordinates had steered quite deliberately into an avoidable war. An entire issue of the periodical *Die Kriegsschuldfrage* was devoted to questions raised by the memoirs.[11] Friedrich Thimme, who had led the attack upon Lichnowsky, now sponsored the attack upon Lichnowsky's mentor. He gathered the various commentaries and replies that scholars and statesmen had issued and published them together in a book entitled *Front wider Bülow*.[12] But in all this there was no attempt to revise the picture Bülow had composed of his friend Prince Lichnowsky.

Hitler's accession to power in 1933 created a new climate for attitudes toward the prince. Soon the war-guilt question was no longer a matter of practical politics. Germany had already ceased to pay reparations in 1932; and when Hitler in 1937 formally withdrew Germany's signature from the Treaty of Versailles, the *Schuldreferat* was transformed into a historical section attached to the Foreign Ministry's archives.[13] But the propagandistic treatment of the question grew, if anything, more vituperative. For the Nazis the war-guilt question was emotionally entwined with their hatred of Jews, Marxists, and pacifists. In the burst of frenzy that accompanied Hitler's accession, the Nazis ransacked the bookstores for copies of Lichnowsky's collected papers and consigned their booty to the flames.[14] Not because of Lichnowsky's attacks upon the Wilhelmstrasse, to be sure, but because he was, in general, soft. Hitler's men had inherited a contempt for amicable diplomacy from the prewar Pan-Germans (who were the "spoiled fathers of all Nazis," said Mechtilde Lichnowsky).[15] In 1939 the Nazi "theorist" Alfred Rosenberg reissued his 1927 collection of polemics against the representative figures of the old Germany who shared the blame for the lost war. Along with Jews and Social Democrats, his culprits included Stresemann, Bethmann, and Lichnowsky.[16]

The Wilhelminian establishment was broader than Rosenberg implies, and its pacesetters were not men like Lichnowsky. It was not until the war broke out that the ambiguity of Lichnowsky's position became clear. He belonged wholeheartedly to the establishment and profited by the advantages the political system gave the aristocracy. The outward circumstances of his life would distinguish him little from his peers. His career conformed to the pattern for the Upper Silesian Catholic nobility; he supported the fleet with Darwinistic theories; and being modern was not in itself unwelcome in Wilhelm II's Germany. Yet his family's uncommon history and his personal qualities established him as an individual apart from the ordinary Wilhelminian. In common opinion he was an honest man who could judge things by natural and unprejudiced reason. But his moral potential was limited. As Theodor Wolff and Max Weber have pointed out, the optimates, who in other countries and times constituted a source of political strength and moderation, had in Prussia-Germany no cohesion or community. At one time Wolff thought that Lichnowsky was the natural leader of those *grands seigneurs* who were strangers "to the terroristic style of the Junkers." But, as Wolff wrote when the prince was appointed to London in 1912, Lichnowsky had "failed to draw the logical conclusion and hesitated to take the steps necessary to create a liberal aristocratic party."[17] Hence when the unavoidable clash of judgment and conception occurred in the summer of 1914, Lichnowsky stood all alone.

In judging Lichnowsky's performance as a diplomat it has been difficult to escape the prejudices and errors of the twenties and thirties. The record does not support the conclusion that for all his good intentions he was professionally weak. We should not be misled by his failure at impossible tasks. Certainly he was not an ingenious opportunist on the order of Bismarck, not a bold calculator with the strength to overcome stubborn opposition. Had he been so, he would not have been an ambassador. Nor did he, as a diplomat, proceed in all situations as the eighteenth-century ideal would have him do—"with a smile on his lips and a visage of brass." (Who in his time could match this classic description?) He did conform, however, to his own model of the successful diplomat—a man who combined "sound commonsense, the faculty of making himself liked and of adapting himself to foreign conditions, ability to understand and appreciate other people's standpoints and, especially in the case of important positions, political judgment."[18] The record shows more than that: skill in presenting proposals to a conference, cleverness in representing his government's attitude on ticklish questions, ability to grasp weaknesses in a colleague's response. His early reports display some of the defects of the literary dispatch; but he always conveyed a vivid and truthful impression of circumstances and events. The analysis he sent Berlin in July 1914, the *summa* of his thought on the condition of Europe, was irrefutably logical, eloquent, and statesmanlike.

For the last fourteen years of his life Lichnowsky was preoccupied with the question of Germany's intentions in 1914, but he was never able to resolve that question in a convenient way. If we follow his history from 1914 to 1927 we see that he could not settle upon a conventional word or phrase to characterize the war. The concept "preventive war" he did not use after 1916. "Aggressive" or "hegemonial" were not in his vocabulary. Of course he saw the deeper sources and the historical meaning of the struggle: the defects in Germany's foreign policy in 1914 sprang from its social and political structure; and the conflict, he recognized during the war, had become a struggle for imperial supremacy. But his concern was to comprehend the scheme of action in 1914. "Did they or did they not want war?" was the question he asked himself in the letter to Solf in December 1914. He did not know then; he thought it possible that they did not. Eventually his answer to this question was "no." It was only partly from a sense of patriotic duty that he expunged from his collected papers wording that would seem to describe the war as willed by Germany for whatever reasons. For he had penetrated the mind of the Wilhelmstrasse. One might indeed suppose that Lichnowsky had before him Riezler's record of Bethmann's colloquies. Riezler paraphrases Bethmann's thoughts on the possibility of forcing an agreement with Russia: "If the Serbian affair goes well without Russia mobilizing and consequently without war, it might be possible to arrive without any danger at an understanding on Austria-Hungary, now appeased, with a Russia that had been disappointed by the Western Powers."[19] This approximates the view Lichnowsky had achieved in the 1920s. As he once told his son, he thought Berlin would have been satisfied if Austria had acquired control of Serbia. Then, Russia, humiliated, would have to seek Germany's friendship. England too would have to come to terms.[20]

In 1927 Lichnowsky did not, in the introduction to his papers, offer any specific reasons why Bethmann, if he did not want war, carried his policy of risk beyond the point of no return. Why did he not turn back before military considerations narrowed and eventually eliminated all choices? It was not for lack of counter-advice. No sooner had Berlin accepted the plan of an Austro-Serbian conflict than Lichnowsky pointed out its folly. Nor was there any lack of evidence that Russia and England would inter-vene. Yet Bethmann, like King Canute, persisted in his efforts to turn back the tide by his own commands. Why? Lichnowsky's answer is that Stumm and Bethmann could not bring themselves to accept the advice of the man they considered a rival and an obstacle to their personal ambitions. "Only those who know Stumm and his prejudice and opposition to everything that came from me can understand [their] attitude," he wrote Solf in De-cember 1914.[21] "The more I pressed, the less they were inclined to come around," he wrote in *My London Mission*, "if only that I in conjunction with Sir Edward Grey might not have the success of averting war."[22] "Indifference is all that I have left since they made world war in order to cause my downfall in London," he wrote Harden in 1918. "In any case, the anger over my successes there contributed to it."[23] Although Lichnowsky, when he pub-lished his papers, suppressed the passage from *My London Mis-sion*, he wrote in the gloss on his appointment that "one man wanted my post, another thought that I wanted his. Finally, too, they even came to believe in what they called the 'localization of the conflict,' merely because I held an opposite view."[24] Lich-nowsky believed that the animosity toward him was the stable element in the mixture of thought and feeling that had impelled Berlin along its dangerous course.

In our effort to reconstruct the atmosphere in Berlin in July 1914 we cannot ignore the element of personal malice suggested by Lichnowsky's experience. The early war-guilt historians dis-missed Lichnowsky's accusations of his colleagues as mere resent-ment due to his own failures. The foregoing chapters, however, provide evidence that Stumm's animosity distorted Berlin's con-duct of affairs and strategic conceptions. Lichnowsky's relations with Bethmann were more complicated. One can only speculate about the effect upon Bethmann of Lichnowsky's apparent candidacy for the chancellorship. Problems were in any case unavoidable. It was not long before Bethmann recognized that he and Lichnowsky envisaged quite different objectives when they spoke of détente and Anglo-German cooperation. But unless Bethmann was willing to listen to Lichnowsky's propositions or clarify his own, he could do nothing about their differences. At the kaiser's insistence he had entered into a partnership with Lichnowsky that was not dissolvable as long as Germany's approach to England was all smiles and relations were improving. And so, as we have seen, he condoned the ad hominem responses to the prince's initiatives and suggestions and slyly belittled him, creating the atmosphere in which the congenial counsel was that proffered by Stumm. In 1921 Stumm, on a walk with Werner von Rheinbaben, suddenly broke out of a state of depressed silence to volunteer that in 1914 he had been mistaken and had given Bethmann the wrong advice.[25]

Lichnowsky bitterly regretted that he had not himself dissolved his partnership with Bethmann. He wrote of his failure as a sin of omission. "I had to support a policy the error of which I recognized," he said in *My London Mission*, "and that took its revenge on me because it was a sin against the Holy Spirit."[26] But is not his failing a more positive one and his suffering, as Maximilian Harden suggested, due rather to human vanity? "To persist in the service of a cause one regards as wrong because that service bestows power and glory and (whatever its drawbacks) is, after all, 'interesting,' is unpardonable," Harden wrote. This, however, was not Lichnowsky's sin. "The crux," Harden proposed instead, "is not that he was acting against conviction but that he thought that at this most important of all foreign posts his political sense, his social position, and the opportunity of direct correspondence with the kaiser would enable him to cope with Berlin's mediocrities, these men sustained only by their routine proficiencies, and somehow himself to guide policy." "He hoped to harness his obstinate superiors to his own policy . . . and thus, formidably equipped, to bridge the chasm between military and political strategy. This is the error that finally exacted its price."[27]

Chapter X
Exodus

The Lichnowsky estates no longer exist, and the prince's family has been dispersed. The events of 1933 to 1945 hastened the dissolution begun with the war of 1914–1918. After Hitler came to power, the prince's son Michael, not wishing to join the Nazi Foreign Ministry, immigrated to Brazil. The prince's daughter Leonore taught at the Peking Government University and then worked for the International Agricultural Institute in Rome. Prince Wilhelm, as the older son, had inherited the properties, which he managed until the end of the Second World War. As Soviet troops approached Kuchelna, the family fled westward, hauling across Bohemia by tractor a few ancient books from their library and other tokens of an historic past. After the loss of property, Prince Wilhelm with his wife and son and two daughters joined his brother in Brazil. Later he acquired a plantation not far from Curitiba where he lived until his death in the spring of 1975 while he was on his way to a visit with his sister Leonore in Italy. Countess Leonore had remained in Germany for some years after the war and taught at the University of Heidelberg. Now she lives in Rome where since 1954 she has been a Far Eastern expert for the Food and Agricultural Organization.

Mechtilde Lichnowsky, surviving her husband by thirty years, has perpetuated through her literature the historic name and memories of her husband's family. After the prince's death she bought a villa in Cap d'Ail on the Riviera, which became her second home. In 1937 she married Ralph Harding Peto, of the family of the baronets Peto of Somerleyton, a major in the British army whom she had met thirty-five years earlier when he was attached to the British legation in Munich. She became a British subject and made her home in London. The outbreak of the Second World War found her in Munich, where she was visiting her sister, Countess Harrach. Unable to return to England, she remained in Germany for the duration of the war, reporting periodically to the police as an enemy alien. Her second husband died in 1945, but in 1946 she returned to London, where she spent her last years, living under the name of Princess Lich-nowsky.[1]

In London she lived as independently as she had everywhere else. (It is not true that she lived in a "working-class district," for she occupied elegant quarters in Mayfair.) In various works she described happy encounters with taxi drivers and street clean-ers. "Most people who belong to the category of 'the man in the street,' as it is known in London, perceive by some sign or other, my receptivity," she wrote in her last published work in 1958, "and, contrary to British custom, they will tell me their life's story and God knows what else." "The exchange of thoughts, of admission of any likes or dislikes is carried on in a conversation with the man in the street as it was when I was seated at the table between Ambassador Cambon and King George V. That is quite a long time ago; but the mold from which the pieces were poured has not yet been shattered."[2]

There are few direct references in Mechtilde Lichnowsky's writings to her husband's career. Politics did not interest her. Only her complete abhorrence of Nazism drew from her an essay on Hitler which she called *Der Werdegang eines Wirrkopfs* (The making of a muddlehead). She wrote this essay during the war and buried it in a tin container to be retrieved when the fighting was over.[3] Most of her fictional works, from her first novella pub-lished in 1917 to her last novel in 1936, evoke situations of the intellectual aristocracy in Wilhelminian Germany, and in some of these there are characters who were clearly suggested by per-sonages she met as Princess Lichnowsky. The oval-faced mi-gnonne with the pretty foreign accent described in the novel *Delaïde* (1935), where there are characters from diplomacy, is obviously Princess Bülow.[4] In the novel *Der Lauf der Asdur* (1936) there is a thin-haired, glassy-eyed north German diplomat who has an astounding memory and can quote entire pages from learned books, and who doubtless represents Prince Bülow.[5] Paul Cambon figures in this novel too, as we have noted,[6] and in the recollections she brought together in the book *An der Leine* (On the leash) in 1930 she writes of Cambon's frequent visits to the German embassy and of discussions that were far removed from politics.[7]

In the 1950s Mechtilde Lichnowsky summed up her life and thought in two collections of miscellanea, *Zum Schauen bestellt* (My life is viewing) and *Heute und vorgestern* (Today and the day before yesterday). In the latter the frontispiece is a profile drawing in pencil of "Carlmax" Lichnowsky done in 1904, the year of their marriage. In answering criticism of her essay on Hitler by those who said she should not venture into political subjects, she wrote that she had lived for twenty-three years with a man of model political intelligence. "In contrast to most Germans, who are ungifted in political matters, he was endowed with an understanding of other peoples and countries. Their way of thinking and their languages were as natural to him as those of his own country, where he saw both the good and the bad and recognized it for what it was."[8]

Note on Usage

Quotations from Prince Lichnowsky's published writings adhere (except where noted) to the translation made by Sefton Delmer for the English edition of the Prince's collected papers published under the title *Heading for the Abyss: Reminiscences* (London: Constable and Sons; New York: Payson and Clarke Ltd., 1928). Quotations from German Foreign Ministry documents that are included in this diverse collection also follow Delmer's translation, though the original German edition of these documents, *Die Grosse Politik (GP)*, will be cited in the notes. There seemed to be two advantages in using Delmer's translation: it is, for one thing, a work that is accessible to English-language readers; and his style would make quotations from Lichnowsky stand out distinctly from the surrounding text. A few deviations from Delmer's rendition were necessary in order to eliminate errors in translation or terms that in present usage would be misleading. The spelling has been Americanized. The title of the prince's best-known writing, *Meine Londoner Mission, 1912–1914,* will be rendered as *My London Mission*, which is the common English translation, though the title given in *Abyss* is "My Mission to London."

Delmer's version of the *Mission* differs slightly from the manuscript signed by the prince on 1 August 1916. The original wording was retained in the clandestine and unauthorized printing in Germany early in 1918. The British propagandists based their 1918 translations on this correct version but eliminated one small and (it was thought) indelicate reference to Sir Edward Grey's consort (as they did in their widely distributed German version issued by the Swiss publishing house of Orell Füssli). For the first authorized publication of the *Mission* (Berlin: Verlag Bund Neues Vaterland, 1919) the prince made several deletions and alterations in the original text, and he made additional ones for the publication in his collected papers in 1927.

Because of the outcry over these unannounced changes, Delmer in the English edition decided to return to the original text. The English version published by Cassell's in 1918 provided him with the English wording for the missing or altered passages (which he rewrote where the syntax seemed faulty to him). But, working from Cassell's edition, he could not reinsert the passage concerning Grey's consort; and, by inadvertence or intention, he deleted the name of the seasick Austrian (Count Felix Thun) on Wilhelm II's yacht *Meteor* who (according to Lichnowsky) suddenly recovered his health when he heard of the assassination of the Austrian crown prince. Otherwise, Delmer's English version of the *Mission* corresponds to the copy of the original manuscript found in the files of the German Foreign Ministry.

The German Auswärtiges Amt is translated throughout as Foreign Ministry.

𝕽otes

Chapter I

1. Ludwig Igálffy-Igály, "Stammtafel der Ritter, Freiherrn, Grafen und Fürsten Lichnowsky v. Woszczyc vom 14. Jahrhundert bis zur Gegenwart," *Adler: Zeitschrift für Genealogie und Heraldik* 3 (17), no. 9/10 (May/Aug. 1954). Unless otherwise noted, the genealogical information in the following pages comes from this compilation. The preferred spelling of the name Woszczyc now is the German phonetic form Woschütz. There are several Czech versions of this name. When the prince became the head of the family in 1901, he dropped the "von" (which is still found in some references), maintaining that "sky" already meant "von." It was family practice to call the firstborn son *Prinz* until he had inherited the property, after which he was known as *Fürst*. (Information from Countess Leonore Lichnowsky.) The prince's full title in German was Karl Max, 6. Fürst Lichnowsky, Graf zu Werdenberg, Edler Herr von Woschütz, Herr auf Grätz. Karl Max is a double name, the two parts always being spoken and written together. His wife, Mechtilde Lichnowsky, preferred to write his name as "Carlmax."

2. As noted in fragment of diary of Karl Max's mother in RAUSL.

3. Information from Countess Leonore Lichnowsky. Some of the letters the prince wrote his mother from Neuchâtel are preserved in RAUSL.

4. Johann Graf von Bernstorff, *Memoirs of Count Bernstorff*, trans. Eric Sutton (New York: Random House, 1936), p. 23.

5. Data on the prince's military career and on his promotions as a diplomat and other administrative actions are from an abstract of the Foreign Ministry's personnel file *(Personalakte)* on Lichnowsky available at the archives of the Foreign Ministry in Bonn. The personnel file itself is not open for study.

6. Bogdan Graf von Hutten-Czapski, *Sechzig Jahre Politik und Gesellschaft*, 2 vols. (Berlin: E. S. Mittler, 1936), 1 : 110.

7. Information from Countess Leonore Lichnowsky.

8. Information from Count Michael Lichnowsky.

9. August Scholtis, *Die Katze im schlesischen Schrank* (Augsburg: Oberschlesischer Heimatverlag, 1958), p. 9.

10. Gottlieb Biermann, *Geschichte der Herzogthümer Troppau und Jägerndorf* (Teschen: Buchholz und Diebel, 1874), pp. 57ff, 399–403, 578–583, 637; Christian Ritter d'Elvert, *Beiträge zur Geschichte der Rebellion, Reformation, des dreissigjährigen Krieges und der Neugestaltung Mährens im siebzehnten Jahrhundert*, 4 vols. (Brünn: A. Nitsch, 1867–1868), 2 : foreword, i–iv.

11. References to the Lichnowskys' eighteenth-century political difficulties in *Politische Korrespondenz Friedrichs des Grossen*, published for the Preussiche Akademie der Wissenschaften by A. Duncker et al., 46 vols. (Berlin, 1879–1939), 7 : 137, 139; and Alfred Ritter von Arneth, *Geschichte Maria Theresia's*, 10 vols. (Vienna: W. Braumüller, 1863–1870), 10 : 590ff, 820.

12. Information on the entailment, the *Fideikommiss*, given in Eberhard von Kahlden, "Die Herrschaft Kuchelna: Ein oberschlesischer Grossgrundbesitz Se. Durchlaucht des Fürsten Lichnowsky: Reisebericht," *Landwirtschaftliche Jahrbücher* 29 (1900) : 3.

13. Karl Kobold, *Beethoven: Seine Beziehungen zu Wiens Kunst und Kultur, Gesellschaft und Landschaft* (Zurich: Almathea-Verlag, 1946), pp. 132, 273, 246–255. The compositions dedicated to the Lichnowskys are listed in Constant von Wurzbach, *Biographisches Lexikon des Kaiserthums Österreich*, s.v. "Lichnowsky."

14. Stephan Ley, "Schloss Grätz bei Troppau: Beethoven und die fürstliche Familie Lichnowsky," *Atlantis* 9, no. 1 (Jan. 1937) : 63.

15. Eduard Marie Lichnowsky, *Geschichte des Hauses Habsburg*, 8 vols. (Vienna: Schaumburg, 1836–1844), 1 : xiv.

16. Ludwig Bergsträsser, "Das unbekannte Leben des bekannten Fürsten Felix Lichnowsky," *Hochland* 21 (1934), passim; C. Reinhold Köstlin, *Auerswald und Lichnowsky: Ein Zeitbild nach den Akten des Appellations-Gerichtes zu Frankfurt a.M.* (Tübingen: Laupp, 1853), passim; Heinz Gollwitzer, "Der erste Karlistenkrieg und das Problem der internationalen Parteigängerschaft," *Historische Zeitschrift* 176, no. 3 (1953), passim. Presentation also based on study of Nachlass Felix Lichnowsky, a collection of source materials gathered by Ludwig Bergsträsser and now deposited with the Bundesarchiv branch in Frankfurt.

17. Presentation based partly on information from Countess Leonore Lichnowsky and Count Michael Lichnowsky. See also Siegfried von Kardorff, *Wilhelm von Kardorff: Ein nationaler Parlamentarier im Zeitalter Bismarcks und Wilhelms II. 1828–1907* (Berlin: E. Mittler, 1936), p. 78; August Wolfstieg, "Die Anfänge der freikonser-

vativen Partei," in *Delbrück-Festschrift: Gesammelte Aufsätze zu seinem sechzigsten Geburtstage (11. November 1908) dargebracht von Freunden und Schülern*, ed. Emil Daniels et al. (Berlin: Georg Stilke, 1908), passim.

18. Information from Countess Leonore Lichnowsky.

19. Bernstorff, *Memoirs*, pp. 29–30; Bernhard von Bülow, *Denkwürdigkeiten*, ed. Franz von Stockhammern, 4 vols. (Berlin: Ullstein, 1930–1931), 4 : 272.

Chapter II

1. Information from Countess Leonore Lichnowsky. Lichnowsky's discovery of the notations in his personnel file is recounted by Plessen's son, Leopold von Plessen, *Begegnungen* (Glückstadt: privately printed, 1964), pp. 35–36.

2. Bernstorff, *Memoirs, pp.* 36–37.

3. Take Ionescu, *Souvenirs* (Paris: Payot, 1919), p. 9.

4. Constantin Dumba, *Dreibund- und Entente-Politik in der Alten und Neuen Welt* (Zurich: Almathea-Verlag, 1931), pp. 27–28.

5. Bülow to Eulenburg, 12 Dec. 1893, Nachlass Eulenburg.

6. There is reference to the liaison in private notes made by Axel Freiherr von Varnbüler, the Württemberg representative in Berlin, who was Lichnowsky's friend (John C. G. Röhl, ed. *Zwei deutsche Fürsten zur Kriegsschuldfrage: Lichnowsky und Eulenburg und der Ausbruch des 1. Weltkriegs: Eine Dokumentation* [Düsseldorf: Droste, 1971], p. 15n16). Lichnowsky was implicated in the story originating with Eulenburg that Holstein had discovered letters compromising Maria Bülow with a certain man and used this knowledge to consolidate his control over Bülow. Some thought this man was the painter Lenbach, one of the princess's admirers. In 1930 the journalist Sigmund Münz published in one of his two books on Bülow notes he had made of a 1911 discussion with Count Anton Monts, once an intimate of Lichnowsky's. Monts told Münz (Bülow, introducing them, made the obvious Wilhelm Busch-style joke on their names) that Bülow and his wife had had scenes because of "L." "Sometimes it was convenient for Bülow to have a Cicisbeo nearby," he said (Sigmund Münz, *Fürst Bülow, der Staatsmann und Mensch: Aufzeichnungen, Erinnerungen und Erwägungen von Sigmund Münz* [Berlin: Verlag für Kulturpolitik, 1930], p. 263). One of Bülow's academic critics who believed the story of the purloined letters then identified "L." as Prince Lichnowsky (Edgar v. Schmidt-Pauli, ed., *Fürst Bülows*

Denk-Unwürdigkeiten: Ein Protest [Berlin: Schlieffen-Verlag, 1931], p. 168. The story of Holstein's blackmail proved to be a falsification (H. O. Meisner, "Gespräche und Briefe Holsteins 1907–1909," *Preussische Jahrbücher* 228 (1932) : n3).

7. Bülow, *Denkwürdigkeiten*, 4 : 529, 585. See further Anna von Helmholtz, *Ein Lebensbild in Briefen*, ed. Ellen von Siemens-Helmholtz, 2 vols. (Leipzig: v. Hase und Koehler Verlag, 1929), 1 : 302; Anton Graf Monts, *Erinnerungen und Gedanken des Botschafters Anton Graf Monts*, ed. K. F. Nowak and F. Thimme (Berlin: Verlag für Kulturpolitik, 1932), pp. 153–154.

8. Hutten-Czapski, *Sechzig Jahre*, 1 : 391.

9. Helmuth Rogge, *Holstein und Harden: Politisch-publizistisches Zusammenspiel zweier Aussenseiter des Wilhelminischen Reichs* (Munich: Verlag C. H. Beck, 1959), p. 453. The phrase is *Damenbedienung*.

10. Lichnowsky was one of the few guests invited to the Bülows' summer quarters in the Austrian Alps (Münz, *Bülow Staatsmann Mensch*, pp. 47–48, 57–58), and he joined Maria Bülow at intimate breakfasts in Vienna (as reported by Eulenburg to Bülow, 23 Oct. 1898, Nachlass Bülow).

11. Maria Bülow to Lichnowsky, 20 Aug. 1918, RAUSL.

12. See Bülow to Monts, 5 July 1894, in Monts, *Erinnerungen*, p. 331. Additional indications in Monts to Bülow, 6 Apr. 1894, in F. Thimme, "Fürst Bülow und Graf Monts: Ein vervollständigter Briefwechsel," part 1, *Preussische Jahrbücher* 231, no. 3 (1932) : 214.

13. Lichnowsky, "Die Denkwürdigkeiten des Botschafters General von Schweinitz," first installment, *Berliner Tageblatt*, 12 July 1927, quoted here from English translation, "The Roots of the Catastrophe," *Abyss*, p. 100.

14. See Walter Wagner, "Kaiser Franz Josef und das Deutsche Reich von 1871–1914," Diss. Vienna (1950), and B. B. Hayes, "The German *Reich* and the 'Austrian Question' 1871–1914," Diss. Yale (1963): Wilhelm Schüssler, *Deutschland zwischen Russland und England: Studien zur Aussenpolitik des Bismarck'schen Reiches* (Leipzig: Koehler und Amelang, 1940).

15. Szögyény to Kálnoky, private, 17 March 1894, MÄ, 145 PA III Preussen 1894, 1895, p. 52.

16. Eulenburg to Bülow, 6 Dec. 1895, quoted in Johannes Haller, *Aus dem Leben des Fürsten Philipp zu Eulenburg-Hertefeld* (Berlin: Gebrüder Paetel, 1924), p. 141.

17. Bülow to Eulenburg, 12 Dec. 1893, Nachlass Eulenburg.

18. *Berliner Neueste Nachrichten*, 18 July 1895. Austrian ambassa-

dor Szögyény forwarded this and a *Vossische Zeitung* article on which this was a comment to the Austrian Foreign Ministry 20 July 1895, MÄ, 146 PA III Preussen 1895, pp. 568–571.

19. The quotations in order are from Lichnowsky to Hohenlohe, 9 July 1895, AA, Österreich 70, vol. 28; Lichnowsky to Hohenlohe, 13 June 1898, *GP* 13, no. 3474, p. 119; Lichnowsky to Hohenlohe, 7 Nov. 1897, Österreich 95, reel 246, 725–730.

20. Based on Lichnowsky to Hohenlohe, 19 July 1895, AA, Österreich 103, vol. 2, reel 253, 171–180; Lichnowsky to Hohenlohe, 9 July 1895, AA, Österreich 70, vol. 28, reel 216, 363–372; Lichnowsky to Hohenlohe, 20 Apr. 1895 and 29 Apr. 1895, AA, Österreich 70, vol. 28, reel 216, 309–329; Lichnowsky to Hohenlohe, 20 Aug. 1896, ibid., vol. 29, reel 216, 415–421; Lichnowsky to Hohenlohe, 23 Sept. 1896, ibid., vol. 30, reel 216, 428–433.

21. Quotation from Lichnowsky to Hohenlohe, 19 July 1895, AA, Österreich 103, vol. 2. Also Lichnowsky to Hohenlohe, 23 Sept. 1896, AA, Österreich 70, vol. 30, reel 216, 428–433; Lichnowsky to Hohenlohe, 19 July 1895, AA, Österreich 103, vol. 2, reel 253, 171–180; Lichnowsky to Hohenlohe, 9 July 1895, AA, Österreich 103, vol. 2, reel 253, 171–180.

22. See especially Lichnowsky to Hohenlohe, 9 July 1895, AA, Österreich 70, vol. 28, reel 216, 363–372; Lichnowsky to Hohenlohe, 19 July 1895, AA, Österreich 103, vol. 2, reel 253, 171–180; Lichnowsky to Hohenlohe, 20 July 1896, ibid. (not filmed).

23. Compare Peter Stein, *Die Neuorientierung der österreichisch-ungarischen Aussenpolitik 1895–1897: Ein Beitrag zur europäischen Bündnispolitik im ausgehenden Jahrhundert* (Göttingen: Musterschmidt, 1972), pp. 56–79.

24. Lichnowsky to Hohenlohe, 30 Oct. 1895, *GP* 10, no. 2492, pp. 147–149; Holstein to Hohenlohe, 12 Nov. 1895, in Fürst Chlodwig zu Hohenlohe-Schillingsfürst, *Denkwürdigkeiten der Reichskanzlerzeit*, ed. Karl Alexander von Müller (Stuttgart-Berlin: Deutsche Verlags-Anstalt, 1931), p. 120; Hohenlohe to Eulenburg, 5 Nov. 1895, *GP* 10, no. 2495, pp. 155–156; Marschall to Bülow, 15 Nov. 1895, *GP* 9, no. 2328, pp. 379–382.

25. Lichnowsky to Hohenlohe, 13 June 1898, *GP* 13, no. 3474, pp. 118–119; Bülow to Lichnowsky, 18 June 1898, ibid., no. 3475, pp. 120–121; Lichnowsky to Hohenlohe, 7 Nov. 1897, AA, Österreich 95, reel 246, 725–730; Lichnowsky to Hohenlohe, 26 June 1897 and Eulenburg to Hohenlohe (prepared by Lichnowsky), 28 Aug. 1897, AA, Österreich 70, vol. 30, reel 216, 0507–0512 and 0547–0550; Lichnowsky to Hohenlohe, 7 Nov. 1897, AA, Österreich 95, vol. 6, reel 246,

725–730; Lichnowsky to Hohenlohe, 2 June 1898, AA, Österreich 97, vol. 4, reel 248, 0286–0287; Lichnowsky to Hohenlohe, 20 Oct. 1897, AA, Österreich 70, vol. 31, reel 276, 573–581. Compare the interpretation in B. B. Hayes, "German Reich and Austrian Question." Believing Lichnowsky to be inclined toward the Pan-Germans, Hayes interprets Lichnowsky's suggestion that Berlin refrain from harsh measures against the Prussian Poles as "a rare appeal [by Lichnowsky] to common sense" (p. 362). Lichnowsky was against harsh measures because he thought they would have a bad effect upon the Austrian Poles, whose favor he thought Berlin should be currying. The formulation of Lichnowsky's attitude in the 1890s in Wilhelm Kosch, *Biographisches Staatshandbuch: Lexikon der Politik, Presse und Publizistik*, 2 vols. (Bern: Francke Verlag, 1963), 1 : 763–764, is more cautious: "Lichnowsky war auch früher der einzige reichsdeutsche Diplomat gewesen (so während seiner Tätigkeit in Wien), der an eine Annäherung an Russland und im Fall einer Auflösung der Donaumonarchie an die Deutschen in Österreich zu gedenken empfahl."

26. Lichnowsky to Hohenlohe, 9 July 1895, Österreich 70, vol. 28.

27. Lichnowsky to Hohenlohe, 17 May 1895, Österreich 86, no. 2, vol. 7, reel 223, 0421–0430.

28. In October 1896 Eulenburg did write Lichnowsky that his reporting had irritated some unnamed persons or person in the Wilhelmstrasse (probably Holstein). The subject of the criticized reports was apparently the Austrian reaction to Bismarck's recent revelation of the Russo-German reinsurance treaty. The complainant said that Lichnowsky had sent too much gratuitous advice and suggested that he limit his pleasantries and make his reports more precise, objective, and labored. "I am not aware," wrote Lichnowsky, "that my style of reporting is different from what it was. If it was good before—and Berlin affirmed that it was—why should it suddenly not be precise, objective, and labored enough? I think there is ill-temper and irritation on account of Friedrichsruh [Bismarck] rather than on my account" (Lichnowsky to Eulenburg, 30 Oct. 1896, Nachlass Eulenburg).

29. Lichnowsky to Hohenlohe, 9 July 1895, AA, Österreich 70, vol. 28, reel 216, 329.

30. Lichnowsky to Hohenlohe, 5 May 1897, *GP* 12 (1), no. 2134, pp. 292–293.

31. Information from Countess Leonore Lichnowsky.

32. Lichnowsky to Eulenburg, 21 Jan. 1899, Nachlass Eulenburg.

33. Elisabeth von Heyking, *Tagebücher aus vier Weltteilen, 1886–1904* (Leipzig: Koehler und Amelang, 1926), p. 284.

34. Figures from Doreen Collins, *Aspects of British Politics, 1904–1919* (Oxford: Oxford University Press, 1965), p. 67, and American Historical Association Committee for the Study of War Documents, "A Catalogue of the Files and Microfilms of the German Foreign Ministry Archives, 1867–1920" (Washington, 1959), esp. p. XVI.

35. Granville to Grey, 14 Oct. 1912, FO 800, Grey Papers, vol. 62.

36. Otto Hammann, *Zur Vorgeschichte des Weltkrieges: Erinnerungen aus den Jahren, 1897–1906* (Berlin: Reimar Hobbing, 1919), p. 125 n1.

37. Lichnowsky to Bülow, 18 Oct. 1900, and Bülow to Lichnowsky, 18 Oct. 1900, Nachlass Bülow.

38. Baronin Spitzemberg geb. Freiin von Varnbüler, *Das Tagebuch der Baronin Spitzemberg geb. Freiin v. Varnbüler: Aufzeichnungen aus der Hofgesellschaft des Hohenzollernreiches,* ed. Rudolf Vierhaus, foreword Peter Rassow, vol. 43 of Deutsche Geschichtsquellen des 19. und 20. Jahrhunderts ed. by Historische Kommission bei der Bayerischen Akademie der Wissenschaften (Göttingen: Vandenhoeck and Ruprecht, 1961), p. 397.

39. His predecessor was Count Friedrich Pourtalès. See Hans von Miquel, "Aus den nachgelassenen Papieren eines deutschen Diplomaten: Aufzeichnungen des Gesandten Hans von Miquel," ed. Friedrich Thimme, *Berliner Monatshefte* 16 (March 1938): 235.

40. "Diplomatie und Demokratie," *Berliner Tageblatt,* 1 July 1917, quoted here from translation in *Abyss,* p. 85.

41. E. Heyking, *Tagebücher,* pp. 301, 387–388; Daisy Princess of Pless, *From My Private Diary,* ed. Major Desmond Chapman-Huston (London: J. Murray, 1931), pp. 63, 133–134; Spitzemberg, *Tagebuch,* p. 397.

42. See Ludwig Raschdau, *In Weimar als Preussischer Gesandter: Ein Buch der Erinnerungen an deutsche Fürstenhöfe, 1894–1897* (Berlin: E. S. Mittler, 1939), pp. 12–13. On 20 March 1895 Monts wrote Bülow: "Pourtalès erledigt mit Hilfe des Professors Krüger sehr gut Holsteins Personaldirektiven" (F. Thimme, "Bülow-Monts," *Preussische Jahrbücher* 232, no. 1 : 33).

43. Bülow, *Denkwürdigkeiten,* 3 : 123; M. H. Fisher and Norman Rich, *The Holstein Papers: The Memoirs, Diaries, and Correspondence of Friedrich von Holstein, 1837–1909,* 4 vols. (Cambridge: At the University Press, 1955–1963), doc. 803, p. 259.

44. Holstein to Pietro Blaserna, 11 Apr. 1900, Fisher and Rich, *Holstein Papers,* 4 : 180; Holstein to vom Rath, 26 May 1909, in H. O. Meisner, "Gespräche und Briefe Holsteins," *Preussische Jahrbücher* 219 (2) (Aug. 1932): 171; Harden, *Zukunft,* 6 Apr. 1918, p. 3.

45. See chap. 2, n24.

46. Friedrich Rosen, *Aus einem diplomatischen Wanderleben*, 2 vols. (Berlin: Transmare Verlag, 1931–1932), 1 : 25; Harden, *Zukunft*, 6 Apr. 1918, p. 3.

47. Herbert von Hindenburg, *Am Rande zweier Jahrzehnte: Momentbilder aus einem Diplomatenleben* (Berlin: Schlieffen-Verlag, 1938), p. 130.

48. All in *Abyss*, pp. 89, 48, 1.

49. Information from Countess Leonore Lichnowsky.

50. Hutten-Czapski, *Sechzig Jahre*, 1 : 418–420.

51. Born on 8 March (the same day as her husband) 1879. Her first name is sometimes given erroneously as Mechtild. This was an error her publisher made in one of her early works (M. Lichnowsky, *Heute und vorgestern* [Vienna: Bergland Verlag, 1958], p. 106n). On the family history see Erwein Aretin, "Geschichte der Herren und Grafen von Arco," MS (1936–1945), deposited at Schloss Moos, Plattling, Lower Bavaria.

52. Information from Countess Leonore Lichnowsky.

53. Based on letters Mechtilde Lichnowsky wrote her sister Helene. Substance supplied by Countess Leonore Lichnowsky.

54. Information from Countess Leonore Lichnowsky.

55. Mary Theresa Olivia (Cornwallis-West) Fürstin von Pless, *Daisy Princess of Pless by Herself*, ed. Major D. Chapman-Huston (New York: Dutton, 1929), p. 172; idem, *Diary*, p. 240.

56. Harden, *Zukunft*, 30 March 1918, pp. 461–464.

57. Karl Kraus, *Fackel* 24, no. 608–612 : 71.

58. Quoted from the English edition in *Abyss*, p. 48.

59. *Hradec: Slezské kulturní Středisko, státní zámek a památky v okolí* [official guidebook to Grätz] (Prague, 1962), pp. 44–45. Description of library also in Ludwig Stein, *Aus dem Leben eines Optimisten* (Berlin: Brückenverlag, 1930), p. 173.

60. Information on reading preference from Countess Leonore Lichnowsky. On Schopenhauer see also Stein, *Leben eines Optimisten*, p. 172.

61. Heine first used the word "Schnapphahnski" in connection with Felix Lichnowsky in his poem Atta Troll, written in the fall of 1841. His poem opens with the description of a vagrant who had once been a monk and then a robber chieftan, and had then united both professions by taking service with Don Carlos. When Don Carlos fled Spain, most of his paladins had taken to honest work. This vagrant had become a bear trainer and exhibited his dancing bear Atta Troll.

"Herr Schnapphahnski," Heine interjected, "became an author" (Heine, *Sämtliche Werke,* ed. Stephen Born, 12 vols. [Berlin-Stuttgart: Cotta, 1886], 2 : 204).

62. Information from Countess Leonore Lichnowsky. German original: "Wenig und einfach, aber in der Vollendung."

63. August Scholtis, *Ein Herr aus Bolatitz: Lebenserinnerungen* (Munich: Paul List Verlag, 1959), p. 159.

64. See esp. ibid., pp. 147–148.

65. Figures from *Schlesisches Güteradressbuch, 1912* (Breslau: W. G. Korn, 1912). Also Kahlden, "Herrschaft Kuchelna," passim: Charlotte Thilo, "Die Bevölkerungs- Siedlungs- und Wirtschaftsverhältnisse im Hultschiner Ländchen," in *Beiträge zur schlesischen Landeskunde,* ed, M. H. Friedrichsen (Breslau: Ferdinand Hirt, 1925), pp. 102–103.

66. Information from Countess Leonore Lichnowsky. See also Scholtis, *Erinnerungen,* pp. 79, 222.

67. Rosen, *Wanderleben,* 1 : 26–27.

68. Stein, *Leben eines Optimisten,* pp. 180–181.

69. Information from Countess Leonore Lichnowsky.

70. Maurice Baumont, "Le prince de Radolin," in *Mélanges Pierre Renouvin: Etudes d'histoire des relations internationales* (Paris: Presses universitaires de France, 1966), p. 175.

71. Information from Countess Leonore Lichnowsky.

72. Hofmannsthal to Schnitzler, 29 Oct. 1910, in Hugo von Hofmannsthal, Arthur Schnitzler, *Briefwechsel,* ed. Theresa Nickel and Heinrich Schnitzler (Frankfurt: S. Fischer Verlag, 1964), p. 255.

73. Daisy of Pless, *Diary,* p. 64.

74. Ibid., p. 240.

75. Daisy of Pless, *Herself,* p. 231.

76. Scholtis, *Erinnerungen,* p. 207.

77. Reported in article on Lichnowsky's appointment to London in the Free Conservative *Die Post,* 17 Oct. 1912.

78. Information from Countess Leonore Lichnowsky.

79. Prussia. Herrenhaus, *Stenographische Berichte über die Verhandlungen des Preussischen Herrenhauses, Session 1908,* 26. bis 30. Juni 1908, XXI. Legislaturperiode, p. 448.

80. Herrenhaus, *Verhandlungen,* Session 1905/06, XX. Sitzung, p. 522.

81. See reaction in Hutten-Czapski, *Sechzig Jahre,* 1 : 530–531; Bülow, *Denkwürdigkeiten,* 2 : 492–493.

82. Lichnowsky to Eulenburg, 27 Apr. 1895, Nachlass Eulenburg.

83. Herrenhaus, *Verhandlungen,* Session 1910, 7. Sitzung, p. 90.

84. Lichnowsky to Bülow, 12 Dec. 1909, Nachlass Bülow.

85. For *Berliner Tageblatt* comment on decline of Free Conservatives see issues of 6 Aug. 1911, Morgen-Ausgabe; 20 Jan. 1912, Abend-Ausgabe; 27 Jan. 1912, Abend-Ausgabe.

86. Wolff, *Der Marsch durch zwei Jahrzehnte* (Amsterdam: Albert de Lange, 1936), pp. 67–68.

87. Wolff, "Nicht einer," *Berliner Tageblatt,* 8 Apr. 1910.

88. David Lloyd George, *War Memoirs of David Lloyd George,* 2 vols. (Boston: Little, Bown, 1935), 1 : 28.

89. Lichnowsky to Bülow, 12 December 1909, Nachlass Bülow.

90. Lichnowsky to Bülow, 8 April 1910, Nachlass Bülow. This letter partially published in Bülow, *Denkwürdigkeiten,* 3 : 91.

91. Lichnowsky to Maria Bülow, 8 Apr. 1910, Nachlass Bülow.

92. Ernst Jäckh, ed., *Kiderlen-Wächter, der Staatsmann und Mensch: Briefwechsel und Nachlass,* 2 vols. (Stuttgart: Deutsche Verlags-Anstalt, 1925), 2 : 173. In 1912 Berlin informed the British embassy that Lichnowsky had been considered for Vienna but would not do there as his father had dual nationality and opted for Prussia in 1866 (Granville to Grey, 14 Oct. 1912, FO 800, Grey Papers, vol. 62). In 1906 and 1908 it was rumored that Lichnowsky would be appointed foreign secretary. Harden thought Lichnowsky was the man favored by the Silesian magnates, while Holstein believed he belonged to a clique headed by the press chief Hammann, whom Holstein considered the truly influential man in the Wilhelmstrasse (Rogge, *Holstein und Harden,* p. 367). Holstein wrote Radolin in 1907 that Hammann had hoped Lichnowsky would become state secretary when Richthofen died in 1906 (Holstein to Radolin, 15 Oct. 1907, Fisher and Rich, *Holstein Papers,* 4 : 501). That Lichnowsky was being considered as a replacement for Richthofen is also indicated in letter of Princess Radziwill to General Robilant, 18 Jan. 1906, in Marie Dorothea Elisabeth (de Castellane) Radziwill, *Lettres de la Princesse Radziwill au Général de Robilant, 1889–1914,* 4 vols. (Bologna: Nicola Zanichelli, 1933), 3 : 218. In the fall of 1908 Holstein and Harden agreed that Hammann was again working for Lichnowsky's appointment to some high position in an effort to establish a combination that Hammann could control if he were to lose his own job in the wake of the crisis following the kaiser's indiscretions about German foreign policy in his interview with the London *Daily Telegraph* (Rogge, *Holstein und Harden,* p. 367).

93. From abstract of personnel file. With the acceptance of his petition for release he was granted the title of true privy councillor

(Wirklicher Geheimer Rat). But the kaiser, whose permission for the release was necessary, refused to condone the address "Excellency," normally used for a councillor of that rank, for this form, he said, was inappropriate for a man who was a prince.

Chapter III

1. Lloyd George, *War Memoirs*, 1 : 28–29.
2. Emil Ludwig, *Wilhelm der Zweite* (Berlin: Ernst Rowohlt Verlag, 1926), p. 270.
3. See George Monger, *The End of Isolation: British Foreign Policy, 1900–1907* (London: Thomas Nelson and Sons, 1963), passim; Norman Rich, *Friedrich von Holstein: Politics and Diplomacy in the Era of Bismarck and Wilhelm II*, 2 vols. (Cambridge: At the University Press, 1965), 2 : passim; Gerhard Ritter, *Staatskunst und Kriegshandwerk: Das Problem des 'Militarismus' in Deutschland*, 3rd ed., 4 vols. (Munich: Verlag K. Oldenbourg, 1965–1968), 2 : 171–209; P. J. V. Rolo, *Entente Cordiale: The Origins and Negotiations of the Anglo-French Agreements of 8 April 1904* (New York: Macmillan, St. Martin's Press, 1969), passim.
4. Ludwig, *Wilhelm II.*, p. 267.
5. See Volker R. Berghahn, *Der Tirpitz-Plan: Genesis und Verfall einer innerpolitischen Krisenstrategie unter Wilhelm II.* (Düsseldorf: Droste Verlag, 1971) and Jonathan Steinberg, *Yesterday's Deterrent: Tirpitz and the Birth of the German Battle Fleet* (London: Macdonald, 1965), passim.
6. Granville to Nicolson, private, 18 Oct. 1912, *BD* 9 (2), no. 47, p. 38.
7. See Konrad H. Jarausch, *The Enigmatic Chancellor: Bethmann Hollweg and the Hubris of Imperial Germany* (New Haven and London: Yale University Press, 1973), pp. 148–207; Fritz Fischer, *Krieg der Illusionen: Die deutsche Politik von 1911 bis 1914* (Düsseldorf: Droste Verlag, 1969), pp. 85–116, 169–206.
8. Theobald von Bethmann Hollweg, *Bethmann Hollwegs Kriegsreden,* ed. Friedrich Thimme (Stuttgart-Berlin: Deutsche Verlags-Anstalt, 1919), p. 19.
9. Quotation from Bethmann to Metternich, 18 March 1912, *GP* 31, no. 11 406, p. 189. See further Ritter, *Staatskunst*, 2 : 205ff.
10. Aufzeichnung Lichnowsky, 13 Apr. 1904, *GP* 20 (1), no. 6516, pp. 202–203.

11. *Abyss*, p. 50. There is testimony concerning an incident not yet verifiable from the files that, if true, would support the interpretation above that Lichnowsky believed in some form of Great Power cooperation *against* Morocco and would have opposed Berlin's posture as the sultan's protector. According to Theodor Wolff, at a dinner at the German embassy in Paris in July 1904 French foreign minister Delcassé took Lichnowsky aside and spoke to him intently of France's desire to reach an agreement with Germany over Morocco (*Das Vorspiel* [Munich: Verlag für Kulturpolitik, 1924], pp. 154–155). Rosen reports that Lichnowsky, who told Rosen about the approach, wrote an account of the conversation for Bülow which later disappeared (*Wanderleben*, 1 : 192). Although Lichnowsky, who mentions the incident in *Abyss* (p. xix), did, as we know from family letters, visit Paris in July 1904, that was not the time Delcassé was interested in a written agreement with Germany. Rosen's statement that Delcassé wished to know what Germany wanted from him suggests that the incident took place in 1905 after Germany decided to intervene in Morocco and was prepared to force Delcassé's dismissal.

12. "Die deutsche Flotte und England," *Berliner Tageblatt*, 28 Aug. 1909. Same ideas further developed in article for *Neues Wiener Tageblatt*, 24 Dec. 1911.

13. See Metternich to Bethmann, 10 Dec. 1911, *GP* 31, no. 11 328, pp. 46–47; Bethmann to Metternich, 12 Dec. 1911, ibid., no. 11 329, p. 48; Metternich to Kiderlen, 17 March 1912, ibid., no. 11 403, pp. 181ff and p. 187n containing Wilhelm II's draft message to Metternich not sent. Example of Widenmann reporting: Widenmann to Tirpitz, 28 Oct. 1911, copy in AA, England 78, no. 3, geheim, vol. 10, reel 71, 0152. Metternich commented on this dispatch in a letter to Bethmann, 1 Nov. 1911, ibid., frames 0155–0161. See further Richard von Kühlmann, "Reichsgraf Paul Wolff Metternich zur Gracht," *Berliner Monatshefte* 13 (1) (Jan. 1935): 20–24; Friedrich-Christian Stahl, "Botschafter Graf Wolff Metternich und die deutsch-englischen Beziehungen," Diss. Hamburg (1951); Richard von Kühlmann, *Erinnerungen* (Heidelberg: Lambert Schneider, 1948), pp. 346–347.

14. Zara S. Steiner, *The Foreign Office and Foreign Policy, 1898–1914* (Cambridge: At the University Press, 1969), pp. 66ff, 76, 180.

15. Minute by Crowe to Granville to Grey, 29 Feb. 1912, FO 371, vol. 1371, Germany 1912, file 9163 of 2 March 1912.

16. Goschen to Nicolson, private, 22 Oct. 1910, FO 800, Grey Papers, vol. 62.

17. Grey to Goschen, private, 5 March 1913, *BD* 10 (2), no. 465, p. 687.

18. *Abyss*, p. 70. See Steiner, *Foreign Office and Foreign Policy*, pp. 147, 150–151.

19. *Abyss*, p. 48.

20. Bethmann to Lichnowsky, 3 Oct. 1912, RAUSL. "Marschalls Tod," wrote Bethmann, "ist ein grosser Verlust, wenngleich ich nicht den Glauben Vieler teilte, dass er in *kurzer* Zeit etwas grosses zu Stande gebracht haben würde. Aber er hätte den Boden geebnet kraft seines Prestiges." Also Wilhelm II to Eisendecher, 12 Dec. 1912, Nachlass Eisendecher, K 159721–159722.

21. Mensdorff to Berchtold, 21 June 1912, MÄ, 148, PA VIII, no. 31, a B, p. 168.

22. Mensdorff to Berchtold, private, 24 May 1912, MÄ, 149, PA VIII, Varia 1912 folio 1–40, p. 4. Crowe's comment: "This is a development characteristic of German methods, which was to be expected, but it is not the less unfortunate. Baron Marschall's presence in London will undoubtedly be used to put our ambassador in the shade" (Crowe minute to German newspaper reports dated 17 May 1912, FO 371, vol. 1371, 1912 Germany, file 21895, 22 May 1912).

23. Kühlmann, *Erinnerungen*, p. 359.

24. Spitzemberg, *Tagebuch*, p. 547.

25. There is reference to the kaiser's proposal in Botho Graf von Wedel, "Diplomatisches und Persönliches," in *Front wider Bülow: Staatsmänner, Diplomaten und Forscher zu seinen Denkwürdigkeiten*, ed. Friedrich Thimme et al. (Munich: F. Bruckmann, 1931), p. 268–269. Wedel says that Lichnowsky stood first on the kaiser's list.

26. "Deutschland und Frankreich," *Deutsche Revue* 37 (July 1912).

27. Goschen to Tyrrell, private, 27 Oct. 1912, FO 800, Grey Papers, vol. 62.

28. Stein, *Leben eines Optimisten*, pp. 134, 197, 210.

29. *Nord und Süd* 142 (July 1912). This issue also published separately as *Krieg oder Frieden: Die deutsch-englische Verständigung* (Breslau: Schles. Buchdr., Kunst- und Verlagsanstalt, 1912).

30. Stein, *Leben eines Optimisten*, pp. 176–178.

31. Granville to Grey, private and confidential, 14 Oct. 1912, FO 800, Grey Papers, vol. 62; Georg Alexander von Müller, *Der Kaiser . . . Aufzeichnungen des Chefs des Marinekabinetts über die Ära Wilhelms II.*, ed. Walter Görlitz (Göttingen: Musterschmidt, 1965), p. 121.

32. Acceptance of invitation to hunt at Grätz indicated in Bethmann to Lichnowsky, 3 Sept. 1912, RAUSL.

33. Bethmann to Wilhelm II, 25 Sept. 1912, DZA Merseburg, Rep. 53 J, Lit. B Nr. 7.

34. Ibid.

35. In a marginal note to Bethmann to Wilhelm II, 3 Oct. 1912, DZA Merseburg, Rep. 53 J, Lit. B Nr. 7.

36. Wilhelm II to Eisendecher, 27 Sept. 1912, copy in Eisendecher's hand, Nachlass Eisendecher, K 45981. "Herzlichsten Dank für treue Teilnahme, bin tief betrümmert über seinen Tod, es ist eine complette Catastrophe, der einzige meiner Zivilbeamten der ein Staatsmann war und Schneid, Tapferkeit und Energie hatte. Would you feel up to replacing him? Wetter hier scheusslich. Grüsse an Mrs."

37. Eisendecher to Wilhelm II, 30 Sept. 1912, Nachlass Eisendecher, K 459782-4. There is a garbled account in Josef Redlich, *Schicksalsjahre Österreichs, 1908–1912: Das politische Tagebuch Josef Redlichs,* ed. Fritz Fellner, 2 vols. (Graz-Köln: Verlag Hermann Böhlaus Nachf., 1953–1954), 2 : 284. Monts told Redlich, according to this account, that Kiderlen first offered the job to him.

38. Kühlmann, *Erinnerungen,* pp. 374–375. When several months later Eisendecher publicly noted that Germany had built her fleet because England had concluded ententes with France and Russia, Crowe noted that "although the Admiral's remarks betray very little insight into the elements of the international situation, and a defective knowledge of the history of the Anglo-French and Anglo-Russian understandings, yet the fact that he was a candidate for the German embassy in London, and his close connection with the Emperor invest his opinion with a vicarious interest. . . . It is these indiscreet outpourings of the amateur diplomats which clearly reveal the inner workings of the mind of the German government." (Minute by Crowe to Acton to Foreign Office, FO 371, vol. 1647, 1913 Germany, files 4-1710, file 7737, 18 Feb. 1913).

39. In English in the original.

40. Wilhelm II to Bethmann, 30 Sept. 1912, DZA Merseburg, Rep. 53 J, Lit. B, Nr. 7. Also Eisendecher diary entry for 27 Oct. 1912: "At Potsdam H. M. most outspoken against England. Who may the Hetzer be? Sat next to Princess, who quite antienglish. Kaiser complained about Goschen. They must send me a better and more prominent man" (Nachlass Eisendecher, K 459543).

41. Kühlmann, *Erinnerungen,* p. 287.

42. Mensdorff to Berchtold, private, 11 Oct. 1912, MÄ, 149, PA VIII, Varia 1912, no. 3, p. 35.

43. Goschen to Grey, private, 12 Aug. 1910, FO 800, Grey Papers, vol. 62.

44. Kühlmann, *Erinnerungen,* pp. 404–405.

45. In the short list the kaiser sent Bethmann on 24 September.

Admiral von Müller's account of the appointment suggests that after Eisendecher declined, the kaiser's candidates were Prince Hatzfeldt and, in second place, Lichnowsky (Müller, *Aufzeichnungen*, p. 121). If Wedel is correct (see chap. 3, n23 above), the kaiser must have reversed his preferences.

46. Bethmann to Wilhelm II, 3 Oct. 1912, DZA Merseburg, Rep. 53 J, Lit. B, Nr. 7.

47. Marginal notes by Wilhelm II to ibid.

48. Ibid.

49. Bethmann to Lichnowsky, 3 Oct. 1912, RAUSL. "Die Nachfolge ist zwischen S.M. und mir noch nicht geregelt. Ich muss ihn dazu sehen, darum kann ich Ihnen über meine Gedanken noch nichts mitteilen."

50. Granville to Grey, private and confidential, 14 Oct. 1912, FO 800, Grey Papers, vol. 62.

The German Minister for Foreign Affairs asked me to telegraph certain points about Prince Lichnowsky, which he cannot send you through the Prince's future staff. The Prince was first suggested by the Emperor, whose attention had been drawn to him afresh by his article in the June [sic] number of "Nord und Süd." After careful consideration of all other possible candidates, MFA said, "they" were unanimously in the Prince's favor. He was attaché in London in '84, was for some years councillor at Vienna, but would not do there as his father had the double nationality and opted for the Prussian in '66. MFA considers that he ought to be acceptable in London, as he is not a "Naval Fanatic," has a great name, plenty of money, and goes with best intentions. His wife, born Arco, is rather eccentric.

51. Lichnowsky to Wilhelm II, 11 Oct. 1912, Brand. Preuss. Hausarchiv, I.a.R. 53 E III no. 8, cited (but not quoted) by Hans Günter Zmarzlik, *Bethmann Hollweg als Reichskanzler: Studien zu Möglichkeiten und Grenzen seiner innerpolitischen Machtstellung* (Düsseldorf: Droste Verlag, 1957), p. 38n1.

52. Information from Prince Wilhelm Lichnowsky.

53. Emil Ludwig, "Der Fürst Lichnowsky," *Die Weltbühne*, 20 March 1928, p. 430. The kaiser probably informed Lichnowsky of his appointment by telegram. The penciled letter may have been the post office's form of the message or a copy done in the prince's home.

54. Bülow, *Denkwürdigkeiten*, 3 : 122–123.

55. These commentaries appeared on 17 or 18 October 1912.

56. Adm. Holleben to Eisendecher, 17 Oct. 1912, Nachlass Eisendecher, K 460272-3.

57. Such comments in *Le Figaro*, 18 Oct. 1912; Georges Louis to Poincaré, 28 Oct. 1912, *DDF*, 3ᵉ série, 4, no. 258, p. 266; Mensdorff to

Berchtold, 25 Oct. 1912, MÄ, England 1912, Berichte, Weisungen, Varia, 149, PA VIII, n. 52 C.

58. Mensdorff to Berchtold, private, 11 Oct. 1912, MÄ, 149, PA VIII, Varia 1912, no. 3, p. 35.

59. Goschen to Tyrrell, private, 27 Oct. 1912, FO 800, Grey Papers, vol. 62.

60. Monts wrote in his memoirs that that was the advice Bülow gave Max Ratibor (Monts, *Erinnerungen*, p. 153), but it was a common cynical manner of speaking.

61. Jäckh, *Kiderlen-Wächter*, 2 : 88.

62. Leopold von Plessen, *Begegnungen*, p. 48. Baron Plessen says that the interview had appeared in the *Berliner Tageblatt*. It was actually the interview carried by the *Berliner Neueste Nachrichten*.

63. *Abyss*, p. 49.

64. Diary entry of 27 Oct. 1912, Nachlass Eisendecher, reel 5158, K 459 544–545. *Oberflächlich* (superficial) was in German in the original. See also Bethmann to Eisendecher, 12 Aug. 1919, ibid., K 459 631.

Chapter IV

1. Harold Nicolson, *Sir Arthur Nicolson, Bart., First Lord Carnock: A Study in the Old Diplomacy* (London: Constable, 1930), pp. 391–392.

2. *Abyss*, p. 69.

3. Ibid.

4. Ibid., pp. 67–68.

5. *Der Lauf der Asdur* (Vienna: Bermann-Fischer Verlag, 1936), p. 191.

6. Wladimir v. Korostovetz, "Graf Alexander Konstantinowitsch Benckendorff," *Berliner Monatshefte* 14 (Nov. 1936), p. 895.

7. *Abyss*, p. 56.

8. *Neue Freie Presse*, 10 March 1906. Found in Nachlass Mensdorff, II: Zeitungsausschnitte 1905–1915.

9. Sir George Franckenstein, *Diplomat of Destiny* (New York: Alliance Book Corp., 1940), p. 142; Kühlmann, *Erinnerungen*, p. 327; Hugo Hantsch, *Leopold Graf Berchtold: Grandseigneur und Staatsmann*, 2 vols. (Graz-Köln: Styria-Verlag, 1963), 1 : 24.

10. This obvious in his efforts to dispel distrust of Marschall, noted above. See also Stumm to Bülow, 1 June 1906, AA, England 87, vol. 5; Kühlmann, *Erinnerungen*, p. 327.

11. Mensdorff to Berchtold, 29 March 1912, MÄ, 148 PA VIII, no. 19B, pp. 288–291; Mensdorff to Berchtold, 5 Dec. 1913, MÄ, PA VIII, Berichte, No. 96 B, geheim, p. 6337.

12. *Abyss*, pp. 66–67.

13. Ibid., p. 65.

14. Luigi Albertini, *The Origins of the War of 1914*, trans. and ed. Isabella M. Massey, 3 vols. (London: Oxford University Press, 1957), 1 : 402–418; A. J. P. Taylor, *The Struggle for Mastery in Europe 1848–1918* (Oxford: At the Clarendon Press, 1954), pp. 483–496.

15. See especially Fischer, *Illusionen*, pp. 223–230.

16. Report of Foreign Secretary Alfred von Kiderlen-Wächter to the Foreign Affairs Committee of the German Bundesrat, 28 November 1912, from *Verhandlungen des Bundesrats des Deutschen Reiches*, abridged translation in Henry Cord Meyer, ed., *The Long Generation: Germany from Empire to Ruin, 1913–1945* (New York: Walker, 1973).

17. Lichnowsky to Bethmann, 4 Dec. 1912, AA, Deutschland 135, no. 2, vol. 3, reel 368, 00750–00751.

18. Lichnowsky to Wilhelm II, 7 Nov. 1912, DZA Merseburg, Rep. 53 J Lit. B Nr. 7.

19. Minute by Wilhelm II to Griesinger to Kiderlen, 25 Oct. 1912, *GP* 33, no. 12 297, p. 253; minute by Wilhelm II to Wolff Telegraph Agency telegram, 4 Nov. 1912, ibid., no. 12 321, p. 277.

20. Wilhelm II to Kiderlen, 7 Nov. 1912, ibid., no. 12 339, p. 295.

21. Wilhelm II to Kiderlen, 9 Nov. 1912, ibid., no. 12 348, and editors' fn., p. 302. Also Kiderlen to Wilhelm II, 3 Nov. 1912, ibid., no. 12 320, pp. 274–276.

22. John C. G. Röhl, *Germany without Bismarck: The Crisis of Government in the Second Reich, 1890–1900* (Berkeley and Los Angeles: University of California Press, 1967), pp. 106–107.

23. As explained by the chancellor in Bethmann to Lichnowsky, 2 Dec. 1912, AA, Deutschland 135, no. 2, vol. 3, reel 368, 00745.

24. Lichnowsky to Kiderlen, 19 Nov. 1912, *GP*, no. 12399, pp. 363–364.

25. Pourtalès to Bethmann, 20 Nov. 1912, forwarded to Lichnowsky on 22 Nov. 1912, ibid., no. 12 413, p. 383.

26. Lichnowsky to Wilhelm II, 23 Nov. 1912, AA, Deutschland 135, no. 2, vol. 3, reel 368, 00737–00739.

27. Bethmann to Kiderlen, interoffice memo., 25 Nov. 1912, ibid., 368, 00740–00741.

28. Kiderlen to Bethmann, interoffice memo., 29 Nov. 1912, ibid., 368, 00742–00743.

29. Bethmann to Lichnowsky, 2 Dec. 1912, ibid., 368, 00745–00747.

30. Lichnowsky to Bethmann, 4 Dec. 1912, ibid., 368, 00750–00751.

31. Lichnowsky to Kiderlen, 27 Nov. 1912, *GP* 33, no. 12 447, pp. 417–418.

32. Benckendorff to Sazonov, 16/29 Nov. 1912, *DS* 2, no. 741, pp. 510–511.

33. Benckendorff to Sazonov, 15/28 Nov. 1912, ibid., no. 738, p. 508.

34. GP 33, fn.**, pp. 445–446.

35. Grey to Goschen, 4 Dec. 1912, BD 9 (2), no. 327. Also Lichnowsky to Kiderlen, 4 Dec. 1912, *GP* 33, no. 12 481, pp. 351ff.

36. Lichnowsky to Bethmann, 9 Dec. 1912, *GP* 33, no. 12 489, p. 405.

37. P. Cambon to Poincaré, 3 Dec. 1912, *DDF*, 3e série, 4, no. 615, p. 634.

38. Lichnowsky to Bethmann, 3 Dec. 1912, *GP* 29, no. 15 612, pp. 119ff.

39. Lichnowsky to Wilhelm II, 23 Nov. 1912, AA, Deutschland 135, No. 2, vol. 3, reel 368, 00737–00739.

40. Kiderlen to Bethmann, interoffice memo., 29 Nov. 1912, ibid., 00742–00743.

41. Lerchenfeld to Hertling, private, 14 Dec. 1912, in *Briefwechsel Hertling-Lerchenfeld: Dienstliche Privatkorrespondenz zwischen dem bayerischen Ministerpräsidenten Georg Graf von Hertling und dem bayerischen Gesandten in Berlin Hugo Graf von und zu Lerchenfeld,* vols. 50 (1 & 2) Deutsche Geschichtsquellen des 19. und 20. Jahrhunderts, ed. Historische Kommission bei der Bayerischen Akademie der Wissenschaften, ed. Ernst Deuerlein, 2 vols. (Boppard am Rhein: Harald Boldt Verlag, 1973), 1 : 189–190.

42. Wilhelm II to Eisendecher, 12 Dec. 1912, Nachlass Eisendecher, K 159721.

43. Minute by Wilhelm II to Kiderlen to Wilhelm II, 19 Nov. 1912, *GP* 33, no. 12 395, p. 359; Wilhelm II to Kiderlen, 21 Nov. 1912, ibid., no. 12 405, pp. 374–375.

44. Fischer, *Illusionen,* pp. 231–241.

45. Quoted ibid., p. 239.

46. Quoted ibid., p. 232.

47. Ibid., pp. 226–241.

48. Lichnowsky to Bülow, 3 Jan. 1913, Nachlass Bülow.

49. For the diplomatic origins of the conference see Ernst C. Helmreich, *The Diplomacy of the Balkan Wars, 1912–1913* (Cambridge, Mass.: Harvard University Press, 1938), pp. 221ff. For the course of the conference see Robert R. Kritt, "Die Londoner Botschafter Konferenz 1912–1913," Diss. Vienna (1960).

50. Harold Nicolson, *King George V* (London: Constable, 1952), p. 176.

51. Lichnowsky to Kiderlen, received 18 Dec. 1912, *GP* 34 (1), no. 12 548, p. 56; Lichnowsky to Kiderlen, 18 Dec. 1912, ibid., no. 12 549, pp. 56–58; Kiderlen to Lichnowsky, 19 Dec. 1912, ibid., no. 12 550, p. 58.

52. The key documents on this question are in *GP* 34 (1), no. 12 615, 12 647, 12 656 (plus fn. on p. 172), 12 658, and 12 681. There was some unjustified suspicion by Benckendorff and Cambon that Lichnowsky and Berlin were encouraging the Rumanians to be intransigent. This question dealt with in ibid., fn.*, p. 153.

53. The key documents on this question are in ibid., no. 12 616, 12 630, 12 637, 12 650, 12 651, 12 662, 12 677.

54. Lichnowsky to Jagow, 26 March 1913, *GP* 34 (2), no. 13 021, pp. 557–558; Zimmermann to Lichnowsky, 28 March 1913, ibid., no. 13 032, pp. 566–567; Lichnowsky to Jagow, 1 Apr. 1913, ibid., no. 13 059, p. 595; Jagow to Lichnowsky, 1 Apr. 1913, ibid., no. 13 061, p. 596; Jagow to Wilhelm II, 1 Apr. 1913, ibid., no. 13 060, pp. 595–596; P. Cambon to Pichon, 3 Apr. 1913, *DDF*, 3ᵉ série, 6, no. 183, p. 222.

55. Lichnowsky to Kiderlen, received 18 Dec. 1912, GP 34 (1), no. 12 548, p. 56.

56. Lichnowsky to Kiderlen, 20 December 1912, ibid., no. 12 557, pp. 62–63.

57. Nikolai Nikolaevich Schebeko, *Souvenirs: Essai historique sur les origines de la guerre de 1914*, preface by Jules Cambon (Paris: Bibliothèque diplomatique, 1936), p. 21.

58. Lichnowsky had informed Berlin of the conference's action in a telegram to Zimmermann, 13 Jan. 1913, *GP* 34 (1), no. 12 677, p. 191. See further Goschen to Grey, private, 17 Jan. 1913, FO 800, Grey Papers, vol. 62; Szögyény to Berchtold, 17 Jan. 1913, *ÖUA* 5, no. 5419, p. 471; J. Cambon to Poincaré, 20 Jan. 1913, *DDF*, 3ᵉ série, 5, no. 237, p. 299; J. Cambon to Joannart, 21 Jan. 1913, ibid., no. 240, p. 304.

59. Zimmermann to Lichnowsky, 20 Jan. 1913, *GP* 34 (1), no. 12 710, pp. 229–230; Lichnowsky to Zimmermann, 22 Jan. 1913, ibid., no. 12 717, p. 236; Benckendorff to Sazonov, 10/23 Jan. 1913, *DS* 3, no. 837, p. 59; Grey to Goschen, 22 Jan. 1913, *BD* 9 (2), no. 542, p. 435; Grey to Goschen, 20 May 1913, ibid., no. 1018, p. 824; J. Cambon to Pichon, 4 June 1913, *DDF*, 3ᵉ série, 7, no. 30, p. 33.

60. Kiderlen to Lichnowsky, 15 Dec. 1912, *GP* 34 (1), no. 12 540, pp. 44–46; Poincaré to P. Cambon, 17 Dec. 1912, *DDF*, 3ᵉ série, 5, no. 75, p. 92.

61. Lichnowsky to Kiderlen, 17 Dec. 1912, *GP* 34 (1), no. 12 545, pp. 53–54; Lichnowsky to Kiderlen, 20 Dec. 1912, ibid., no. 12 556, p. 62.

62. Marginal note to Lichnowsky to Kiderlen, 20 Dec. 1912, ibid., no. 12 556, p. 62.

63. Lichnowsky to Bethmann, 20 Dec. 1912, ibid., no. 12 561, pp. 70–71.

64. Aufzeichnung Lichnowsky, 22 Dec. 1912, ibid., no. 12 562, pp. 74–75.

65. Klaus Meyer, *Theodor Schiemann als politischer Publizist* (Frankfurt/Main: Rütten und Loening, 1956), pp. 173, 187 n. 577.

66. Lichnowsky to Kiderlen, 26 Nov. 1912, *GP* 33, no. 12 438, pp. 408–409; Kiderlen's reply cited in fn.***, ibid., p. 408.

67. Fn.***, ibid., pp. 408–409.

68. Benckendorff to Sazonov, *DS* 2, no. 363, 31 Nov./4 Dec. 1912, pp. 516f.

69. Szögyény to Berchtold, 20 Jan. 1913, *ÖUA* 5, no. 5454, p. 497. Benckendorff said the same thing to the Italian ambassador, according to Mensdorff to Berchtold, 20 Jan. 1913, ibid., no. 5462, p. 561.

70. Lichnowsky to Zimmermann, 19 Jan. 1913, *GP* 34 (1), no. 12 707, pp. 224ff; Bethmann (draft by Stumm) to Lichnowsky, 20 Jan. 1913, ibid., no. 12 708, p. 228; Lichnowsky to Bethmann, 22 Jan. 1913, ibid., no. 12 740, pp. 260ff; Benckendorff to Sazonov, 6/19 Jan. 1913, *DS* 3, no. 831, pp. 49–50; Bethmann (draft by Stumm) to Lichnowsky, 20 Jan. 1913, *GP* 34 (1), no. 12 763, p. 283.

71. Pourtalès to Jagow, 6 Feb. 1913, *GP* 34 (1), no. 12 805, pp. 330ff.

72. Benckendorff to Sazonov, 5/18 Dec. 1912, *DS* 2, no. 767, pp. 541–542; Lucius to Kiderlen, 21 Dec. 1912, *GP* 34 (1), no. 12 559, p. 68; Aufzeichnung Lichnowsky, 22 Dec. ibid., no. 12562, p. 74; Benckendorff to Sazonov, 20 Dec. 1912/2 Jan. 1913, *DS* 3, no. 795, p. 6.

73. Lichnowsky to Bethmann, 26 Jan. 1913, *GP* 34 (1), no. 12 748, pp. 270–271; Jagow to Lichnowsky, 28 Jan. 1913, ibid., no. 12 747, p. 269; Jagow to Lichnowsky, 30 Jan. 1913, ibid., no. 12 760, p. 279. On 22 Jan. Berlin had sent Lichnowsky more detailed information on the border desired by Austria, which Tschirschky had reported to Jagow on 21 Jan. 1913, ibid., no. 12 715, pp. 234–235.

74. Mensdorff to Berchtold, 6 Feb. 1913, *ÖUA* 5, no. 5694, pp. 649–650; Lichnowsky to Jagow, 6 Feb. 1913, *GP* 34 (1), no. 12 799, pp. 326–327; Benckendorff to Sazonov, 24 Jan./6 Feb. 1913, *DS* 3, no. 857, pp. 83ff.

75. Berchtold to Szögyény et al., 7 Feb. 1913, *ÖUA* 5, no. 5712, pp. 667–668.

76. Jagow to Lichnowsky, 8 Feb. 1913, *GP* 34 (1), no. 12 803, p. 329;

Lichnowsky to Jagow, 9 Feb. 1913, ibid., no. 12 817, pp. 345–346; Lichnowsky to Jagow, 10 Feb. 1913, ibid., no. 12 820, pp. 349–350; Jagow to Lichnowsky, 11 Feb. 1913, ibid., no. 12 822, p. 350.

77. Mensdorff to Berchtold, 15 Feb. 1913, *ÖUA* 5, no. 5815, pp. 743–744.

78. Lichnowsky to Jagow, 11 Feb. 1913, *GP* 34 (1), no. 12 826, pp. 355–356.

79. Nicolson, *Lord Carnock*, p. 394.

80. Mensdorff to Berchtold, 23 May 1913, *MÄ*, 149 PA VIII, Varia, p. 159.

81. Mensdorff to Berchtold, 15 Feb. 1913, *ÖUA* 5, no. 5814, p. 740.

82. Mensdorff to Berchtold, private, 15 Feb. 1913, ibid., no. 5818., p. 743.

83. Bethmann to Eisendecher, 23 March 1913, Nachlass Eisendecher, K 4599588–91.

84. Bethmann to Berchtold, private, 10 Feb. 1913, *GP* 34 (1), no. 12 818, p. 348.

85. Bethmann to Eisendecher, 23 March 1913, Nachlass Eisendecher, K 4599588–91.

86. Jagow to Lichnowsky, 26 Apr. 1913, RAUSL. This letter is faded and only partly legible. The pertinent passage is as follows: "S.M. schimpft über die Politik 'die ihm aufgezwungen' sei (namentlich die Londoner Conferenz) . . . Er vergisst, dass unsere allgemeine Position sich [word missing] durch die Londoner [faint: probably Beratungen] insgesamt gebessert hat."

87. G. v. Müller, *Aufzeichnungen*, p. 202.

88. Grey to Goschen, private, 25 Dec. 1912, FO 800, Grey Papers, vol. 62.

89. Grey to Goschen, private, 6 Jan. 1913, ibid.

90. Lichnowsky to Bülow, 30 Apr. 1913, Nachlass Bülow.

Chapter V

1. Lichnowsky to Bethmann, 1 Dec. 1912, *GP* 34 (1), no. 12 512, p. 18.

2. *Abyss*, p. 50. There is no conclusive or complete study of the 1911–1914 Anglo-German negotiations on the division of the Portuguese colonies. Arnold Springborn, *Englands Stellung zur deutschen Welt-und Kolonial-politik in den Jahren 1911–1914* (Würzburg-Aumühle: Konrad Triltsch Verlag, 1939), employs limited sources and is inaccurate. Though interesting for the analogy between the 1910s and

the 1930s, Pierre Renouvin, "L'Afrique centrale dans les relations anglo-allemandes en 1912–14," in *Etudes maghrébines: Mélanges Charles-André Julien*, vol. 11, Publications de la Faculté des lettres et Sciences Humaines de Paris, Série d'Etudes et Mélanges (Paris: Presses universitaires de France, 1964), is careless about sequences; and the same is true of Jacques Willequet, "Anglo-German Rivalry in Belgian and Portuguese Africa," in *Britain and Germany in Africa*, ed. Prosser Gifford and W. R. Louis (New Haven: Yale University Press, 1967).

3. Metternich to Bethmann, 21 July 1911, *GP* 29, no. 10 617, pp. 202–203.

4. Grey to Goschen, private, 29 Dec. 1911, *BD* 10 (2), no. 266, p. 424.

5. Lichnowsky to Bethmann, 30 Nov. 1912, *GP* 37 (1), no. 14 652, p. 10.

6. Bethmann to Metternich, 3 Apr. 1912, *GP* 31, no. 11 440, pp. 264–267.

7. Jacques Willequet, *Le Congo belge et la Weltpolitik* (Brussels: Universitaire libre de Bruxelles, 1962), pp. 342–346. See also Metternich to Bethmann, 11 March 1912, *GP* 31, no. 11 437, pp. 255–260.

8. Sir Raymond Beazley, "Britain, Germany, and the Portuguese Colonies 1898–99," *Berliner Monatshefte* 14 (Nov. 1936): 867–885; Rich, *Holstein*, 2 : 586-590.

9. Metternich to Bethmann, 21 July 1911, *GP* 29, no. 10 617, pp. 202–203; Metternich to Bethmann, private, 9 Dec. 1911, *GP* 31, no. 11 339, p. 724; Grey to Goschen, private, 29 Dec. 1911, *BD* 10 (2), no. 266, p. 424; Metternich to Bethmann, 4 June 12, *GP* 31, no. 11 449, pp. 281–284.

10. See *BD* 10 (2), docs. 270, 271, 272, 273, 274, 275, 280, 281, 282, 284, 286, 288, 290, 291, 294, 295, 296, pp. 429–468.

11. Letter quoted in Fischer, *Illusionen*, p. 443. On public discussion see Klaus Wernecke, *Der Wille zur Weltgeltung: Aussenpolitik und Öffentlichkeit im Kaiserreich am Vorabend des Ersten Weltkrieges* (Dusseldorf: Droste Verlag, 1970), pp. 288–310. Also: Bethmann to Metternich, 3 Apr. 1912, *GP* 31, no. 11 440, p. 265; Kiderlen to Metternich, 29 May 1912, ibid., no. 11 448, pp. 279–281; Marschall to Bethmann, 19 July 1912, ibid., no. 11 456, pp. 294–296.

12. Bethmann to Metternich, 3 Apr. 1912, *GP* 31, no. 11 440, p. 267.

13. Lichnowsky to Jagow, 2 July 1913, *GP* 37 (1), no. 14 671, p. 59.

14. Lichnowsky to Bethmann, 17 Jan. 1913, *GP* 37 (1), no. 14 656, pp. 16–19.

15. Lichnowsky to Bethmann, 18 July 1913, *GP* 37 (1), no. 14 674, p. 604.

16. Grey to Goschen, 10 Apr. 1912, *BD* 10 (2), no. 287, p. 456; Zimmermann to Marschall, 25 June 1912, *GP* 31, no. 11 455, pp. 291ff; Aufzeichnung Zimmermann, 24 July 1912, GP 31, no. 11 457, pp. 300–302.

17. See K. Wernecke, *Wille zur Weltgeltung*, pp. 288–310.

18. Fundamental arguments for publication in memo by Sir Eyre Crowe, 26 Jan. 1912, *BD* 10 (2), no. 270, pp. 429ff. Also Lichnowsky to Bethmann, 20 Nov. 1912, *GP* 37 (1), no. 14 652, pp. 9–11; Lichnowsky to Bethmann, 1 Apr. 1914, *GP* 37 (1), no. 14 705, pp. 115–116.

19. Zimmermann to Marschall, 25 June 1912, *GP* 31, no. 11 455, pp. 291ff; Marschall to Bethmann, 19 July 1912, ibid., no. 11 456, pp. 294ff; Grey to Goschen, 4 July 1912, *BD* 10 (2), no. 312, p. 482; Kiderlen to Lichnowsky, *GP* 37 (1), no. 14 654, pp. 13ff; Jagow to Lichnowsky, ibid., no. 14 686, pp. 88ff.

20. *Abyss*, p. 61.

21. Grey to Granville, 13 Aug. 1913, *BD* 10 (2), no. 342, pp. 540–541; ed. note, ibid., p. 544.

22. The various drafts of the treaty are reproduced in *BD* 10 (2) and *GP* 31.

23. Rosen to Bethmann, 23 Oct. 1913, *GP* 37 (1), no. 14 684, pp. 83ff; Jagow to Lichnowsky, 12 Dec. 1913, ibid., no. 14 686, pp. 88ff; Lichnowsky to Jagow, 7 Feb. 1914, ibid., no. 14 696, pp. 101–102.

24. Grey to Goschen, private, 29 Dec. 1911, *BD* 10 (2), no. 266, p. 424.

25. Grey to Goschen, 13 June 1913, ibid., no. 337, p. 535.

26. Bertie to Nicolson, private, 6 Aug. 1911, *BD* 7, no. 464, p. 441.

27. Bertie to Grey, 12 Jan. 1912, *BD* 10 (2), no. 268, pp. 425–427.

28. Crowe minute to Harcourt to Grey, 26 May 1912, ibid., no. 299, pp. 470–472.

29. Schoen to Jagow, 30 Oct. 1913, AA, England 78, no. 1, *secr.*, vol. 26, reel 59, 0419 (not in *GP*).

30. Metternich to Bethmann, 11 March 1912, *GP* 31, no. 11 437, p. 257; Grey to Goschen, 4 June 1912, *BD* 10 (2), no. 305, p. 477.

31. Grey to Bertie, 29 Oct. 1913, ibid., no. 345, pp. 544–545; Grey to Granville, 28 Nov. 1913, ibid., pp. 547–548; P. Cambon to Doumergue, private, 8 Jan. 1914, *DDF*, 3ᵉ série, 9, no. 35, pp. 39ff; Doumergue to P. Cambon et al., 20 Jan. 1914, ibid., no. 116, pp. 135ff; P. Cambon to Doumergue, 27 Jan. 1914, ibid., no. 171, pp. 196–203; Doumergue to P. Cambon, 10 Feb. 1914, ibid., no. 256, pp. 316ff; Doumergue to P. Cambon, 18 Feb. 1914, ibid., no. 326, pp. 419f.

32. Bertie to Grey, 11 Feb. 1914, and Crowe and Nicolson minutes, *BD* 10 (2), no. 361, pp. 556–558.

33. Lichnowsky to Bethmann, 3 March 1914, *GP* 37 (1), no. 14 699, pp. 106ff; Lichnowsky to Bethmann, 1 Apr. 1914, ibid., no. 14 705, pp. 115–116; Grey to Goschen, Apr. 1914, *BD* 10 (2), no. 372, p. 568.

34. Lichnowsky to Jagow, private, 7 March 1914, *GP* 37 (1), no. 14 700, pp. 108ff.

35. Jagow to Lichnowsky, 30 March 1914, ibid., no. 14 704, pp. 114–115, Jagow to Lichnowsky, 14 Apr. 1914, ibid., no. 14 707, p. 118; Grey to Goschen, private, 7 Apr. 1914, *BD* 10 (2), no. 373, p. 569; Goschen to Grey, private, 10 Apr. 1914, FO 800, Grey Papers, vol. 62.

36. Lichnowsky to Bethmann, 26 May 1914, *GP* 37 (1), no. 14, 708, pp. 119–120.

37. Goschen to Grey, 29 March 1914, *BD* 10 (2), no. 371, p. 567.

38. Bethmann to Lichnowsky, 29 May 1914, *GP* 37 (1), no. 14 709, pp. 120–121.

39. Lichnowsky to Bethmann, 4 June 1914, *GP* 37 (1), no. 14 761, pp. 128ff.

40. Stumm to Jagow, private, 8 June 1914, ibid., no. 14 712, pp. 131–132; unsigned minute in Stumm's hand, dated 6 June 1914, attached to memorandum by Rosen dated 30 May 1914, AA, England 78, no. 1, *secr.*, vol. 27, reel 59, 0611–0619. Rosen's memorandum·published in *GP* 37 (1), no. 14 710, pp. 121ff, but Stumm's minute deleted. Lichnowsky to Bethmann, 14 July 1914, *GP* 37 (1), no. 14 715, pp. 135–136; Fischer, *Illusionen*, pp. 451–456. Finally admitting that publication was necessary, Stumm and Jagow would not, however, give up their original doubts. These seemed confirmed by an opinion on the German reaction prepared by the Wilhelmstrasse's press chief Otto Hammann, who noted that if the benefits this agreement conferred seemed to be of doubtful value, he would have to take special precautions in alerting the press. The newspapers would obviously wonder why the British had insisted upon publication of the treaty with Portugal. He predicted that French newspapers would endeavor to "sharpen the thorn" this question bore; and, he said, "as our Pan-German papers always fall into the Parisian traps, there will be no end to the hue and cry about perfidiousness and dupery, which will inevitably have an undesirable echo in the English press" (quoted in memorandum on the colonial agreement by Wedel prepared early in 1918, AA Lichnowsky, vol. 2, reel 373, 00224–00225).

41. Minute by Stumm, 6 June 1914, cited above, AA, England 78, no. 1, *secr.*, vol. 27, reel 59, 0611–0619; Jagow to Lichnowsky, private, 27 July 1914, AA, England 78, no. 1, *secr.*, reel 59, 0631, final draft *GP* 37 (1), no. 14 716, p. 138.

42. Minutes by Eyre Crowe and Grey to Goschen to Grey, 21 Apr.

1914, *BD* 10 (2), no. 374; p. 571; minutes by Eyre Crowe and Grey to Carnegie to Grey, 23 June 1914, ibid., no. 376, p. 576; Foreign Office to Colonial Office, 10 July 1914, ibid., no. 378, pp. 577–578.

43. See p. 93–94.

44. *Abyss*, p. 61. In *My London Mission* Lichnowsky provides an essentially accurate account of the negotiations though it does not follow the shifts on both sides in exact detail. Bernhard Schwertfeger defends Stumm in "Fürst Lichnowsky und das deutsch-englische Kolonial-abkommen," *Tägliche Rundschau*, 29 Dec. 1927.

45. J. B. Wolf, *The Diplomatic History of the Bagdad Railway*, University of Missouri Studies: A Quarterly of Research 9 (April 1936), no. 2 passim; Maybelle Kennedy Chapman, *Great Britain and the Bagdad Railway, 1888–1914*, vol. 31, Smith College Studies in History (Northampton, Mass., 1948), passim; Kühlmann, *Erinnerungen*, pp. 365ff.

46. John G. Williamson, *Karl Helfferich, 1872–1924: Economist, Financier, Politician* (Princeton: Princeton University Press, 1971), pp. 102, 107.

47. *Abyss*, p. 63.

48. "When Lichnowsky arrived an intimation was relayed to me on his behalf that it was hoped in the interest of good relations between the two countries that I should not mention naval expenditures to him (memorandum by Grey, 25 May 1914, *BD* 10 [2], no. 512, p. 748). "I had been given to understand, indirectly, that when Lichnowsky came here he hoped that I would not raise the question of naval expenditure with him" (Grey to Goschen, private, 5 March 1913, ibid., no. 465, p. 687).

49. Jagow to Tirpitz, AA, England 78, no. 3, vol. 17, reel 59, 0377. Jagow did appear before the budget committee on 7 Feb. 1913 and spoke about the improvement of relations with England. He asked the deputies to be moderate in their discussions of the naval budget in order to protect the tender shoots of Anglo-German cooperation (*GP* 39, fn., pp. 16–17).

50. Footnote *, *GP* 39, p. 16–17; Alfred von Tirpitz, *Politische Dokumente*, 2 vols. (Stuttgart-Berlin, Cotta, 1924–1926), 1 : 380–381.

51. Footnote *, *GP* 39, p. 17.

52. Jagow to Lichnowsky, Easter 1913, RAUSL. Main passage in original: "Was Tirpitz mit seiner Erklärung 10:16 eigentlich gemeint hat, ist mir noch nicht ganz klar. Hintergedanken hat er ja [word missing]. Möglich ist, dass er die Morgenluft einer englischen Annäherung gewittert und es vorgezogen hat, diesen Wind in seine Segel zu nehmen." Partially illegible sentences following this passage indicate that

Jagow also suspected that Tirpitz was devising a means to increase the size of the German fleet.

53. Lichnowsky to Bethmann, 15 Feb. 1913, AA, England 78, no. 3, vol. 17, reel 59, 0523 (not published in *GP*).

54. Goschen to Nicolson, private, 22 Feb. 1913, *BD* 10 (2), no. 463, p. 683.

55. Goschen to Grey, 10 Feb. 1913, ibid., no. 457, p. 669.

56. Grey to Goschen, private, 5 March 1913, ibid., no. 465, pp. 687–688.

57. Lichnowsky to Bethmann, 27 March 1913, *GP* 39, no. 15 568, pp. 24ff; Kühlmann to Bethmann, 20 Oct. 1913, ibid., no. 15 580, pp. 53ff (reporting that Churchill would have excluded from the moratorium British colonial ships and ships that might be needed in the Mediterranean): footnote *, ibid., pp. 35ff; Lichnowsky to Bethmann, 30 Apr. 1913, ibid., no. 15 573, pp. 38–39; Müller to Naval Ministry, ibid., no. 15 574, pp. 39ff (written after consultation with Tirpitz, who had Müller add that Churchill proposed the holiday because he had realized that he could otherwise not maintain the desired naval superiority over the Germans); Lichnowsky to Bethmann, 23 June 1913, ibid., no. 15 574, p. 48 (and marginal note by Wilhelm II, of which Lichnowsky informed by cable on 29 June); Goschen to Grey, private, 3 July 1913, *BD* 10 (2), no. 480, pp. 705–706. Both Grey and Churchill made public but not entirely explicit reference to the kaiser's wish that the naval holiday not be discussed further. In his speech in Manchester on 18 October, Churchill said that the British government "had no intention of taking steps in the matter if the German government did not consider them useful, for she must avoid the appearance of striving for the honor of proposing a limitation on armaments to place Germany in the position of having to reject it" (reported by Kühlmann, 20 Oct. 1913, *GP* 39, no. 15 580, p. 53). In a speech in Manchester on 3 Feb. 1914, Grey said: "It is no good making to them appeals which they will not welcome and are not prepared to receive" (reproduced in the original in footnote *, ibid., pp. 75–76).

58. Churchill to Grey, minute sent privately, 8 July 1913, *BD* 10 (2), no. 481, p. 706.

59. Footnote *, *GP* 39, pp. 74–75.

60. Grey to Goschen, 5 Feb. 1914, *BD* 10 (2), no. 498, pp. 734–735; Goschen to Grey, 10 Feb. 1914, ibid., no. 501, p. 737; Goschen to Nicolson, private, 6 Feb. 1914, ibid., no. 500, p. 736.

61. Crowe, minute to Goschen to Grey, 10 Feb. 1914, ibid., no. 501, p. 737.

62. Tirpitz, *Politische Dokumente*, 1 : 359, 360, 383–384, 403. Fisch-

er, *Illusionen,* p. 195, is in error when he writes: "Auch Lichnowsky erhielt seine Instruktionen oft von Tirpitz."

63. Jagow to Lichnowsky, private, 26 Feb. 1914, *GP* 37 (1), no. 14 697, p. 105.

64. Tirpitz, *Politische Dokumente,* 1 : 366, 404. Müller attributes this opinion to Kühlman, who reportedly said the same of Metternich (ibid., p. 191).

65. Lichnowsky to Harden, 8 June 1917, Nachlass Harden. Original reads: "Was hat denn der 'schöne Müller' aus London über mich verbreitet? Er war kein angenehmes Element, sehr alldeutsch, 'Tageszeitung.' " By Tageszeitung Lichnowsky meant that his political attitudes were those of Reventlow's Pan-German *Deutsche Tageszeitung,* known for its extreme anti-English views.

66. Lichnowsky to Bethmann, 18 May 1914, *GP* 39, no. 15 875, p. 615.

67. Lichnowsky to Jagow, private, 26 May 1914, *GP* 39, footnote **, pp. 101–102.

68. Lichnowsky to Jagow, private, 7 March 1914, *GP* 37 (1), no. 14 700, p. 109.

69. Reported in *Times* (London), 17 Oct. 1913.

70. See Tirpitz, *Politische Dokumente,* 2 : 404; Bülow, *Denkwürdigkeiten,* 1 : 183. Fischer, *Illusionen,* p. 107, says that Lichnowsky was the Kaiser's candidate to replace Bülow in 1909 but gives no source for this and apparently has misunderstood the passages on Bülow's proposed successors in Friedrich Freiherr Hiller von Gaertringen, *Fürst Bülows Denkwürdigkeiten: Untersuchungen zu ihrer Entstehungsgeschichte und ihrer Kritik* (Tübingen: J. C. B. Mohr [Paul Siebeck], 1956), pp. 200–201.

71. Lerchenfeld to Hertling, private, 21 Jan. 1914, *Briefwechsel Hertling-Lerchenfeld,* 1 : 269.

72. *Fürstliche Reuss-Geraer-Zeitung, Tageblatt und Anzeiger,* 5 Feb. 1914. This notice found in Nachlass Bülow.

73. Peter-Christian Witt, *Die Finanzpolitik des Deutschen Reiches von 1903 bis 1913* (Lübeck: Matthiesen Verlag, 1970), p. 373.

74. *Abyss,* pp. 33, 38.

75. Ibid., p. 62.

Chapter VI

1. *Abyss,* p. 71.
2. Ibid., p. 58.

3. Ibid.

4. Lichnowsky to Bethmann, 10 March 1914, *GP* 39, no. 15 847, p. 557, Benckendorff wrote Sazonov that he had never seen Lichnowsky so vexed (Benckendorff to Sazonov, private, 15 March/28 Feb. 1914, *MO*, ser. 3, 1 : 585).

5. Buchanan to Grey, 3 Apr. 1914, *BD* 10 (2), no. 537, p. 783.

6. Crowe minute of 16 Jan. 1914 to Townley to Grey, 12 Jan. 1914, FO 371, Persia 1914, vol. 2071, file 1492. On this question see especially Herbert Butterfield, "Sir Edward Grey in July, 1914," in Irish Conference of Historians, *Historical Studies* 5 (London: Bowes and Bowes, 1965).

7. Grey to Bertie, 1 May 1914, *BD* 10 (2), no. 541, pp. 788–789. Zhurnal soveschaniia u nachal'nika morskogo general'nogo shtaba, *MO*, ser. 3, no. 86, pp. 98–100.

8. Wolff, *Pontius Pilatus*, pp. 273–275. On p. 275 the date of the first article is erroneously given as May 29. *Berliner Tageblatt*, 23 May 1914; ibid., 24 May 1914; ibid., 2 June 1914. On 27 May 1914 Prof. Theodor Schiemann, translator of the Siebert documents, lent his voice to the campaign, demanding in an article in the *Neue Preussische (Kreuz-) Zeitung* that the British give a straightforward account of their dealings with France and Russia. This had a very bad effect in England, Lichnowsky reported to Bethmann, 29 May 1914, *GP* 39, no. 15 878, pp. 619–620.

9. Crow minute to Goschen to Grey, 23 May 1914, *BD* 10 (2), no. 544, p. 792; Crowe minute of 9 June 1914 to Goschen to Grey, 2 June 1914, FO 371, Russia 1914, vol. 2092, file 25526 (dispatch not published in *BD*).

10. *BD* 10 (2), no. 548, p. 801.

11. Bethmann to Lichnowsky, 16 June 1914, *GP* 39, no. 15 833, pp. 628–630.

12. Lichnowsky to Bethmann, 24 June 1914, ibid., no. 15 884, pp. 630–633. Grey's record of this discussion is in Grey to Goschen, 24 June 1914, BD 11, no. 4, pp. 4–6.

13. Lichnowsky to Bethmann, 18 May 1914, *GP* 39, no. 15 874, p. 614.

14. Lichnowsky to Bethmann, 10 June 1914, ibid., no. 15 880, pp. 621–623.

15. Fischer, *Illusionen*, pp. 231–257, 483–501.

16. Hugo Hantsch, *Berchtold*, 2 : 545–549.

17. Note by Zimmermann, 27 June 1914, *GP* 39, no. 15 884, p. 633n.

18. Franz Joseph to Wilhelm II, n.d., *DD* 1, no. 13, p. 21.

19. Szögyény to Berchtold, 5 July 1914, *ÖUA* 7, no. 10 058; Szögyény to Berchtold, 6 July 1914, ibid., no. 10 076, p. 319.

20. Quotation based on translation in *Abyss*, pp. 4–6. Passages not found in 1914 original are eliminated. The original German is found in "England vor dem Kriege," published in Friedrich Thimme, "Fürst Lichnowskys 'Memoirenwerk,'" *Archiv für Politik und Geschichte* 7, no. 1 (1928), pp. 39–57. Bethmann left no record of this discussion. See page 000 below for dispute over extent of Wilhelmstrasse's revelations to Lichnowsky. Lichnowsky's account agrees with the impression of Bethmann's concerns preserved in Kurt Riezler, *Tagebücher, Aufsätze, Dokumente,* ed. Karl Dietrich Erdmann, vol. 48 Deutsche Geschichtsquellen des 19. und 20. Jahrhunderts, ed. Historische Kommission bei der Bayerischen Akademie der Wissenschaften (Göttingen: Vandenhoeck und Ruprecht, 1972), and as presented in Konrad H. Jarausch, *The Enigmatic Chancellor,* pp. 152–157. Although Jarausch refers to Lichnowsky's account of the 29 June discussion with Bethmann in a paragraph in which he is trying to show that the initial response of the German government to the assassination was "hesitant, groping, and generally peaceful," he says (p. 153) that in this discussion Bethmann "attempted to disabuse the Austrophobe Count [sic] Lichnowsky of his all too sanguine picture of the international situation."

21. Information from Count Michael Lichnowsky.

22. *Abyss*, p. 72.

23. Grey to Goschen, 6 July 1914, *BD* 11, no. 32, pp. 24–25. The record shows that Lichnowsky was much more concerned by what he heard in Berlin than he remembered when he wrote *My London Mission,* where he said that he thought "nothing would come of it this time either" (*Abyss*, p. 72).

24. Jagow to Lichnowsky, 12 July 1914, *DD* 1, no. 36, p. 57; Lichnowsky to Jagow, 14 July 1914, ibid., no. 43, pp. 68–69; Jagow to Lichnowsky, 15 July 1914, ibid., no. 48, p. 73.

25. Lichnowsky to Bethmann, 16 July 1914, ibid., no. 62, pp. 88–90.

26. Jagow to Lichnowsky, private, 18 July 1914, ibid., no. 72. Compare Bethmann's utterances recorded by Riezler, *Tagebücher,* pp. 185ff.

27. Lichnowsky to Jagow, private, 27 July 1914, *DD* 1, no. 161, pp. 175–177.

28. Lichnowsky to Jagow, 25 July 1914, ibid., no. 163, p. 178; Thimme, "Memoirenwerk," p. 49; Lichnowsky to Jagow, 28 July 1914, *DD* 2, no. 301, p. 23. In *My London Mission* Lichnowsky wrote that after returning to London from his holiday in Germany he had "ascer-

tained that at the decisive conference at Potsdam on the 5th July, the
Vienna enquiry received the unqualified assent of all the leading
people, and with the rider that no harm would be done if a war with
Russia should result. Thus it was expressed, at any rate, in the Austrian protocol which Count Mensdorff received in London" (*Abyss*,
p. 72). The Austrian record of the meetings in Berlin on 5 and 6 July
consisted of two cables from ambassador Szögyény, one reporting the
audience with Wilhelm II, the other the conference with Bethmann,
and an informal penciled account by the head of the Austrian special
mission, Count Hoyos. See Jan Opocenský, "A War-time Discussion of
Responsibility for the War: Documents," *Journal of Modern History* 4
(March-Dec. 1932): 419–420. Writers intent upon destroying Lichnowsky's credibility have insisted that Mensdorff received nothing resem-
bling a "protocol" of those discussions, and Mensdorff himself, when
questioned about the alleged protocol, stated that while he had received no report of this discussion he had received a copy of the letter
Franz Joseph sent to Wilhelm II (Opocenský, pp. 422–423). He did
not say whether he had received any comment on this letter or an account of the circumstances under which it was delivered, but Lichnowsky's description adheres so closely to the content of Szögyény's
cabled report of the discussion that followed upon his presentation of
the Austrian emperor's note to the German kaiser that the prince must
have seen or been given orally some reliable account of that meeting.
Kühlmann, who returned to London from vacation on 29 July, writes
in his memoirs that in London the Austrian councillor of embassy,
Trauttmansdorff, opened to him files containing information unknown in Germany concerning the Austrian ultimatum and the special
mission to Berlin (Kühlmann, *Erinnerungen*, pp. 299, 404). In a dispatch to Jagow, 28 July 1914, *DD* 2, no. 301, p. 23, Lichnowsky wrote
further: "Auch erzählten die genannten Herren, man beabsichtige,
Teile von Serbien an Bulgarien (und vermutlich auch an Albanien)
zu verschenken. Ich möchte aber dringend bitten diese Äusserungen
nicht in Wien zu verwerten, da ich meine freundschaftlichen Beziehungen zu Graf Mensdorff nicht aufs Spiel setzen will. Ob die Herren
sich auch anderen Personen gegenüber in ihren Gesprächen so äusser-
ten, weiss ich nicht, die Annahame dürfte aber nicht unberechtigt sein,
dass es sich nicht bloss um so harmlose, pädagogische Monita handeln
sollte, zu denen die nagelhafte Vigilanz des polnischen Schwätzers Biliński den Anstoss gab." Biliński, the Austro-Hungarian minister of
finances, was a strong proponent of military action against Serbia. Lichnowsky must have known that information on the confidential

discussions within the Austrian government was leaking from his ministry. See Hantsch, *Berchtold*, 2 : 591.

29. Ionescu, *Souvenirs*, p. 15.

30. Benckendorff to Sazonov, private, 22/9 July, *MO*, ser. 3, 4, pp. 289–291. Nicolson heard of Lichnowsky's anxiety from Benckendorff but was not ready to credit it. On 20 July he wrote de Bunsen, British ambassador in Vienna, that "the German ambassador here, so Benckendorff tells me, is very anxious, and mysteriously so, over the situation, and thinks that Austria is preparing some coup which she intends to put into execution. I daresay he is very largely influenced by the reports of his German colleague in Vienna, who, I expect, takes a very exaggerated view of the situation" (FO 800, vol. 375, Nicolson Papers). On 28 July Nicolson wrote to Buchanan that "for the past three weeks the German ambasasdor here has been exceedingly anxious and perturbed, and on more than one occasion has said to some of his colleagues that if they knew all that he did they would be equally disquieted" (Nicolson to Buchanan, private, 28 July 1914, *BD* 11, no. 239, p. 157).

31. Lichnowsky to Jagow, 23 July 1914, *DD* 1, no. 129, pp. 148–149; Lichnowsky to Jagow, 24 July 1914, ibid., no. 157, p. 171; Lichnowsky to Jagow, 26 July 1914, ibid., no. 237, p. 233.

32. Bethmann to Pourtalès et al., 21 July 1914, ibid., no. 100; Pourtalès to Jagow, 23 July, 1914, ibid., no. 130, pp. 149–150; Pourtalès to Bethmann, 25 July 1914, ibid., no. 204, pp. 208–210. In *My London Mission* Lichnowsky attacked Pourtalès for his lack of concern and alleged that he had reported "Russia would not move under any circumstances" (*Abyss*, p. 73). After 29 July Pourtalès did attempt, strenuously, to defend Austria's determination to punish Serbia and then to persuade the Russians to withdraw their order of mobilization. Compare [Friedrich] Graf Pourtalès, *Am Scheideweg zwischen Krieg und Frieden: Meine letzten Verhandlungen in Petersburg, Ende Juli 1914* (Charlottenburg: Deutsche Verlagsgesellschaft für Politik und Geschichte, 1919). See also ch. 7, note 118.

33. Riezler, *Tagebücher*, pp. 188–189.

34. Ibid.

35. Bülow, *Denkwürdigkeiten*, 3 : 159; Alfred von Wegerer, "Weitere Irrtümer des Fürsten Bülow über den Kriegsausbruch," *Berliner Monatshefte* 9, no. 4 (Apr. 1931), pp. 374–375.

36. Riezler, *Tagebücher*, p. 188.

37. Gottlieb von Jagow, "Die deutsche politische Leitung und England bei Kriegsausbruch," *Preussische Jahrbücher* 213, no. 1 (July

1928), p. 9. Jagow seems to be attributing this attitude in part to what he says was Lichnowsky's reversal as to Britain's intentions. Cf. Erdmann, introduction to Riezler, *Tagebücher*; Fischer, *Illusionen*, pp. 635, 734; Egmont Zechlin, "Die Illusion vom begrenzten Krieg," *Die Zeit*, no. 38, 21 Sept. 1965; Zechlin, "Bethmann Hollweg, Kriegsrisiko und SPD 1914," *Der Monat* 18, no. 208 (Jan. 1966); note by Geiss, Hermann Kantorowicz, *Gutachten zur Kriegsschuldfrage 1914*, ed. Imanuel Geiss (Frankfurt/Main: Europäische Verlagsanstalt, 1967), p. 276; Jarausch, *The Enigmatic Chancellor*, pp. 169–170.

38. See note by Geiss, Kantorowicz, *Gutachten*, p. 276.

39. Jagow to Lichnowsky (drafted by Stumm), 13 May 1914, *GP* 39, no. 15 874, p. 614.

40. Bethmann to Wilhelm II, 23 July 1914, AA, Weltkrieg, vol. 3, quoted in Konrad H. Jarausch, "The Illusion of Limited War: Chancellor Bethmann Hollweg's Calculated Risk, July 1914," *Central European History* 2, no. 1 (March 1969), p. 62.

41. Georg von Müller, *Regierte der Kaiser? Kriegstagebücher, Aufzeichnungen und Briefe des Chefs des Marine-Kabinetts Admiral Georg von Müller, 1914–1918*, ed. Walter Görlitz (Göttingen: Musterschmidt, 1959), p. 36. In a letter to Friedrich Thimme, 24 December 1927, Theodor Wolff wrote: "On the main point Lichnowsky saw clearly, more clearly than the Foreign Ministry, which, as I know because I heard it myself, clung to the illusion that in a war between Germany and France England would remain neutral" (Nachlass Thimme).

42. Reports of the discussion in Grey to Rumbold, 6 July 1914, *BD* 11, no. 32; Lichnowsky to Bethmann, 6 July 1914, *GP* 39, no. 15 886. Grey first discussed this question with Nicolson, who advised him not to walk into the trap the Germans were setting (Nicolson, *Lord Carnock*, p. 407). Lichnowsky to Bethmann, 9 July 1914, *GP* 39, no. 15 887, pp. 638–640; Grey to Rumbold, 9 July 1914, *BD* 11, no. 41, pp. 33–34.

43. Jagow to Ballin, private, 15 July 1914, *GP* 39, no. 15 888, pp. 640–642; Ballin to Jagow, private, 24 July 1914, ibid., no. 15 889, pp. 643–645.

44. Müller to the German Naval Ministry, 26 July 1914, *DD* 1, no. 207, p. 211; Prince Heinrich to Wilhelm II, private, 28 July 1914, ibid., 2, no. 374, pp. 96–97. See discussion of incident in Nicolson, *George V*, p. 246n.

45. Lichnowsky to Bethmann, 26 July 1914, *DD* 1, no. 201, p. 204.

46. Lichnowsky to Jagow, 25 July 1914, ibid., no. 180, pp. 191–192; Jagow to Lichnowsky, 25 July 1914, ibid., no. 192, p. 200; Bethmann

to Lichnowsky, 27 July 1914, ibid., no. 248, pp. 241–242; Lichnowsky to Jagow, 27 July 1914, ibid., no. 266, p. 256.

47. Lichnowsky to Jagow, 26 July 1914, ibid., no. 236, pp. 231–232.

48. Lichnowsky to Jagow, 24 July 1914, ibid., no. 157, pp. 169–171; Lichnowsky to Jagow, 25 July 1914, ibid., no. 180, pp. 191–192; Grey to Rumbold, 24 July 1914, *BD* 11, no. 99, p. 78; Grey to Rumbold, 25 July 1914, ibid., no. 115, p. 88; Lichnowsky to Jagow, 27 July 1914, *DD* 1, no. 258, pp. 250–251.

49. Lichnowsky to Jagow, 27 July 1914, *DD* 1, no. 265, pp. 254–255.

50. Jagow to Lichnowsky, 25 July 1914, ibid., no. 192, p. 200; Bethmann to Lichnowsky, 27 July 1914, ibid., no. 248, pp. 241–242; Goschen to Grey, 27 July 1914, *BD* 11, no. 185, p. 128.

51. Lerchenfeld to Hertling, private, 28 July 1914, *Briefwechsel Hertling-Lerchenfeld*, 1, no. 105, pp. 315–316.

52. Riezler, *Tagebücher*, p. 191.

53. Record of 28 July 1914, quoted in John Alfred Spender and Cyril Asquith, *Life of Henry Asquith, Lord Oxford and Asquith*, 2 vols. (London: Hutchinson, 1932), 2 : 80–81.

54. Bethmann to Tschirschky, 27 July 1914, *DD* 1, no. 277, pp. 267–268.

55. Not knowing this, Lichnowsky accepted Berlin's report that it had taken the desired steps toward mediation (Bethmann to Lichnowsky, 27 July 1914, ibid., no. 278, p. 268) and informed Grey in a personal note that he had begun "to hope that it has once more been possible owing to Anglo-German collaboration to save the peace of Europe" (Lichnowsky to Grey, private, undated, probably 28 July 1914, *BD* 11, no. 236, p. 155). Nicolson wrote Buchanan that "Lichnowsky's interpretation of the word 'co-operation' must be totally different from that which is usually accepted" (Nicolson to Buchanan, private, 28 July 1914, ibid., no. 239, p. 157).

56. Bethmann to Lichnowsky, 28 July 1914, *DD* 2, no. 279, pp. 1–2.

57. Lichnowsky to Jagow, 29 July 1914, ibid., no. 368, pp. 86–89.

58. Grey to Goschen, 29 July 1914, *BD* 11, no. 286, p. 183. Grey may have been influenced in his choice of words to Lichnowsky by Nicolson's report on the twenty-sixth that Benckendorff had said Lichnowsky was convinced that Britain would remain neutral in the event of a European conflict (Nicolson to Grey, private, 20 July 1914, ibid., no. 144, p. 102). Benckendorff knew better, and if he actually spoke as Nicolson said, he did so purposely to encourage the British to show their colors, just as he seems to have done before the opening of the Conference of Ambassadors in 1912 (see p. 58 above). Nicolson told Grey that this was an unfortunate conviction "as were they to understand

that our neutrality was by no means to be counted upon and that we could not be expected to remain indifferent when all Europe was in flames, a restraining influence would be exercised in Berlin."

59. Goschen to Grey, 29 July 1914, ibid., no. 293, p. 186. Jarausch, *The Enigmatic Chancellor*, pp. 169–170, writes that Bethmann made this offer because "he was unable to derive a clear picture of London's intentions from the conflicting reports of Lichnowsky, Albert Ballin, and Prince Heinrich." He therefore "proposed to Goschen a formula reminiscent of the Haldane negotiations of 1912." Ballin's 24 July report of his discussions with Grey and Haldane (Ballin to Jagow, private, 24 July 1914, *GP* 39, no. 15 889, pp. 643–645) did indeed picture the British as very friendly and not overly disturbed by the Austrian ultimatum. But by the twenty-ninth Bethmann had reason, if only from Benckendorff's reports, to believe that the British attitude had stiffened. Riezler noted on the twenty-seventh that London had changed its tone (*Tagebücher*, p. 191). The occasion of the démarche on 29 July was of course Austria's declaration of war, which was followed by Russia's mobilization, which made the question of British neutrality of immediate interest to Bethmann, who, for the purpose of his representations to Goschen, accepted Lichnowsky's long-standing view that England would not allow France to be crushed. Jarausch remarks further, p. 473n31, quoting Riezler's statement that "Lichnowsky was trembling like a leaf," that Lichnowsky "failed to communicate effectively with Berlin." This failure is not due, however, to any lack in Lichnowsky's communications of clarity, cogency, eloquence, or timeliness.

60. Goschen to Grey, 30 July 1914, *BD* 11, no. 305, p. 195; Goschen to Nicolson, private, July (no day given) 1914, ibid., no. 677, p. 362.

61. Lerchenfeld to Hertling, private, 30 July 1914, *Briefwechsel Hertling-Lerchenfeld*, 1, no. 111, p. 320.

62. Sir Horace Rumbold, *The War-Crisis in Berlin July-August 1914* (London: Constable, 1940), p. 220.

63. G. v. Müller, *Kriegstagebuch*, p. 37.

64. Minutes by Wilhelm II to Lichnowsky to Jagow, 29 July 1914, *DD* 2, no. 368, pp. 86–88. Forwarded under Bethmann to Wilhelm II, 30 July 1914, ibid., no. 407, pp. 137–138.

65. Kantorowicz, *Gutachten*, p. 93.

66. Kühlmann, *Erinnerungen*, p. 396.

67. Riezler, *Tagebücher*, p. 191.

68. Wolff, *Pontius Pilatus*, p. 345.

69. Grey to Goschen, 29 July 1914, *BD* 11, no. 285, 181–182.

70. Grey to Buchanan, 30 July 1914, ibid., no. 309, p. 197.

71. Bethmann to Lichnowsky, 30 July 1914, *DD* 2, no. 393, p. 123.

72. John Viscount Morley, *Memorandum on Resignation* (New York: Macmillan, 1928), p. 6.

73. Lichnowsky to Jagow, 31 July 1914, *DD* 2, no. 484, p. 4.

74. Nicolson to Grey, 31 July 1914, *BD* 11, no. 368, p. 227.

75. *BD* 11, no. 372, pp. 230–231.

76. The best attempt to reconstruct the "misunderstanding" of 1 August 1914 is Albertini, *The Origins of the War of 1914*, 3 : 171–178, 380–386. He does not see, however, that Lichnowsky and Grey were temporarily confused about the extent of the proposed military stand-off. Other helpful discussions are August Bach, "Das angebliche Miss-verständnis des Fürsten Lichnowsky vom. 1. August 1914," *Berliner Monatshefte* 7 (Apr. 1930), and J. V. Bredt, "Das 'Missverständnis' des Fürsten Lichnowsky vom 1. August 1914," *Preussische Jahrbücher* 230 (Nov. 1932). The notion that Lichnowsky misunderstood Grey's purpose was assiduously fostered by his enemies and the early war-guilt historians, and that wrong view persists in recent works—in Fischer, *Illusionen*, p. 724, Erdmann's introduction to Riezler, *Tage-bücher*, p. 194n2, and Imanuel Geiss, ed., *Julikrise und Kriegsausbruch 1914: Eine Dokumentensammlung*, 2 vols. (Hanover: Verlag für Liter-atur und Zeitgeschehen, 1964), 2 : 530.

77. Lichnowsky to Jagow, 1 Aug. 1914, *DD* 3, no. 562, p. 66.

78. From the original form of "England before the War," published in Thimme, "Memoirenwerk," p. 54.

79. *BD* 11, no. 419, p. 250n.

80. Lichnowsky to Jagow, 1 Aug. 1914, *DD* 3, no. 570, p. 70.

81. The records of the discussions this afternoon left by the partici-pants are collected in Geiss, *Julikrise und Kriegsausbruch*, 2 : 555ff.

82. G. v. Müller, *Kriegstagebuch*, p. 39.

83. Bethmann to Lichnowsky, 1 Aug. 1914, *DD* 3, no. 578, p. 76.

84. Wilhelm II to George V, 1 Aug. 1914, ibid., no. 575, p. 74.

85. Morley, *Memorandum*, p. 3.

86. Goschen to Grey, 31 July 1914, *BD* 11, no. 383, pp. 234–235.

87. Morley, *Memorandum*, p. 13.

88. Lichnowsky to Jagow, 1 Aug. 1914, *DD* 2, no. 596, p. 89.

89. In an account of the crisis sent to French foreign minister Del-cassé on 22 December 1914, Cambon wrote of the Grey-Lichnowsky discussions as follows: "C'est après le Conseil qu'il vit l'ambassadeur d'Allemagne et qu'il s'aperçut du malentendu. Il ne me donna aucune indication sur cet incident que j'appris par la suite et il se contenta de me dire, quand je le vis dans l'après-midi, que le Cabinet britta-nique n'avait encore pris aucune décision" (Adrien Thierry, *L'Angle-*

terre au temps de Paul Cambon [Paris-Geneva: La Palatine, 1961], Annexe II [Relation de P. Cambon, 22 déc. 14], p. 202).

90. Grey to Bertie, 1 Aug. 1914, *BD* 11, no. 426, p. 253.

91. Ibid.

92. Bertie to Grey, 2 Aug. 1914, ibid., no. 453, p. 263.

93. Grey to Bertie, 2 Aug. 1914, ibid., no. 460, p. 266.

94. H. Nicolson, *George V*, pp. 328–329. Nicolson saw Grey's note in the Royal Archives.

95. George V to Wilhelm II, 1 Aug. 1914, *DD* 3, no. 612, p. 103.

96. The kaiser, however, who received the cable on the second, filled the margins with uncomplimentary remarks about Grey.

97. Bethmann to Lichnowsky, 1 Aug. 1914, *DD* 3, no. 605, p. 96.

98. Jagow to Tschirschky, 1 Aug. 1914, ibid., no. 607, p. 97.

99. Bethmann to ambassadors, 2 Aug. 1914, ibid., no. 613, p. 104.

100. Lichnowsky to Jagow, 1 Aug. 1914, *DD* 2, no. 603, p. 95. Some German historians, notably Bach, "Das angebliche Missverständnis," believed Lichnowsky blundered in withholding this cable from the British because it would have proved Germany's willingness to spare France. Bredt, "Missverständnis," points out, however, that the British knew this from the kaiser's cable.

101. Lichnowsky to Jagow, 2 Aug. 1914, *DD* 3, no. 630, p. 113.

102. Lichnowsky to Jagow, 2 Aug. 1914, ibid., no. 631, p. 113. Bredt, "Missverständnis," interprets this to mean that Lichnowsky saw Grey again sometime late on 1 August. There is no record of this.

103. H. H. Asquith (the Earl of Oxford and Asquith), *Memories and Reflections, 1852–1927*, 2 vols. (London: Cassell, 1928), 2 : 8. Margot Asquith, the prime minister's wife, recounts in her gossipy and personal memoirs the visit she paid the Lichnowskys on the afternoon of 2 August. "Oh! say there is surely not going to be war!" she records him as saying. Of the kaiser he allegedly said: "He is ill-informed—impulsive, and must be *mad*! He never listens, or believes one word of what I say; he answers none of my telegrams." Mechtilde Lichnowsky, whose eyes "were starved and swollen from crying," spoke of the kaiser's friends as brutes. When she said goodbye to Lichnowsky, tears were running down his cheeks (Margot Asquith, *An Autobiography*, 4 vols. [New York: George H. Doran, 1920–1922], 4 : 26–29).

104. Lichnowsky to Jagow, 2 Aug. 1914, *DD* 3, no. 641, p. 119.

105. Tagebücher, Heft IV, folio 1–69, Nachlass Mensdorff.

106. Lichnowsky to Jagow. 2 Aug. 1914, *DD* 4, no. 764, p. 17. In his memoirs Grey said that he would not tell Lichnowsky of the cabinet's decision because "the German Government, of all people, must not

know an hour in advance of others abroad what was to be said" [in his speech to the House] (Viscount Grey of Fallodon [Sir Edward Grey], *Twenty-five Years*, 2 vols. [New York: Frederick A. Stokes, 1925], 2 : 13). Grey's speech, however, was a plea for the support of the House for an action that might be forced upon the government and not the announcement of a decision by the cabinet to go to war.

107. Lerchenfeld to Hertling, private, 3 Aug. 1914. *Briefwechsel Hertling-Lerchenfeld*, 1, no. 116, pp. 325–326.

108. Herbert Asquith, *Moments of Memory: Recollections and Impressions* (London: Hutchinson, 1937), p. 199.

109. Bethmann to Lichnowsky, 3 Aug. 1914, *DD* 4, no. 790, pp. 37–38.

110. Naval Ministry to Jagow, 3 Aug. 1914, ibid., no. 808, p. 50.

111. Jagow to Lichnowsky, 4 Aug. 1914, ibid., no. 810, p. 51.

112. Jagow to Lichnowsky, 4 Aug. 1914, ibid., no. 829, p. 64.

113. P. Cambon to Viviani. 3 Aug. 1914, *DDF*, 3ᵉ série, 9, no. 670, p. 505.

114. Lichnowsky to Jagow, 3 Aug. 1914, *DD* 4, no. 801, pp. 44–45.

115. Lichnowsky to Jagow, 4 Aug. 1914, ibid., no. 820, pp. 57–58.

116. Lichnowsky to Jagow, 4 Aug. 1914, ibid., no. 835, p. 68.

117. See discussion in Albertini, *Origins*, 3 : 498–500.

118. *BD* 11, no. 643, p. 330.

119. Nicolson, *Lord Carnock*, pp. 425–426.

120. A reference to Bethmann's proposal to Goschen on 29 July.

121. Copy prepared 7 Aug. 1914, sent 8 Dec. 1914, by Zimmermann to Jagow at General Headquarters, AA, Grosses Hauptquartier 25, England no. 4, vol. 1.

122. *Abyss*, p. 76.

123. Burton J. Hendrick, *Life and Letters of Walter Hines Page*, 3 vols. (New York: Doubleday, Page, 1922), 1 : 306.

124. Tagebücher, Heft IV, Folio. 1–69, p. 53, Nachlass Mensdorff.

125. Mensdorff to Berchtold, 7 Aug. 1914, quoted in Grey, *Twenty-five Years*, 2 : 239–240.

126. *Abyss*, p. 76.

127. Thierry, *L'Angleterre au temps de Paul Cambon*, p. 114. Kühlmann writes, *Erinnerungen*, p. 394, that during the last stages of the crisis while he was trying to convince Lichnowsky that England would enter the war, Princess Lichnowsky, listening to the conversation from the next room, kept repeating, "like a parrot," "Don't believe him!" In a letter published in the 10 March 1951 issue of the *Schwäbische Illustrierte*, which had described this scene in an earlier issue, Prin-

230 Notes to Chapter VII

cess Lichnowsky denied the occurrence. What Kühlmann described was wholly inconsistent with her own strict observances, the manners of the time, and the conditions under which official conversations took place. Besides, the ambassador's work rooms were completely separate from the family's private quarters.

128. Shane Leslie, *Long Shadows* (London: J. Murray, 1966), p. 170.

129. As recalled by Bernhard Guttmann, "Lichnowskys Erinnerungen," *Frankfurter Zeitung*, 17 Jan. 1928.

130. As he told his daughter Leonore. Cf. Plessen, *Begegnungen*, p. 47.

Chapter VII

1. Thus reported by Jagow, "Die deutsche politische Leitung und England bei Kriegsausbruch," *Preussische Jahrbücher* 213, no. 1 (July-Sept. 1928), p. 9.

2. F. Thimme, "Memoirenwerk," p. 58. Thimme seems to have had access to the personnel files.

3. *Abyss*, p. 16.

4. Wilhelm II, Hohenzollern, *Ereignisse und Gestalten aus den Jahren 1878–1918* (Leipzig: K. F. Koehler, 1922), p. 279.

5. Tirpitz, *Politische Dokumente*, 1 : 348.

6. Egmont Zechlin, "Deutschland zwischen Kabinettskrieg und Wirtschaftskrieg," *Historische Zeitschrift* 199, no. 2 (Oct. 1964), pp. 347–385; Ritter, *Staatskunst*, 3 : 26–29. Bethmann's belief in the value of forbearance toward England was shared by Lichnowsky, as explained below, and Professor Schiemann, the anti-Russian commentator for the conservative *Neue Preussische (Kreuz-) Zeitung* who had worked for the Foreign Ministry as translator of the documents Siebert took from the Russian embassy in London. Schiemann had long encouraged good relations with England as a counterweight to Russia, and when the fighting began he still believed it was necessary to continue working for an understanding with England (K. Meyer, *Theodor Schiemann*, pp. 191–196).

7. Zechlin, "Kabinettskrieg und Wirtschaftskrieg," pp. 347–385; Ritter, *Staatskunst*, 3 : 26–29.

8. *Deutsche Tageszeitung*, Morgen Ausgabe, 7 Aug. 1914; Abend Ausgabe, 8 Aug. 1914.

9. *Deutsche Tageszeitung*, Morgen Ausgabe, 12 Aug. 1914. Reventlow also attacked T. Schiemann's pro-English attitude (K. Meyer, *Theodor Schiemann*, pp. 191–196).

10. Lichnowsky to Wilhelm II, 11 Aug. 1914, DZA Merseburg, Rep. 53 J, Lit. L No. 5.

11. A note at the top of Lichnowsky's letter indicates he was summoned the day the letter was written.

12. Jagow to Zimmermann, 31 Aug. 1914, AA, Krieg, 1914, Sammlung von Schriftstücken zur Vorgeschichte des Krieges, reel 382, 00271–00272.

13. Jagow to Lichnowsky, 15 Aug. 1914, RAUSL. The letter is very faded and partly illegible. German text (missing words or undecipherable passages shown by brackets):

Graf R. ist, wie Sie wissen, immer Ihr Kritiker gewesen und [?] einmal noch ist [ ] seine [ ] Stellung England gegenüber, also Flottenmann und Marineoffizier [ ], bewogen haben, [ ] hauptsächlich Ihre Reden [four faint lines] recht, muss schliesslich auch mit einer öffentlichen Kritik rechnen. Und Ihre Reden haben auch in Kreisen von ganz anderen [ ] als die des Grafen R. viel Kopfschütteln erregt. Wir haben Ihnen das oft geschrieben, Sie haben es uns aber nicht glauben wollen. R. hat jetzt mit seinem steten Misstrauen gegen England ja—scheinbar oder wirklich—recht behalten; kein Wunder, dass er das hervorhebt. Ob [ ] eine amtliche Entgegnung möglich wäre [ ] möchte ich [ ] mit dem Pressereferat besprechen. Sie wird wohl ganz [ ] neue und [ ] begreift auch unsere Politik und [ ] Diplomatie im allgemeinen oder ein allgemeines gezeitigt wurden. Ich theile Ihnen [ ] und sende Ihnen den Ausschnitt zurück. Ob Sie selbst antworten wollen, stelle ich Ihnen anheim, *machen* kann ich nichts dazu. Denn in einer Polemik so allgemeiner Natur [last four lines of letter not completely decipherable].

In a memorandum on *My London Mission* dated 16 July 1918, Stumm wrote that he had Count Wedel (Botho Wedel) speak to Reventlow to stop the attacks (AA Lichnowsky). Lichnowsky's letter requesting support from Jagow is not in the files, but in a letter to Bethmann on 22 Aug. 1914 Lichnowsky, answering Bethmann's reproaches about his publications, says, "Im übrigen hatte ich Herrn von Jagow davon in Kenntnis gesetzt, dass ich nicht den öffentlichen Angriffen gegenüber zu schweigen beabsichtige" (AA Lichnowsky, vol. 3, reel 373, 434).

14. "Fürst Lichnowsky," *Vossische Zeitung*, Abend Ausgabe, 19 Aug. 1914.

15. Bethmann to Foreign Ministry, 16 Aug. 1914, AA, Weltkrieg, no. 7, Akten betreffend den Krieg 1914: Deutsche Weissbücher und andere Veröffentlichungen, vol. 2, reel 409, 0009.

16. *Norddeutsche Allgemeine Zeitung*, zweite Ausgabe, 20 Aug. 1914.

17. Theodor Wolff, "Das Telegramm des Fürsten Lichnowsky," *Berliner Tageblatt*, Abend Ausgabe, 21 Aug. 1914. In the morning edition of the *Berliner Tageblatt* Wolff had remarked that "Grey may

have later told the king that he had been misunderstood by the ambassador. But it is probable that he simply withdrew the suggestion when he no longer believed in its practicality."

18. Bethmann to Lichnowsky, 21 Aug. 1914; Lichnowsky to Bethmann, 22 Aug. 1914; Bethmann to Zimmermann, 23 Aug. 1914; Zimmermann to Bethmann, 24 Aug. 1914; Bethmann to Lichnowsky, 25 Aug. 1914; Lichnowsky to Bethmann, 27 Aug. 1914; Bethmann to Zimmermann, 29 Aug. 1914, AA Lichnowsky, vol. 3, reel 373, 433–441.

19. Lichnowsky to unknown, probably Mechtilde Lichnowsky, from Vauxcillon (?), date given as "24"—probably October 1914—RAUSL. The letter is torn and badly faded. Original German of cited passages:

Hier bin ich eben ganz ausgeschieden, kalt gestellt, was sonst in der Welt vorgeht weiss ich nicht, kann auch nichts tun um den Angriffen gegen mich zu begegnen. Zu tun habe ich Nichts, ich fahre täglich aus und sehe mir eine Stellung an, wo gekämpft wird. . . . Du solltest auch zu Brockdorff gehen und nachher zu T.W. und dann zur Kronprinzessin. Es wäre ganz gut sie über die Sache aufzuklären, ihnen zu sagen, ich hätte dringend gewarnt und den Weltkrieg für unvermeidlich gehalten wenn wir uns [words missing] in den Dienst österr. Orientpolitiken stellen.

20. G. v. Müller, *Kriegstagebuch*, p. 369.

21. Information from Countess Leonore Lichnowsky. German original: "Du hattest natürlich ganz recht, der Bethmann ist ein Esel."

22. *BD* 11, no. 419, note 2, p. 250.

23. *Norddeutsche Allgemeine Zeitung*, erste Ausgabe, 6 Sept. 1914.

24. Ibid., erste Ausgabe, 16 Oct. 1914.

25. Von Schoen to Hertling, 12 Aug. 1917, Ges. Berlin 1093, Geh. Staatsarchiv München. In a report about *My London Mission* von Schoen wrote: "Derartige Darlegungen, durch die er sich bei den Offizieren äusserst missliebig gemacht, waren auch der Grund, weshalb der Fürst das Armeeoberkommando Kluck, dem er bald nach Kriegsbeginn zugeteilt worden war, nach kurzer Zeit wieder verlassen musste."

26. Bethmann to Lichnowsky, 29 Oct. 1914, AA Lichnowsky, vol. 3, reel 373, 446–447.

27. Lichnowsky to Jagow, ibid., frame 443.

28. Thimme, "Memoirenwerk," p. 58. Thimme apparently established the date from the personnel file.

29. Zechlin, "Kabinettskrieg und Wirtschaftskrieg," pp. 347–385.

30. Lichnowsky to Tirpitz, 26 Dec. 1914, in Tirpitz, *Politische Dokumente*, 2 : 179–180. Also letter of Tirpitz to Admiral von Capelle, 17 Aug. 1914, ibid., p. 57. Further G. v. Müller, *Kriegstagebuch*, p. 59.

31. Ritter, *Staatskunst*, 3 : 552.

32. Otto Brunner, *Adeliges Landleben und europäischer Geist: Leben und Werk Wolf Helmhards von Hohberg 1612–1688* (Salzburg: Otto Müller, 1959), p. 95.

33. August Scholtis, *Erinnerungen*, p. 139.

34. A. Scholtis, "Die Denkschrift des Fürsten Lichnowsky nach Ausbruch des Ersten Weltkrieges, " 1967, Scholtis Papers. This is an impressionistic remembrance of the circumstances of the writing and circulation of *My London Mission* adding interesting details to Scholtis's *Erinnerungen*.

35. Letter of 28 Oct. 1914, quoted in Ludwig Maenner, *Prinz Heinrich zu Schoenaich-Carolath: Ein parlamentarisches Leben der wilhelminischen Zeit (1852–1920)* (Stuttgart: Deutsche Verlags-Anstalt, 1931), p. 172.

36. Letter of 21 May 1915, quoted in Eduard Bernstein, "In Sachen des Fürsten Lichnowsky," *Berliner Tageblatt*, 18 July 1918.

37. Scholtis, *Erinnerungen*, p. 79.

38. Princess of Pless, *Herself*, p. 394.

39. Tschirschky to Jagow, 8 Dec. 1915, AA Lichnowsky, vol. 3, reel 373, 442.

40. Entry of 14 July 1915, Tagebücher, Heft 5, Nachlass Mensdorff.

41. The Foreign Ministry's report on this article by Erik Juel, which appeared in the *Dagens Nyheter* on 26 March 1918 under the title "A Visit to the Tactless Prince," is in AA Lichnowsky, vol. 2. Juel is probably the source of the information of an allegedly secret meeting at Lichnowsky's house sent to London by Sir Esmé Howard, the British ambassador in Stockholm, in August 1916, quoted in Röhl, ed., *1914: Delusion or Design?: The Testimony of two German Diplomats*, translation and revision of *Zwei deutsche Fürsten* (London: Elek, 1973), p. 46. According to this report, the meeting had taken place about five weeks earlier. There were about sixty prominent guests, and the prince delivered an address, "the main characteristic of which was its conciliatory tone toward England." It is wrong to conclude from this and from the suggestion that Lichnowsky or Bernstorff might at that moment have been a good choice for chancellor, made by Ludendorff's factotum Max Hoffmann in private in 1917, that "Lichnowsky was the leader of a secret but influential peace movement" (Röhl, *Delusion or Design?*, p. 47).

42. Otto Lehmann-Russbüldt, *Der Kampf der Deutschen Liga für Menschenrechte vormals Bund Neues Vaterland für den Weltfrieden 1914–1927* (Berlin: Hensel, 1927), p. 23; Willy Brandt and Richard Lowenthal, *Ernst Reuter, ein Leben für die Freiheit: Eine politische Biographie* (Munich: Kindler, 1957), p. 72.

43. *Abyss*, pp. 83–92.

44. Lichnowsky to Harden, 8 June 1917, Nachlass Harden. "Das bisherige Regime ist jedenfalls unhaltbar geworden. Wir gehen dem Reichsparlamentarismus entgegen, der aber mit dem Föderalismus unvereinbar ist, schon wegen Preussen und dessen Stellung zu einer parl. Reichsregierung. Das bedeutet den Einheitsstaat und dieser die ————. Man kann nicht alle Dynastien abschaffen und nur eine lassen."

45. "The Unitary State," *Abyss*, p. 453.

46. Harry F. Young, *Maximilian Harden, Censor Germaniae: Ein Publizist im Widerstreit von 1892 bis 1927*, vol. 6 of Dialog der Gesellschaft, Schriftenreihe für Publizistik-und Kommunikationswissenschaft, ed. Henk Prakke (Münster: Regensberg, 1971), passim.

47. Lichnowsky to Harden, 1 Nov. 1916, Nachlass Harden.

48. Harden to Dr. Späth, 27 Feb. 1915, AA, Deutschland 122, no. 3^g, "Der Schriftsteller Maximilian Harden und die Wochenschrift die Zukunft." Harden: "Es ist der Schulfall eines Präventivkrieges, den zu führen nationale Pflicht sein konnte."

49. Bethmann Hollweg, *Kriegsreden*, pp. 14–15. The contention of England's primary responsibility had been gaining strength for some time and was furthered by the discovery in Belgian files of documents on Anglo-Belgian prewar military conversations.

50. Lichnowsky to Solf, 24 Dec. 1914, Nachlass Solf.

51. The original version now available in Röhl, *Zwei deutsche Fürsten* (translated as *1914: Delusion or Design?*). This is the copy found in the papers of Freiherr v. Varnbüler. The prince deleted many passages before he published this essay under the new title "Wahn, nicht Wille" in *Auf dem Wege zum Abgrund*. In the English translation of *Auf dem Wege* (*Abyss*) this bears the title "Delusions." I have worked from the original version found in Nachlass Bülow. In the family archives there is a version differing from both the original and the one published in 1927, but the title page is missing. This could be the version F. Thimme found in Monts's papers under the title "Wahn, nicht Wille" (Monts, *Erinnerungen*, pp. 536–537).

52. Passages that are the same in the original version and in that published in *Auf dem Wege* follow the Delmer translation in *Abyss*. Translations of passages found only in the original are my own.

53. Lichnowsky to Delbrück, 21 Nov. 1916, Nachlass Delbrück.

54. Lichnowsky to Solf, 23 Dec. 1916, Nachlass Solf. German original: Der Fehler der Präventivkriege liegt eben darin, dass sie kein positives, sondern nur ein negatives Ziel enthalten und dass es un-

möglich ist, nachträglich ein Ergebnis ausfindig zu machen, das den gebrachten Opfern entspräche.

55. *Abyss*, p. 81.

56. See correspondence with Friedrich Naumann, partly published in *Abyss*, pp. 131–139; Theodor Heuss, *Friedrich Naumann: Der Mann, das Werk, die Zeit* (Stuttgart-Berlin: Deutsche Verlags-Anstalt, 1937), pp. 500–501; quoted passages in "Wahn oder Wille?" *Zwei deutsche Fürsten*, p. 63.

57. See Hiller, *Fürst Bülows Denkwürdigkeiten*, pp. 56–57, 62–63, 78.

58. Bülow marginal note to "Wahn oder Wille?", Nachlass Bülow.

59. Hans Gatzke, *Germany's Drive to the West (Drang nach Westen): A study of Germany's Western War Aims during the First World War* (Baltimore: The Johns Hopkins Press, 1950), p. 131.

60. Bülow marginal note to "Wahn oder Wille?", Nachlass Bülow.

61. Lichnowsky to Bülow, 11 July 1915, Nachlass Bülow. Bethmann had also come to realize that Germany could not achieve the goal of Continental domination without world domination. See Fritz Stern, "Bethmann Hollweg and the War: The Limits of Responsibility," in *The Responsibility of Power: Historical Essays in Honor of Hajo Holborn*, ed. Leonard Krieger and Fritz Stern (New York: Doubleday, 1967), pp. 272–273.

62. Lichnowsky to Harden, 1 Nov. 1916, Nachlass Harden.

63. Lichnowsky to Bernstorff, 12 June 1917, in Bernstorff, *Memoirs*, pp. 156–157.

64. Lichnowsky, "Das selbständige Polen," *Berliner Tageblatt*, 2 Sept. 1917.

65. Lichnowsky to Solf, 23 Dec. 1916, Nachlass Solf.

66. Heinrich Mann, *Ein Zeitalter wird besichtigt* (Berlin: Aufbau-Verlag, 1947), p. 316.

67. T. Wolff told F. Thimme he had seen another wartime essay by the prince entitled "Der Frieden" (Wolff to Thimme, 5 March 1928, Nachlass Thimme). See chap. 8n58. There is no record of this essay in any of the files or papers consulted for this work.

68. It is wrongly assumed in Röhl, *Delusion or Design?*, p. 47, that *My London Mission* was the amended version of a speech Lichnowsky gave at the allegedly secret meeting in his house. See chap. 7n41.

69. Lichnowsky to Wolff, 14 June 1916, AA Lichnowsky, vol. 1, reel 373, 39.

70. Bethmann to Lichnowsky, 17 June 1916; Lichnowsky to Beth-

mann, 24 June 1916; Bethmann to Lichnowsky, 9 July 1916, ibid., frames 40–44, 51–56.

71. *Abyss*, pp. 74–75. As to the British impression that Germany wanted war, the prince wrote: "It was impossible to interpret our attitude on a question that did not concern us directly in any other way." As this follows a sentence concerning Grey's view that Russia would not suffer the reduction of Serbia to vassalage, the impression of a German desire for war seems to refer to a war with Russia. Yet the sentences following the above-quoted sentence are concerned with Berlin's insistence on the chastisement of Serbia, that is, on military action by Austria against Serbia—an Austro-Serbian war.

72. Citations from *My London Mission* all follow the version presented in *Abyss*.

73. Scholtis, *Erinnerungen*, p. 168.

74. Statement by Prince Lichnowsky to geheimer Legationsrat Eckhardt, 27 Aug. 1917, AA Lichnowsky, vol. 1, reel 373, 128–130; Memorandum of the state attorney on discussion with Lichnowsky, 30 March 1918, ibid., vol. 2, frame 327. The prince did not name Harden as one of the recipients, but Harden always maintained that he was the first to read *My London Mission* (H. F. Young, *Harden*, p. 200). It is possible that Lichnowsky distributed his copies at Harden's urging. Harden makes an apparent reference to *My London Mission* in a letter to Lichnowsky on 29 October 1916:

Ich kann nur wiederholen, dass ich das von Eurer Durchlaucht damals Geschriebene ungemein stark, bis ans Ende durchgedacht und von einem Menschenherzen durchwärmt finde; seit Bismarck nicht mehr spricht, habe ich derart "majestätischem Menschenverstand" so Nahes von einem Deutschen nicht gehört. Ich möchte auch nicht zweifeln, dass die Stunde E.D. kommt, und bin deshalb froh, dass Sie Sich nach keiner Richtung "verbrauchen." Die Bogen würde ich benutzen, um hier und da sie einem unbedingt Zuverlässigen zu zeigen und ihm zu sagen [word missing, hole in paper]: Da suchst Du den verschrienen Mann.

75. Scholtis, "Die Denkschrift."

76. Statement by Richard Witting to geheimer Legationsrat Eckhardt, 28 Aug. 1917, AA Lichnowsky, vol. 1, reel 373, 130–132.

77. H. Young, *Harden*, pp. 11–12. Additional private information from Witting's son Klaus. Also Arthur Holitscher, *Mein Leben in dieser Zeit: Der 'Lebensgeschichte' eines Rebellen zweiter Band (1907–1925)* (Potsdam: G. Kiepenheuer, 1928), pp. 130ff; Heinrich Mann, *Ein Zeitalter wird besichtigt*, pp. 316–317.

78. Wolff, "Fürst Lichnowsky," *Berliner Tageblatt*, 28 Feb. 1928.

79. From a series of pamphlets he edited in the 1920s under the title *Gewaltige Wirklichkeit*.

80. Witting statement to Eckhardt, 28 Aug. 1917, and Beerfelde statement to same, 29 Aug. 1917, AA Lichnowsky, vol. 1, reel 373, 130–135. Essentially the same story in Beerfelde, "Der wahre Lichnowsky," *Welt am Montag*, 23 Apr. 1928.

81. Lichnowsky statement to Eckhardt, AA Lichnowsky, vol. 1, reel 373, 68–69.

82. Deutelmoser to Michaelis, 6 Aug. 1917, ibid., frames 68–69. F. Thimme believed the Allies learned of the Austro-German consultations on 5 and 6 July 1914 from Lichnowsky's loose talk in the Berlin salons. See Kurt Jagow, "Der Potsdamer Kronrat: Geschichte und Legende," *Süddeutsche Monatshefte* 25, no. 11 (Aug. 1928). This is supposition. Jan Opočenský, "War-Time Discussion of Responsibility," noting that Stumm in March 1917 queried Vienna about the Hoyos mission, surmises that Stumm had already received a copy of *My London Mission*. But he had not.

83. Michaelis to Lichnowsky, 8 Aug. 1917, AA Lichnowsky, vol. 1, reel 373, 65–66.

84. Von Schoen to Hertling, 12 Aug. 1917, postscript of 13 Aug. 1917, Geh. Staatsarchiv München, Ges. Berlin 1093.

Vertraulich äusserte sich Herr von Kühlmann dahin, dass ihm der ehemalige Botschafter den Eindruck eines, gelinde ausgedrückt, stark nervösen Menschen mache. Fürst Lichnowsky habe sich offenbar von seinem "Zusammenbruch" in London von August 1914 nicht erholt und leide an Monomanie.— Dass die Denkschrift authentisch ist, ist auch mir nicht zweifelhaft, denn Fürst Lichnowsky hat sich mir gegenüber wiederholt genau in den gleichen Gedankengängen geäussert.

85. Hermann Freiherr von Eckardstein, *Lebenserinnerungen und politische Denkwürdigkeiten*, 2 vols. (Leipzig: Paul List, 1920), 2 : 399. On Eckardstein's performance see Rich, *Holstein*, 2 : 576–582, 626–662; Monger, *Isolation*, pp. 22–37; H. Nicolson, *Lord Carnock*, p. 137.

86. Wolff, *Vorspiel*, p. 72; AA, Deutschland 122, no. 17, Freiherr von Eckardstein, reel 373, 00390–00396. See further Rogge, *Holstein und Harden*, pp. 307, 425.

87. This story in AA, Deutschland 122, no. 17, Freiherr von Eckardstein, reel 373, 00383–00764.

88. Lichnowsky statement to Eckhardt, 27 Aug. 1917, AA Lichnowsky, vol. 1, reel 373, 128–130.

89. Protokolle des Haushaltausschusses, 172. Sitzung, 22 Aug. 1917, pp. 55, 62ff, Staatsarchiv Stuttgart.

90. Foreign Ministry memorandum on discussion with representatives of Stellvertretender-Generalstab IIIb Abwehr, 1 Sept. 1917, AA Lichnowsky, vol. 1, reel 373, 140–144; memorandum on discussion with political police, 3 Sept. 1917, ibid., frames 145–146; von dem Bussche to Lichnowsky, 29 Aug. 1917, ibid., frames 123–124; Lichnowsky to von dem Bussche, 30 Aug. 1917, ibid., frame 136.

91. Auszug aus den Gerichtsakten, 29 March 1918, AA, Nachlass Luetgebrune, reel 1, 452613.

92. Karl Max Fürst von Lichnowsky, *Die Schuld der deutschen Regierung am Kriege: Meine Londoner Mission* [underground printing allegedly published in Görlitz, 1918], p. 30. A copy of this version is in the Columbia University Library.

93. Stellvertretender Generalstab IIIb Abwehr to Foreign Ministry, 15 Feb. 1918, AA Lichnowsky, vol. 1, reel 373, 194–195.

94. Hans Peter Hanssen, *Diary of a Dying Empire*, trans. of *Fra Krigstiden* (Copenhagen, 1924) by O. O. Winther, ed. Ralph H. Lutz, Mary Schofield, and O. O. Winther, intro. Ralph H. Lutz (Bloomington: Indiana University Press, 1955), pp. 249, 259–260.

95. "Wie die Denkschrift Fürst Lichnowskys verraten wurde: Eine Erklärung Hanssens," *Hamburger Fremdenblatt*, 30 Nov. 1928.

96. Dr. Wilhelm Carlgren of the Swedish Foreign Office archives informs me that the *Politiken* archives no longer exist.

97. Stockholm 766, 19 March 1918, FO 395, News Miscellaneous (General), vol. 241, file 51283.

98. Edited by C. A. McCurdy, M.P.

99. Hans Thimme, *Weltkrieg ohne Waffen: Die Propaganda der Westmächte gegen Deutschland: Ihre Wirkung und ihre Abwehr* (Stuttgart: Cotta, 1932), p. 125.

100. George Creel, *How We Advertised America* (New York: Harper, 1920), p. 457.

101. Ibid., p. 312.

102. Full title: *Meine Londoner Mission, 1912–1914*, von Fürst Lichnowsky, ehemaliger deutscher Botschafter in England (Originaltext), mit einem Vorwort von Prof. Dr. O. Nippold und einem Porträt des Fürsten Lichnowsky. Anhang: Erklärungen Sir Edward Greys am 3. August 1914, Denkschrift von Dr. Mühlon, Erklärungen von Minister Pichon am 1. März 1918. The introduction by Nippold was signed

Thun, April 1918. On Muehlon's activity during the war see Wolf-gang Benz, "Der 'fall Muehlon': Bürgerliche Opposition im Obrig-keitsstaat während des Ersten Weltkriegs," *Vierteljahrshefte für Zeitgeschichte* 18, no. 4 (Oct. 1970), pp. 543–565.

103. Thimme, "Memoirenwerk," p. 30.

104. From FO 395, News Miscellaneous (General), vol. 241. For-eign Office to Rumbold, 21 March 1918, file 52847, 23 March 1918: "Lichnowsky's revelations should be written up as much as possible. We will send full text in English by early bag. We are trying to get from Sweden German text for ultimate issue in pamphlet form." Rum-bold to Foreign Office, 28 March 1918, file 56631, 29 March 1918: "Mühlon when previously approached on the subject objected to our publishing his memo but now that it has appeared in German press there can be no objection to our reproducing it from 'Berliner Tage-blatt.'" Foreign Office to Rumbold, 9 April 1918, file 56631: "Ok three together, suggest also Jagow's reply [published refutation of *Mission*]. Try get Swiss writer introduce all four. Herr Zurlinden or Prof. Nippold may be willing to write this. If so please telegraph amount of honorarium likely to be required." Rumbold to Foreign Office, 9 Apr. 1918, file 64102, 11 Apr. 1918: "We find it impossible to put together here satisfactory edition of Lichnowsky's memorandum and must rely therefore on your sending us complete text." Rumbold to Foreign Office, 24 Apr. 1918, file 73286, 26 April 1918: "In German text of Lichnowsky page 25 lines 21 and 22 we have left out eight words from 'trotzdem to war.' Would suggest you omitting them whenever manuscript is used."

105. Some biographical information on Nippold in Pierre Grappin, *Le Bund Neues Vaterland (1914–1916): Ses rapports avec Romain Rolland*, vol. 7, Bibliothèque de la Société des Etudes Germaniques (Lyon-Paris: Imprimerie artistique en couleurs, 1952), p. 40.

106. Rumbold to Foreign Office, 16 April 1918, FO 395, News Mis-cellaneous (General), vol. 241, file 67473, 17 Apr. 1918: "Publishers urge the necessity of spending 5,000 francs on advertising pamphlet in Swiss press." Foreign Office to Rumbold, 15 Apr. 1918, ibid.: "Ex-penditure authorized." For honorarium see chap. 7n104.

107. Kühlmann (drafted by von dem Bussche) to Rosen (The Hague), 19 March 1918, AA, Krieg. Die Presse, reel 2818, 6282/H 050721. Here as attachment to dispatch to Stockholm. Kühlmann to Lucius v. Stoedten, 17 March 1918, ibid., frames 6262/HO 50720; Lucius v. Stoedten to Kühlmann, 6 May 1918, ibid., frame 50722.

108. Rumbold to Foreign Office, 3 May 1918, FO 395, News, vol.

Notes to Chapter VII

241, file 796580, 6 May 1918; *Die Denkschrift des Fürsten Lichnowsky: Der vollständige Wortlaut: Meine Londoner Mission 1912–1914* (Bern: Paul Haupt, 1918), ed. "eine Gruppe von Friedensfreunden."

109. Copenhagen to Foreign Office, 11 June 1918, FO 395, News, vol. 241, file 105000, 12 June 1918; Rotterdam to Foreign Office, 25 June 1918, ibid., file 112764, 26 June 1918.

110. Eduard Bernstein, "In Sachen des Fürsten Lichnowsky," *Berliner Tageblatt*, 18 July 1918. Lichnowsky also appealed to *Politiken* personally. Minute of discussion with state attorney, 30 March 1918, AA Lichnowsky, vol. 2, reel 373, 326–349.

111. Hansi (Jean Jacques Waltz) and Ernest Tonnelat, *A travers les lignes ennemies: Trois années d'offensive contre le moral allemand* (Paris: Payot, 1922), pp. 167–168.

112. Ibid., pp. 36, 158. There is a copy of the French military propaganda edition of the *Mission* in the Mönkmöller Collection of Propaganda Leaflets at the Hoover Institution on War, Revolution, and Peace.

113. "Protokoll der Besprechung in Grossen Hauptquartier in Spa am 14. August 1918," in Herbert Michaelis, Ernst Schraepler, Günter Scheel, ed., *Ursachen und Folgen vom deutschen Zusammenbruch 1918 und 1945 bis zur staatlichen Neuordnung Deutschlands in der Gegenwart*, 5 vols. (Berlin: Dokumenten-Verlag, 1958–1960), 2 : 280. Also Erich Ludendorff, *Meine Kriegserinnerungen* (Berlin: E. S. Mittler, 1920), pp. 516–517.

114. H. Thimme, *Weltkrieg ohne Waffen*, pp. 194–195.

115. Memorandum of the Foreign Ministry dated 29 Aug. 1918, AA Lichnowsky, vol. 3, reel 373, 421–423. "[Saenger] ist nach Mitteilung des Oberst v. Haeften mit der Abfassung einer Gegenschrift gegen die von unseren Feinden in die deutschen Schützengräben abgeworfene Lichnowsky'sche Denkschrift beauftragt."

116. Alwin Saenger, *Die Schuld der deutschen Regierung am Kriege: Ein Nachtrag zu der Schrift: Meine Londoner Mission von Fürst Lichnowsky* (Berlin: Verlag für Sozialwissenschaft, 1918), pp. 3, 5. In a meeting of the German War Cabinet on 19 October 1918, under the government of Prinz Max von Baden, Socialist leader Scheidemann complained that the military information services were following a line contrary to that adopted by the new government. He mentioned as an example Saenger's brochure against Lichnowsky. What he specifically objected to is not clear from the records of this meeting. See Erich Matthias and Rudolf Morsey, eds., *Die Regierung des Prinzen Max von Baden*, vol. 2 of Quellen zur Geschichte des

Parlamentarismus und der politischen Parteien: Erste Reihe: Von der konstitutionellen Monarchie zur parlamentarischen Republik, ed. Werner Conze et al. (Düsseldorf: Droste Verlag, 1962), p. 271.

117. Stresemann to Kühlmann, 11 Jan. 1918, AA Lichnowsky, vol. 1, reel 373, 179; memorandum of chancellor Hertling, 11 Jan. 1918, ibid., frame 172.

118. Pourtalès to Hertling, 5 Feb. 1918, ibid., frames 180–188. On 30 March Hertling sent Pourtalès a letter stating officially that he had not reported, as Lichnowsky had said, "that Russia would not move under any circumstances," and that his dispatches in the years 1913 and 1914 had pointed repeatedly to the growing power of the Pan-Slavic agitators. Pourtalès published this letter in *Am Scheideweg*. See ch. 6, note 32.

119. Kühlmann to Wedel (Vienna), 17 Feb. 1918, ibid., frame 196; Wedel to Kühlmann, 18 Feb. 1918, ibid., frame 197; Wedel to Kühlmann, 18 Feb. 1918, ibid., frame 198. "Graf Czernin bittet dringend das Thema nicht anzuschneiden," wrote Wedel. Lichnowsky's memoir was already known in Vienna. Redlich refers to the memoir in his diary on 27 Nov. 1917 (*Schicksalsjahre*, 2 : 247), and the Austrian ambassador Hohenwarte wrote Czernin on 7 March 1918 that after the publication in "Copenhagen" there would be discussion of the prince's memoir, a copy of which he had already forwarded to Czernin (MÄ, PA rot 1050, Krieg 62–66, Mappe Krieg 65 [Spezielles über Schuld am Kriege]).

120. Entry in Berchtold's diary, 21 Feb. 1918, quoted in Hantsch, *Berchtold*, 2 : 811.

121. Schulthess', 34 (59): 120–124.

122. Jagow, "Bemerkungen zu der Schrift des Fürsten Lichnowsky 'Meine Londoner Mission,'" manuscript dated 3 Oct. 1917, AA Lichnowsky, vol. 1, reel 373, 151–168; copy dated 2 Oct. 1917 in Nachlass Jagow, reel 15, 873–890.

123. Memorandum by Jagow on changes in his manuscript, 2 March 1918, AA Lichnowsky, vol. 2, not microfilmed. Excised: "Aber wenn ein Krieg unvermeidlich wurde, war der jetzige Zeitpunkt günstiger als später, dies war auch die Auffassung des Generals von Moltke."

124. See p. 101.

125. *Norddeutsche Allgemeine Zeitung*, 23 March 1918.

126. Foreign Office to Rumbold, 9 Apr. 1918, FO 395, News Miscellaneous (General), file 56631.

127. Stumm to Jagow, 24 March 1918, Nachlass Jagow, reel 15, 181–182.

128. Stumm to Jagow, 18 July 1918, ibid., frames 905–907. "Entwurf einer Erwiederung auf die Denkschrift des Fürsten Lichnowsky: 'Meine Londoner Mission,' " dated 27 Nov. 1918, but completed at least as early as July 1918, AA, Aktenstücke zum Kriegsausbruch herausgegeben vom AA, reel 408, 00360–00382; memorandum by Deutelmoser, 25 Aug. 1918.

129. Speech of 26 Oct. 1916, Reichstag, vol. 308, p. 1822.

130. Protokolle des Haushaltausschusses, 173. Stizung, 23 Aug. 1917, p. 25, Staatsarchiv Stuttgart.

131. Reichstag, vol. 313, p. 5658.

132. *Vorwärts*, 20 March 1918.

133. Georg Bernhard, "Fürst Lichnowskys Schrift," *Vossische Zeitung*, 20 March 1918.

134. Von dem Bussche to Freiherr von Grünau (*Grosses Hauptquartier*), 15 March 1918; Grünau to Foreign Ministry, 20 March 1918; Foreign Ministry to Grünau, 20 March 1918; Grünau to Foreign Ministry, 22 March 1918, in AA Lichnowsky, vol. 2, reel 373, 235, 250–251. Beerfelde was arrested in August and released in the fall of 1917 when the courts-martial found he had not disobeyed a command in participating in political action. Arrested again in March 1918 (ibid., vol. 1, reel 373, 133, 171–174; Nachlass Luetgebrune, reel 1, 452613).

135. Ministry of Justice to Hertling, 23 March 1918; Foreign Ministry to Grünau, 28 March 1918; General von Kessel to Hertling, 25 March 1918; Hertling to von Kessel, 26 March 1918, AA Lichnowsky, vol. 2, reel 373, 276–278 and 284–287.

136. Draft of minute of discussion in the Ministry of Justice, 24 Aug. 1918, ibid., vol. 3, reel 373, 481–491. At a session of Prince Max von Baden's war cabinet on 10 Oct. 1918, Scheidemann, appealing for release of imprisoned left Socialists, averred that the people did not understand why Lichnowsky should be free while Dittmann and Liebknecht were still in jail (E. Matthias and R. Morsey, *Regierung des Prinzen Max von Baden*, p. 96).

137. AA Lichnowsky, vol. 3, reel 373, 433–449.

138. *Abyss*, pp. 144–145.

139. Four articles by Harden in *Zukunft*: "Die Töchter der Nacht," 23 March 1918 (beginning p. 458); "Der alte Sauerteig," 30 March 1918; "Diplomatarium," 6 Apr. 1918; "Wider Lichnowsky," 27 Apr. 1918.

140. Lichnowsky to Harden, 23 March 1918, Nachlass Harden.

141. Lichnowsky to Harden, Easter 1918, ibid.

142. Lichnowsky to Harden, 21 May, 18 June, and 24 June 1918, ibid.

143. Lichnowsky to Harden, 16 March 1918, ibid.

144. Schulthess', 34: 144, 157, 243, 254. Also Hutten-Czapski, *Sechzig Jahre*, 2: 487ff., and Bülow, *Denkwürdigkeiten*, 2: 256.

145. Information from Countess Leonore Lichnowsky.

Chapter VIII

1. Entry 14 July 1915, Tagebücher, Heft 5, Nachlass Mensdorff.

2. Wolff, *Marsch*, pp. 68–69.

3. Lichnowsky to Harden, 16 Oct. 1918, Nachlass Harden.

4. Lichsowsky to Harden, 26 Nov. 1918, ibid.

5. Information from Countess Leonore Lichnowsky.

6. *Zukunft*, 1 Feb. 1919, p. 145.

7. Lichnowsky to Harden, 16 Oct. 1918, Nachlass Harden.

8. Lichnowsky to Solf, 19 Nov. 1918 (first telegram that date), AA Lichnowsky, vol. 3 (not filmed). Also Hetta Gräfin Treuberg, *Zwischen Politik und Diplomatie: Memoiren*, ed. M. J. Bopp (Strasbourg: Imprimerie Strasbourgeoise, 1921), p. 256. Lichnowsky to Solf, 19 and 22 Nov. 1918, AA Lichnowsky, vol. 3 (not filmed). This is the second telegram Lichnowsky sent Solf 19 Nov.

9. The appeal, published in *Abyss*, pp. 46ff, first appeared in *Vorwärts*.

10. The negative British reaction reported in *Deutsche Allgemeine Zeitung*, 22 Nov. 1918.

11. Lichnowsky to Bernstorff, 26 March 1919, in Bernstorff, *Memoirs*, pp. 259–260.

12. Lichnowsky to Bülow, 24 May 1919, Nachlass Bülow.

13. Ibid.

14. Golo Mann, "Fürst Lichnowsky," *Du* 20, no. 9 (Sept. 1960), republished in *Geschichte und Geschichten* (Frankfurt/Main: S. Fischer Verlag, 1962), p. 518.

15. Information from Countess Leonore Lichnowsky.

16. Information from Prince Wilhelm Lichnowsky.

17. Information from Prince Wilhelm Lichnowsky and Countess Leonore Lichnowsky.

18. Lichnowsky to Harden, 26 Dec. 1918, Nachlass Harden. "If the enemy demands self-determination for our Polish provinces," he wrote, "we should demand it for Alsace and northern Bohemia. . . . Wilson the ideologue cannot say no. Equal rights for all!"

19. "Should the Large Estates be Split up?" *Abyss*, pp. 440ff.

20. E. Ludwig, "Der Fürst Lichnowsky," *Weltbühne,* 20 March 1928, p. 433.

21. Scholtis, *Erinnerungen,* p. 207.

22. G. Mann, *Geschichte und Geschichten,* p. 518.

23. As Count Max Montgelas, one of the editors of the *Deutsche Dokumente zum Kriegsausbruch,* lost the originals of these four or five letters before copies were made, they were not published. See *Abyss,* p. 157; Max Graf Montgelas, "Persönliche Bemerkungen zu Fürst Lichnowskys 'Auf dem Wege zum Abgrund,' " *Die Kriegsschuldfrage* 5 (Nov. 1927); and Mechtilde Lichnowsky, *Heute und vorgestern,* pp. 83–84. One private letter from Jagow, that of 18 July 1914, was published in the *DD,* however.

24. Germany, *Official German Documents Relating to the World War,* trans. under the supervision of the Carnegie Endowment for International Peace, 2 vols. (New York: Oxford University Press, 1923), 1 : 34.

25. *Meine Londoner Mission 1912–1914 und Eingabe an das Preussische Herrenhaus* (Berlin: Verlag Neues Vaterland, 1919), foreword, n.p.

26. Count Michael Lichnowsky to the author; information on Metternich from Countess Leonore Lichnowsky.

27. He described these circumstances to his daughter, Countess Leonore Lichnowsky. Also in letter to Bülow, 30 Aug. 1926, Nachlass Bülow. He wrote:

Es wird Sie vielleicht interessieren zu erfahren, dass Berchtold mir in Meran unaufgefordert sagte, er würde keine so schroffe Haltung gegen Serbien eingenommen haben, wäre er nicht von Berlin aus dauernd dazu gedrängt worden. Mitte Juli sei Tschirschky erschienen und habe erklärt, dass wenn Österreich sich weigere gegen Serbien vorzugehen, das Bündnis erledigt sei. Erst darauf hin sei Tisza umgefallen. . . . Die Sprache des Auswärtigen Amtes habe zur Annahme berechtigt, dass uns damals der allgemeine Krieg nicht unerwünscht wäre.

28. Lichnowsky to Fritz Kern, 9 Dec. 1926, copy in RAUSL.

29. Herbert von Hindenburg, "Der Grandseigneur als Diplomat: Erinnerungen und Bemerkungen zum Fall Lichnowsky," *Frankfurter Zeitung,* 25 Nov. 1928.

30. Information from Countess Leonore Lichnowsky. In 1924 the princess visited London twice, once in the spring and then again late in the year. Her daughter, Countess Leonore, has provided copies of two letters to the Princess from Tyrrell, dated 6 Feb. 1924 and 16 Dec. 1924, and one letter from Pamela Grey, dated 8 Feb. 1924. In his letter

of 16 Dec., Tyrrell wrote: "May I enclose a letter from Lord Grey to your husband which he gave me the other day when we both talked a great deal about you and him."

31. See Werner Frauendienst, "Das Kriegsschuldreferat des Auswärtigen Amtes," *Berliner Monatshefte* 15 (March 1937); Friedrich Thimme, " 'Die grosse Politik der europäischen Kabinette 1871–1914': Persönliche Erinnerungen," *Berliner Monatshefte* 15 (March 1937).

32. Flyleaf in AA Schuldreferat 56/180 (F. Thimme), reel 3409, E 616 382.

33. Thimme to Wilhelm von Stumm, 7 March 1927, Nachlass Thimme.

34. Alma Luckau, ed., *The German Delegation at the Paris Peace Conference: History and Documents* (New York: Columbia University Press for the Carnegie Endowment for International Peace, Division of Economics and History, 1941), doc. 52, pp. 272–287.

35. Note by Thimme in AA Schuldreferat, Veröffentlichung Lichnowsky (not filmed). Compare admission that there was no misunderstanding with Thimme, "Memoirenwerk," p. 32, and Monts, *Erinnerungen und Gedanken*, p. 530.

36. Richard Kirchner, "Die Berichte Lichnowskys," *Frankfurter Zeitung*, erstes Morgenblatt, 22, 25, 27, and 29 Feb. 1920.

37. Johannes Victor Bredt, "Lichnowsky und Grey," *Preussische Jahrbücher* 212, no. 1 (Apr. 1928), p. 15.

38. Lichnowsky to Bethmann, 24 June 1914, *GP* 39, no. 15 884, pp. 630ff, p. 633n.

39. *Abyss*, pp. 152ff.

40. Lichnowsky to Thimme, 4 Jan. 1927, in *Abyss*, pp. 154ff. A copy of the original is in RAUSL.

41. Thimme to Lichnowsky, 7 Jan. 1927, copy in AA Thimme, reel 3409, E 616643–616646.

42. Thimme to Foreign Ministry, 23 Apr. 1927; undated typed interoffice memorandum, ibid., reel 3409, E 616651–616654.

43. Lichnowsky to Thimme, 28 Apr. 1927, answering Thimme to Lichnowsky, 26 Apr. 1927, ibid., E 616655–616657.

44. Thimme to Lichnowsky, 29 Apr. 1927, ibid., E 61658. In vol. 40 of the *GP*, the last volume, which completed the index for the series and contained the errata, the editors published a communication from Friedrich Rosen, who had objected to three passages in the notes to his correspondence. The editors also noted that there had been an exchange of letters with Lichnowsky concerning the footnotes in vol. 39 but that as they were unable to reach an agreement on the wording, a rectification was not possible (*GP* 40, p. 168).

246 Notes to Chapter VIII

45. Lichnowsky to Schubert, 3 May 1927, AA Thimme, reel 3409, E 61660.

46. The earliest letter concerning the publication is from Harry Schuhmann to Lichnowsky, 16 July 1927, RAUSL.

47. *Abyss*, pp. xxii–xxiii.

48. Schuhmann to Lichnowsky, 9 Sept. 1927, RAUSL. This letter is mutilated and faded and difficult to read. The main passages are these:

Dennoch ist es mir eine selbstverständliche Freude, den [word missing] Ew. Durchlaucht zu erfüllen, und an Herrn Stresemann in der Angelegenheit nochmals heranzutreten, sobald er aus Genf zurückkommt. Hierbei werde [word missing] nicht verfehlen, die Eröffnung weiterzugeben, zu der mich Ew. Durchlaucht ermächtigen. Freilich gestatte ich mir, darauf hinzuweisen, dass ich in durchaus dem gleichen Sinn bereits von fünf Wochen geschrieben habe. Denn entgegen der Annahme Ew. Durchlaucht hatte ich den Brief so gefasst, dass ich Herrn Stresemann dem Sinne nach gebeten habe, sich nicht mit einer Antwort zu bemühen, wenn er keine Bedenken habe, sodass ich ihn um eine Nachricht nur bat, wenn er eine gegenteilige Anschauung habe, die von meiner Meinung abweicht, derzufolge ein solches Werk durch [word missing] offene Kritik der deutschen Sache nur zu nützen vermag. Ich vermochte also nicht deutlicher zu sein als in diesen Darlegungen an Herrn Stresemann, die sowohl mit Rücksicht auf die Stellung Ew. Durchlaucht als auch mit Rücksicht auf meine verlegerische Unabhängigkeit fast schon zu weit gingen. Wenn nun Herr Stresemann auf diesen meinen Brief mir eine ausführliche Antwort aus seinen Ferien sandte [six illegible lines follow]. . . . *Auf keinen Fall könnte er später sagen, er habe die Veröffentlichung des Werkes etwa nicht gebilligt.* Denn angesichts [words and letters missing] wäre ihm dies durchaus unmöglich, eben weil ich ihm, womit [word missing] die Zustimmung Ew. Durchlaucht voraussetzen durfte, die Möglichkeit [word missing] Verschiebung dieser Veröffentlichung damals durchaus geboten hatte. . . . Dennoch wiederhole ich aber, dass ich in einem neuen eindringlichen Schreiben nach der Rückkehr aus Genf an Herrn Stresemann wunschgemäss herantreten werde. Nur von einem bitte ich mich gütigst zu entbinden: von der Anregung, die Korrekturbogen ihm zu übersenden. . . . Zwischen ihm und mir ist ein Generalvertrag zustande gekommen, demzufolge Herr Stresemann die Verpflichtung übernommen hat, alle literarischen Veröffentlichungen ausschliesslich in meinem Verlag erscheinen zu lassen, sofern ich ihm die gleichen finanziellen Vorteile einräume, die ihm etwa von anderer Seite geboten würden. . . . Wenn ich nun aber Herrn Stresemann die Vorkorrektur vorlegen würde, so würde ich hiermit mich einer Art Vorzensur unterwerfen, die in erster Linie doch Ew. Durchlaucht völlig unwürdig wäre, da Ew. Durchlaucht die politische Wirkung doch am besten selbst zu beurteilen vermag.

49. Lichnowsky to Schuhmann, 15 Sept. 1927 (copy), and Schuhmann to Lichnowsky, 16 July 1927, RAUSL.

50. *Abyss*, p. xxi.

51. Ibid., p. xvii.

52. Ibid., p. xx.

53. E. Ludwig, "Ehrenrettung eines Toten," *Vossische Zeitung*, Abend-Ausgabe, 28 March 1928.

54. "Bemerkungen zum 17. Abschnitt des Buches des Fürsten Lichnowsky 'Auf dem Wege zum Abgrund,' II. Bd., S. 229, ff.," AA Veröffentlichung Lichnowsky.

55. Other deletions: from a telegram of 4 Aug. 1914 the words "in all probability" from the sentence: "We therefore in all probability must soon count upon opposition of England"; from the same telegram the word *alsdann* (then, thus) from the sentence: "Conversation with Sir W. Tyrrell confirms my impression that after receiving news of serious German-Belgian collisions, continuance of English neutrality can no longer be counted on and that a rupture of relations is *thus* imminent."

56. Thimme's articles and notices concerning *Heading for the Abyss* are listed in the Bibliography.

57. See pp. 140, 142–144.

58. Thimme had finished writing his article before Theodor Wolff recalled the original title in a letter to Thimme of 5 March 1928, Nachlass Thimme. Thimme exchanged several letters with Wolff between Dec. 1927 and March 1928 concerning the public discussion of Lichnowsky's memoirs. The correspondence, friendly in tone, began with Wolff's refusal to publish Thimme's rejoinder to Lichnowsky's reply (which had appeared in the *Berliner Tageblatt*) to Thimme's first article on the memoirs in the *Kölnische Zeitung*. Wolff thought that Lichnowsky had a right to answer Thimme's charges, but he did not want to open the columns of the *Tageblatt* to a polemic that had started elsewhere (which had begun, in fact, with Thimme's footnotes in the *GP*). In a letter to Wolff on 29 Feb. 1928, Thimme noted that Wolff in his obituary article on the prince had confused *My London Mission* with "England before the War." Answering this on 5 March, Wolff wrote: "Lichnowsky hat mir drei Denkschriften im Manuskript gegeben: 'Wahn oder Wille?' (jetzt in seinem Buche 'Wahn, nicht Wille!') vom Januar 1915, 'Der Frieden' vom Ende Dezember 1915 und die Denkschrift vom August 1916. Ausserdem habe ich in seinem Arbeitszimmer die Denkschrift vom August 1914 gelesen und zwar, wie ich glaube, den zweiten Text. Da nach so langer Zeit meine Erinnerungen schwankend sind, werde ich nicht unterlassen, nach dem Erscheinen Ihres angekündigten Artikels von Ihren Ausführungen Notiz zu nehmen."

59. *Berliner Tageblatt*, 24 Dec. 1927.
60. *Kölnische Zeitung*, 17 Feb. 1928.
61. Wolff, "Fürst Lichnowsky," *Berliner Tageblatt*, 28 Feb. 1928.
62. Thimme, "Memoirenwerk," pp. 33, 64.

Chapter IX

1. "An Introductory Letter from Prince Lichnowsky," n.p., *Abyss*.
2. Ibid., p. vi.
3. Lichnowsky to Constable and Sons, [no day] Dec. 1927, RAUSL.
4. Information from Countess Lichnowsky.
5. The newspaper reports of the burial are scanty. This information is from Countess Leonore Lichnowsky who recalls that neither Rosen nor Bülow, Lichnowsky's closest associates from the Wilhelminian corps of diplomats, was present at the ceremony.
6. *Völkischer Beobachter* (Bayernausgabe), 29 Feb. 1928.
7. *Berliner Tageblatt*, 28 Feb. 1928.
8. *Times* (London), 28 Feb. 1928.
9. Bülow, *Denkwürdigkeiten*, 1 : 183, 3 : 123–124.
10. Ibid., 3 : 149–150, 151–161.
11. For a summary of the criticism see Hiller, *Bülows Denkwürdigkeiten*, pp. 1–7.
12. F. Thimme, ed., *Front wider Bülow: Staatsmänner, Diplomaten und Forscher zu seinen Denkwürdigkeiten* (Munich: F. Bruckmann, 1931).
13. Frauendienst, "Kriegsschuldreferat," p. 204.
14. Information from Countess Leonore Lichnowsky.
15. *Heute und vorgestern*, p. 61.
16. Alfred Rosenberg, *Novemberköpfe*, 2nd. ed. (Munich: Eher, 1939), p. 55.
17. Wolff, "Fürst Lichnowsky Botschafter in London," *Berliner Tageblatt*, 17 Oct. 1912.
18. "Diplomacy and Democracy," *Abyss*, pp. 87–88.
19. Riezler, *Tagebücher*, pp. 188–189.
20. Information from Count Michael Lichnowsky.
21. Lichnowsky to Solf, 24 Dec. 1914, Nachlass Solf.
22. *Abyss*, p. 75.
23. Lichnowsky to Harden, 17 Apr. 1918, Nachlass Harden.
24. *Abyss*, p. 3.
25. Werner Freiherr von Rheinbaben, *Kaiser Kanzler Präsidenten: Erinnerungen* (Mainz: v. Hase und Koehler Verlag, 1968), p. 96.

26. *Abyss,* p. 77.

27. Harden, *Zukunft,* 30 March 1918.

Chapter X

1. Information from Countess Leonore Lichnowsky.

2. *Heute und vorgestern,* pp. 129–130.

3. Published in *Zum Schauen bestellt* (Esslingen: Bechtle Verlag, 1953). Information on circumstances from Franz Brill, "Mechtilde Lichnowsky: Zu ihrem siebzigsten Geburtstage," *Tagesspiegel* (Berlin), 8 March 1949.

4. *Delaïde* (Berlin: S. Fischer Verlag, 1935), p. 11.

5. *Der Lauf der Asdur,* p. 191.

6. See p. 49.

7. *An der Leine: Roman* (Berlin: S. Fischer Verlag, 1930), pp. 157–159.

8. *Heute und vorgestern,* pp. 60–61.

Bibliography

I. Unpublished Sources
(with abbreviations)

A. *Government Documents*

1. Documents of German Auswärtiges Amt in Politisches Archiv, Foreign Ministry of the German Federal Republic, Bonn (cited as AA; citations of AA documents available on microfilm at the National Archives, Washington, D.C., will include microfilm reel and frame numbers).

   Deutschland 122, no. 17, Freiherr von Eckardstein; Deutschland 122, no. 22, betr. den Kaiserlichen Botschafter z.D. Fürsten Lichnowsky, 3 vols. (cited as AA Lichnowsky). This is a special dossier on Lichnowsky's wartime activity; it contains copies of his correspondence with the chancellors and other officials, copies of his essays, and various documents concerning governmental efforts to suppress *My London Mission*. (German Foreign Ministry personnel files are closed to research; abstracts at the Politisches Archiv provide skeleton data on promotions and other administrative actions.)

   Deutschland 135, nos. 2 and 3, Die Botschaft in London.

   Deutschland 135, no. 6, Die Botschaft in Wien.

   England 78, Beziehungen Deutschlands zu England, vol. 17 (1902–1904), vol. 96 (1910–1914).

   England 78, secretissima, Beziehungen Dtlds. zu Engld., vols. 5–6 (1901–1903).

   England 78, no. 1, geh., Beziehungen Dtlds. zu Engld., vols. 10–27.

   England 78, no. 3, geh., Frage einer Verständigung Deutschlands mit England über Flottenbauten.

   England 79, England innere Angelegenheiten.

   England 81, Englische Staatsmänner.

   England 83, geh., Russland und England.

   England 87, Diplomatisches Korps in London.

   Grosses Hauptquartier 25, England no. 4, Zeitungsausschnitte, Berichte, Weissbücher, vol. 1.

Grosses Hauptquartier 206, Europäischer Krieg: Dokumente und Weissbücher über den Beginn des Krieges, vols. 1–2.

Der Weltkrieg adh. 4. Sammlung von Schriftstücken zur Vorgeschichte des Krieges.

Handakten betr. Vorwürfe unserer Gegner, die zu widerlegen sind, vol. 3 (Defensivmappe Legationssekretär v. Bülow).

Aktenstücke zum Kriegsausbruch herausgegeben vom Auswärtigen Amt.

Akten betr. den Krieg 1914: Deutsche Weissbücher und andere Veröffentlichungen.

Der Krieg: Die Presse.

Friedrich Thimme.

Schuldreferat 49/141, Veröffentlichung H. J. von Beerfelde.

Schuldreferat Veröffentlichung Lichnowsky (cited: AA Veröffentlichung Lichnowsky). This is a second AA file on Lichnowsky; it is concerned with publication of his collected papers 1927–1928.

Österreich 70, Allgemeine Angelegenheiten Österreichs, vols. 27–34, 43.

Österreich 86, no. 2, Österreichische Staatsmänner.

Österreich 94, Angelegenheiten Galiziens und der Bukowina, vol. 3.

Österreich 95, Beziehungen Österreichs zu Deutschland (1901–1905).

Österreich 97, Acta betr. den Österreichisch-ungarischen Ausgleich, vols. 1–3 (1896–1897).

Österreich 103, die allgemeine österreichische Politik auch im Hinblick auf die zukünftige Gestaltung Österreich-Ungarns, vol. 2.

2. Documents of Austro-Hungarian Ministerium des Äussern in Österreichisches Staatsarchiv, Abteilung Haus-, Hof- und Staatsarchiv, Vienna (cited as MÄ): 143 PA III Preussen, Weisungen Varia 1892, Berichte 1893; 145 PA III Preussen, 1894, 1895; 146 PA III Preussen 1895; PA rot 1050, Krieg 62–66, Mappe Krieg 65 (Spezielles über die Schuld am Kriege); 148 PA VIII England, Berichte 1912 III–VII; 149 PA VIII England (1912 VIII–XII), Berichte, Weisungen, Varia 1912–1913; 150 PA VIII, England, Berichte 1913 (VI–XII) Weisungen, Varia 1914.

3. Documents of the British Foreign Office in Public Record Office, Foreign Office Records, London (cited as FO). Series 371: Germany 1912, vols. 1371, 1373, 1377, 1379; Germany 1914, vols. 1986, 1987, 1991, 1992; Germany 1918, vol. 3226; Persia 1914, vol. 2071; Russia 1914, vols. 2091, 2092, 2094; Political Intelligence Department 1918, vols. 4360, 4363; The War 1914, vols. 2160, 2165, 2167; The War 1918, vol. 3442. Series 372: Germany 1912, vol. 364. Series 395: News

1917 (Scandinavia files), vol. 115; News 1918 (Switzerland file), vols. 198, 199; News Miscellaneous (general) 1918, vols. 241, 242.
4. Documents from Brand. Preuss. Hausarchiv in Deutsches Zentralarchiv, Historische Abteilung II, Merseburg: Rep. 53 J Lit. B. Nr. 7.
5. Diplomatic correspondence in Geheimes Staatsarchiv München: MA 3084, Ges. Berlin 1093.

B. *Private Papers*

1. Rodinny archiv a ústřední správa Lichnovských [Lichnowsky family and administrative archives] in CSSR State Archives in Opava (cited as RAUSL). These are the remnants of the Lichnowsky family archives. The family was unable to remove this large collection of papers when, at the end of the Second World War, the front drew near. Soviet troops sacked the chateau at Kuchelna and scattered the papers about. A few months later the village school teacher taking a walk near the village came upon some sheaves of paper with Latin words visible on them protruding from a shell crater. When he dug them out and found documents in many languages, he realized that he had come upon the remains of the Lichnowsky family archives. These papers are now housed in the CSSR State Archives in Opava. Among them are the mutilated remnants of the paper deposited by the prince. They range from letters he wrote his mother from Switzerland when he was away at school as a child of nine to his correspondence with Constable and Sons in London concerning the English edition of his collected papers.
2. Nachlässe in the Bundesarchiv, Koblenz (cited as Nachlass and name of person): Oberst Bauer, Bülow, Delbrück, Eulenburg, Harden, Heinrichs, Schwertfeger, Solf, Thimme.
3. Nachlässe in Politisches Archiv, Bonn: Bethmann Hollweg, Eisendecher, Jagow, Luetgebrune.
4. Private Papers in Foreign Office Series 800, Public Record Office, London (cited as FO 800): Sir Edward (Viscount) Grey, Sir Arthur Nicolson.
5. Nachlass Albert Graf Mensdorff-Pouilly-Dietrichstein in Haus-, Hofund Staatsarchiv, Vienna (Nachlass Mensdorff).

II. Official Documents Publications
(with abbreviations)

A. *Austria-Hungary. Österreich-Ungarns Aussenpolitik von der bosnischen Krise 1908 bis zum Kriegsausbruch 1914: Diplomatische*

Aktenstücke des Österreichisch-Ungarischen Ministeriums des Äussern. Edited by Ludwig Bittner, Alfred Francis Pribram, Heinrich Srbik, and Hans Uebersberger. 8 vols. Vienna-Leipzig, 1930. *(ÖUA)*

B. *France.* Ministère des Affaires Etrangères. Commission de publication des documents relatifs aux origines de la guerre. *Documents diplomatiques français 1871–1914.* Paris, 1929–1959. *(DDF)*

C. *Germany.* *Die Deutschen Dokumente zum Kriegsausbruch 1914.* 2nd enlarged ed. 4 vols. Berlin: Deutsche Verlagsgesellschaft für Politik und Geschichte, 1922. *(DD)*

D. ———. *Die Grosse Politik der Europäischen Kabinette: Sammlung der diplomatischen Akten des Auswärtigen Amtes.* Edited by J. Lepsius, A. Mendelssohn-Bartholdy, and F. Thimme. 40 vols. Berlin: Deutsche Verlagsgesellschaft für Politik und Geschichte, 1922–1927. *(GP)*

E. ———. Nationalversammlung. *Official German Documents Relating to the World War.* The Reports of the First and Second Subcommittees of the Committee appointed by the National Constituent Assembly to inquire into the Responsibility for the War, together with the stenographic minutes of the Second Subcommitee and Supplements thereto. Translated under the supervision of the Carnegie Endowment for International Peace, Division of International Law. 2 vols. New York, Oxford University Press, 1923.

———. Reichstag. *Stenographische Berichte über die Verhandlungen des Reichstages.*

———. Prussia. Herrenhaus. *Stenographische Berichte über die Verhandlungen des Preussischen Herrenhauses.*

F. *Great Britain.* *British Documents on the Origins of the War, 1898–1914.* Edited by G. P. Gooch and H. Temperley. 11 vols. London: His Majesty's Stationery Office, 1926–1936. *(BD)*

G. *Italy.* Ministero degli: Affari Esteri. Commissione per la pubblicazione dei Documenti Diplomatici. *I Documenti diplomatici italiani.* Quarta Serie; Quinta Serie. Rome: Libreria dello Stato, 1954; 1964. *(DDI)*

H. *Russia.* Kommissiia po izdanii dokumentov epokhi imperializma. *Mezhdunarodnye otnosheniia v epokhu imperializma: Dokumenty iz arkhivov tsarskogo i Vremmenogo pravitel'stv 1878–1917 gg* [International relations in the epoch of imperialism: documents from the archives of the czarist and the provisional governments 1878–1917]. Edited by M. N. Pokrovskii. Moscow, 1930–1938. *(MO)*

III. Other Collections of Diplomatic Correspondence

A. Geiss, Imanuel, ed. *Julikrise und Kriegsausbruch: Eine Doku-mentensammlung.* 2 vols. Hanover: Verlag für Literatur und Zeit-geschehen, 1963–1964.
B. Siebert, Benno A. von, ed. *Graf Benckendorffs diplomatischer Schriftwechsel.* Rev. ed., 3 vols. Berlin-Leipzig: Walter de Gruyter, 1928. (*DS*)

IV. Prince Lichnowsky's Works

Most of Lichnowsky's essays were published in Lichnowsky, Karl Max Fürst von. *Auf dem Wege zum Abgrund: Londoner Berichte, Erinner-ungen und sonstige Schriften.* 2 vols. Dresden: Carl Reissner Verlag, 1927. See note on Usage and p. ooo for revisions undertaken for 1928 English edition. Works not included in this selection are: "Die deutsche Flotte und England," *Berliner Tageblatt,* 28 Aug. 1909; ar-ticle on Anglo-German relations, *Neues Wiener Tageblatt,* 24 Dec. 1911; "Deutsch-englische Missverständnisse," *Nord und Süd* 142 (July 1912) (also published separately as *Krieg oder Frieden: Die deutsch-englische Verständigung,* Breslau: Schles. Buchdr., Kunst, und Ver-lagsanstalt, 1912) ; "Deutschland und Frankreich," *Deutsche Revue* 37 (1 July 1912); "Das selbständige Polen," *Berliner Tageblatt,* 2 Sept. 1917; "Der Wahlkampf," *Nord und Süd* 140 (Jan. 1912). Since the prince's wartime essays were published in *Auf dem Wege* in amended form, it is necessary to turn to other publications for the original ver-sions. A copy of the original manuscript of *Meine Londoner Mission 1912–1914* is in AA, Deutschland 122, no. 22 (Fürst Lichnowsky). The Orell Füssli edition (Zurich, 1918) corresponds to the manuscript in all respects except that it eliminates the passage concerning Grey's consort. There are three extant versions of "Wahn oder Wille?"— the apparently original version of January 1915 which I found in Nachlass Bülow, a slightly different but incomplete version found in RAUSL, and the greatly amended version, retitled "Wahn, nicht Wille!" published in *Auf dem Wege.* John C. G. Röhl has published the origi-nal version which he found in the papers of Freiherr von Varnbüler in *Zwei deutsche Fürsten zur Kriegsschuldfrage: Lichnowsky und Eulen-*

burg und der Ausbruch des 1. Weltkriegs. Düsseldorf: Droste Verlag, 1971, revised and translated as *1914: Delusion or Design? The Testimony of Two German Diplomats.* London: Paul Elek, 1973. The original version of "England vor dem Kriege" was published in Friedrich Thimme: "Fürst Lichnowskys 'Memoirenwerk,'" *Archiv für Politik und Geschichte* 7, no. 1 (1928).

V. Works on Prince Lichnowsky

Willis, Edward F. *Prince Lichnowsky Ambassador of Peace: A Study of Prewar Diplomacy, 1912–1914.* University of California Publications in History, vol. 25. Berkeley and Los Angeles: University of California Press, 1942. This is based on a doctoral dissertation written between 1931 and 1935 and revised slightly in 1936 (according to preface). A creditable and objective piece of work, it is based on limited published sources and, as the title indicates, concentrates narrowly on the diplomacy of the two years preceding the war. Its primary defect is that it ignores the most gripping and revealing part of the prince's history—his fourteen-year struggle for an answer to the question of who or what was responsible for the war. There is a sixteen-page chapter on Lichnowsky in Heinz Günther Sasse's history of the Prussian and German representatives in England, *100 Jahre Botschaft in London: Aus der Geschichte einer deutschen Botschaft.* Sonderdruck aus dem Mitteilungsblatt der Vereinigung der Angestellten des Auswärtigen Dienstes e.V. Bonn, 1963. Sasse examined some of the pertinent unpublished materials in the German Foreign Ministry archives but his account is far from complete and it breathes an animosity toward the prince reminiscent of the early war-guilt discussion. The biographical information on Lichnowsky is scanty and there is no attempt at an *Entstehungsgeschichte* on "Wahn oder Wille?" or the other wartime essays in J. C. G. Röhl's *Zwei deutsche Fürsten* (English edition: *1914: Delusion or Design?*).

VI. Memoirs and Editions of Letters or Papers Cited

Asquith, Herbert. *Moments of Memory: Recollections and Impressions.* London: Hutchinson, 1937.

Asquith, Herbert H. (The Earl of Oxford and Asquith). *Memories and Reflections, 1852–1927*. 2 vols. London: Cassell's, 1928.

Asquith, Margot. (Margot, Countess of Oxford and Asquith). *An Autobiography*. 4 vols. New York: George H. Doran, 1920–1922.

Bethmann Hollweg, Theobald von. *Bethmann Hollwegs Kriegsreden*. Edited by Friedrich Thimme. Stuttgart-Berlin: Deutsche Verlags-Anstalt, 1919.

Bernstorff, Graf Johann Heinrich. *Memoirs of Count Bernstorff*. Translated by Eric Sutton. New York: Random House, 1936.

Bülow, Bernhard Fürst von. *Denkwürdigkeiten*. 4 vols. Berlin: Ullstein, 1930–1931.

———. "Fürst Bülow und Graf Monts: Ein vervollständigter Briefwechsel." Edited by Friedrich Thimme. *Preussische Jahrbücher* 231 and 232 (1932/1933).

Dumba, Constantin. *Dreibund- und Entente- Politik in der Alten und Neuen Welt*. Zurich-Leipzig-Vienna: Almathea-Verlag, 1931.

Eckardstein, Hermann Freiherr von. *Lebenserinnerungen und politische Denkwürdigkeiten*. 2 vols. Leipzig: Paul List, 1920.

Eulenburg-Hertefeld, Fürst Philipp zu. *Aus 50 Jahren: Erinnerungen, Tagebücher und Briefe aus dem Nachlass des Fürsten Philipp zu Eulenburg-Hertefeld*. Edited by Johannes Haller. Berlin: Gebrüder Paetel, 1925.

Franckenstein, Sir George. *Diplomat of Destiny*. New York: Alliance, 1940.

Friedrich II (Hohenzollern). *Politische Korrespondenz Friedrichs des Grossen*. 46 vols. Berlin: published for the Preussische Akademie der Wissenschaften by A. Duncker et al., 1879–1939.

George, David Lloyd. *War Memoirs of David Lloyd George*. 2 vols. Boston: Little, Brown, 1935.

Grey of Fallodon, Viscount (Sir Edward Grey). *Twenty-five Years, 1892–1916*. 2 vols. New York: Frederick A. Stokes, 1925.

Hammann, Otto. *Zur Vorgeschichte des Weltkrieges: Erinnerungen aus den Jahren 1897–1906*. Berlin: Reimar Hobbing, 1919.

Hanssen, Hans Peter. *Diary of a Dying Empire*. Translation of *Fra Krigstiden* (Copenhagen, 1924). Translated by O. O. Winther. Edited by Ralph H. Lutz, Mary Schofield and O. O. Winther. Introduced by Ralph H. Lutz. Bloomington: Indiana University Press, 1955.

Helmholtz, Anna von. *Ein Lebensbild in Briefen*. Edited by Ellen von Siemens-Helmholtz. 2 vols. Leipzig: v. Hase and Koehler, 1929.

Hertling, Georg Graf von. *Briefwechsel Hertling-Lerchenfeld 1912–1917: Dienstliche Privatkorrespondenz zwischen dem bayerischen*

Ministerpräsidenten Georg Graf von Hertling und dem bayerischen Gesandten in Berlin Hugo Graf von und zu Lerchenfeld. Edited by Ernst Deuerlein. 2 vols., Deutsche Geschichtsquellen des 19. und 20. Jahrhunderts, ed. by the Historische Kommission bei der Bayerischen Akademie der Wissenschaften, vol. 50 (1–2). Boppard am Rhein: Harald Boldt Verlag, 1973.

Heyking, Elisabeth von. *Tagebücher aus vier Weltteilen, 1886–1904.* Leipzig: Koehler und Amelang, 1926.

Hindenburg, Herbert Alexander Otto Wladimir von Benckendorff und von. *Am Rande zweier Jahrzehnte: Momentbilder aus einem Diplomatenleben.* Berlin: Schlieffen-Verlag, 1938.

Hohenlohe-Schillingsfürst, Fürst Chlodwig zu. *Denkwürdigkeiten der Reichskanzlerzeit.* Edited by Karl A. v. Müller. Stuttgart-Berlin: Deutsche Verlagsanstalt, 1931.

Holitscher, Arthur. *Mein Leben in dieser Zeit: Der "Lebensgeschichte" eines Rebellen zweiter Band (1907–1925).* Potsdam: G. Kiepenheuer, 1928.

Holstein, Friedrich von. "Gespräche und Briefe Holsteins 1907–1909." Edited by Heinrich Otto Meisner. *Preussische Jahrbücher* 228 and 229 (1932).

———. *The Holstein Papers: The Memoirs, Diaries, and Correspondence of Friedrich von Holstein, 1837–1909.* Edited by Norman Rich and M. H. Fisher. 4 vols. Cambridge: At the University Press, 1955–1963.

———. *Holstein und Harden: Politisch-publizistisches Zusammenspiel zweier Aussenseiter des Wilhelminischen Reiches.* Edited by Helmuth Rogge. Munich: Oldenbourg, 1959.

Hutten-Czapski, Bogdan Graf von. *Sechzig Jahre Politik und Gesellschaft.* 2 vols. Berlin: E. S. Mittler, 1936.

Ionescu, Take. *Souvenirs.* Paris: Payot, 1919.

Jagow, Günther Gottlieb Karl von. "Die deutsche politische Leitung und England bei Kriegsausbruch." *Preussische Jahrbücher* 213, no. 1 (1928).

———. *Ursachen und Ausbruch des Weltkrieges.* Berlin: Reimar Hobbing, 1919.

Kiderlen-Wächter, Alfred von. Ernst Jäckh. *Kiderlen-Wächter: Der Staatsmann und Mensch.* 2 vols. Berlin-Leipzig: Deutsche Verlagsanstalt, 1925.

Kühlmann, Richard von. *Erinnerungen.* Heidelberg: Lambert Schneider, 1948.

Lerchenfeld, Hugo Graf von und zu. See Hertling, Georg Graf von.

Leslie, Shane. *Long Shadows*. London: J. Murray, 1966.

Lichnowsky, Mechtilde. *An der Leine: Roman*. Berlin: S. Fischer Verlag, 1930.

———. *Heute und vorgestern*. Vienna: Bergland Verlag, 1958.

———. *Zum Schauen bestellt*. Esslingen: Bechtle Verlag, 1953.

Ludendorff, Erich von. *Meine Kriegserinnerungen 1914–1918*. Berlin: E. S. Mittler, 1920.

Mann, Heinrich. *Ein Zeitalter wird besichtigt*. Berlin: Aufbau-Verlag, 1947.

Miquel, Hans von. "Aus den nachgelassenen Papieren eines deutschen Diplomaten: Aufzeichnungen des Gesandten Hans von Miquel." Edited by Friedrich Thimme. *Berliner Monatshefte* 16 (March 1938).

Monts, Anton Graf. *Erinnerungen und Gedanken des Botschafters Anton Graf Monts*. Edited by Karl F. Nowak and Friedrich Thimme. Berlin: Verlag für Kulturpolitik, 1932.

Morley, John Viscount. *Memorandum on Resignation*. New York: Macmillan, 1928.

Müller, Georg Alexander von. *Der Kaiser . . . Aufzeichnungen des Chefs des Marinekabinetts Admiral Georg Alexander von Müller über die Ära Wilhelms II*. Edited by Walter Görlitz. Göttingen: Musterschmidt-Verlag, 1965.

———. *Regierte der Kaiser? Kriegstagebücher, Aufzeichnungen und Briefe des Chefs des Marinekabinetts Admiral Georg Alexander von Müller*. Edited by Walter Görlitz. Göttingen: Musterschmidt-Verlag, 1959.

Münz, Sigmund. *Fürst Bülow, der Staatsmann und Mensch: Aufzeichnungen, Erinnerungen und Erwägungen*. Berlin: Verlag für Kulturpolitik, 1930.

Page, Walter Hines. Burton Jesse Hendrick. *The Life and Letters of Walter H. Page*. 3 vols. New York: Doubleday, Page, 1922.

Pless, Mary Theresa Olivia (Cornwallis-West) Fürstin von. *Daisy Princess of Pless by Herself*. Edited by Major Desmond Chapman-Huston. New York: Dutton, 1929.

———. *From My Private Diary*. Edited by Major Desmond Chapman-Huston. London: J. Murray, 1931.

Plessen, Leopold von. *Begegnungen*. Glückstadt: private printing, 1964.

Pourtalès, [Friedrich] Graf. *Am Scheideweg zwischen Krieg und Frieden: Meine letzten Verhandlungen in Petersburg, Ende Juli 1914*. Charlottenburg: Deutsche Verlagsgesellschaft für Politik und Geschichte, 1919.

Radziwill, Marie Dorothea Elisabeth (de Castellane). *Une grande dame d'avant guerre: Lettres de la Princesse Radziwill au Général de Robilant 1889–1914*. Bologna: Nicola Zanichelli, 1933.

Raschdau, Ludwig. *In Weimar als Preussischer Gesandter: Ein Buch der Erinnerungen an deutsche Fürstenhöfe 1894–1897*. Berlin: E. S. Mittler, 1939.

Rheinbaben, Werner Freiherr von. *Kaiser Kanzler Präsidenten: Erinnerungen*. Mainz: v. Hase und Koehler Verlag, 1968.

Riezler, Kurt. *Tagebücher, Aufsätze, Dokumente*. Edited by Karl Dietrich Erdmann. Deutsche Geschichtsquellen des 19. und 20. Jahrhunderts, ed. by Historische Kommission bei der Bayerischen Akademie der Wissenschaften, vol. 48. Göttingen: Vandenhoeck und Ruprecht, 1972.

Rosen, Friedrich. *Aus einem diplomatischen Wanderleben*. 2 vols. Berlin: Transmare Verlag, 1931–1932.

Rumbold, Sir Horace. *The War-Crisis in Berlin July-August 1914*. London: Constable, 1940.

Schebeko, Nikolai Nikolaevich. *Souvenirs: Essai historique sur les origines de la guerre de 1914*. Preface by Jules Cambon. Paris: Bibliothèque Diplomatique, 1936.

Scholtis, August. "Die Denkschrift des Fürsten Lichnowsky nach Ausbruch des Ersten Weltkrieges." MS Scholtis Papers, 1967.

———. *Ein Herr aus Bolatitz: Lebenserinnerungen*. Munich: Paul List Verlag, 1959.

———. *Die Katze im schlesischen Schrank*. Augsburg: Oberschlesischer Heimatverlag, 1958.

Spitzemberg geb. Freiin von Varnbüler, Baronin. *Das Tagebuch der Baronin Spitzemberg geb. Freiin v. Varnbüler: Aufzeichnungen aus der Hofgesellschaft des Hohenzollernreiches*. Edited by Rudolf Vierhaus. Deutsche Geschichtsquellen des 19. und 20. Jahrhunderts, ed. by Historische Kommission bei der Bayerischen Akademie der Wissenschaften, vol. 43. Göttingen: Vandenhoeck und Ruprecht, 1960.

Stein, Ludwig. *Aus dem Leben eines Optimisten*. Berlin: Brückenverlag, 1930.

Thierry, Adrien. *L'Angleterre au temps de Paul Cambon*. Paris-Geneva: La Palatine, 1961.

Tirpitz, Alfred von. *Politische Dokumente*. 2 vols. Stuttgart-Berlin: J. G. Cotta'sche Buchhandlung Nachf., 1924–1926.

Wilhelm II (Hohenzollern). *Ereignisse und Gestalten aus den Jahren 1878–1918*. Leipzig: K. F. Koehler, 1922.

Wolff, Theodor. *Der Marsch durch zwei Jahrzehnte*. Amsterdam: Albert de Lange, 1936.

VII. Other Works Cited

Albertini, Luigi. *The Origins of the War of 1914.* Translated and edited by Isabella M. Massey. 3 vols. Oxford: At the University Press, 1957.

Aretin, Erwein. "Geschichte der Herren und Grafen von Arco." MS (1936–1945). Deposited at Schloss Moos, Plattling, Lower Bavaria.

Arneth, Alfred Ritter von. *Geschichte Maria Theresias.* 10 vols. Vienna: W. Braumüller, 1879.

Bach, August. "Das angebliche Missverständnis des Fürsten Lichnowsky vom 1. August 1914." *Berliner Monatshefte* 8, no. 4 (Apr. 1930).

Baumont, Maurice. "Le Prince de Radolin," in *Mélanges Pierre Renouvin: Etudes d'histoire des relations internationales.* Paris: Presses universitaires de France, 1966.

Beazley, Sir Raymond. "Britain, Germany, and the Portuguese Colonies 1898–1899." *Berliner Monatshefte* 14 (Nov. 1936).

Beerfelde, Hans Georg (Jürgen) von. "Der wahre Lichnowsky." *Die Welt am Montag* (Berlin), 23 Apr. 1928.

Benz, Wolfgang. "Der 'Fall Muehlon': Bürgerliche Opposition im Obrigkeitsstaat während des Ersten Weltkriegs." *Vierteljahrshefte für Zeitgeschichte* 18, no. 4 (Oct. 1970).

Berghahn, Volker R. *Der Tirpitz-Plan: Genesis und Verfall einer innenpolitischen Krisenstrategie unter Wilhelm II.* Düsseldorf, Droste Verlag, 1971.

Bergsträsser, Ludwig. "Das unbekannte Leben des bekannten Fürsten Felix Lichnowsky." *Hochland* 31 (1934).

Bernstein, Eduard. "In Sachen des Fürsten Lichnowsky." *Berliner Tageblatt,* 18 July 1918.

Biermann, Gottlieb. *Geschichte der Herzogthümer Troppau und Jägerndorf.* Teschen: Buchholz und Diebel, 1874.

Brandt, Willy, and Lowenthal, Richard. *Ernst Reuter, ein Leben für die Freiheit: Eine politische Biographie.* Munich: Kindler, 1957.

Bredt, Johann Victor. "Das 'Missverständnis' des Fürsten Lichnowsky vom 1. August 1914." *Preussische Jahrbücher* 230, no. 2 (Nov. 1932).

———. "Lichnowsky und Grey." *Preussische Jahrbücher* 212, no. 1 (Apr. 1928).

Brunner, Otto. *Adeliges Landleben und europäischer Geist: Leben und Werk Helmhards von Hohberg 1612–1688.* Salzburg: Otto Müller Verlag, 1949.

Butterfield, Herbert. "Sir Edward Grey in July 1914," in Irish Conference of Historians. *Historical Studies* 5. London: Bowes and Bowes, 1965.

Chapman, Maybelle Kennedy. *Great Britain and the Bagdad Railway 1888–1914*. Smith College Studies in History, vol. 31. Northampton, Mass., 1948.

Collins, Doreen. *Aspects of British Politics, 1904–1919*. Oxford: At the University Press, 1965.

Cord Meyer, Henry. *The Long Generation: Germany from Empire to Ruin, 1913–1945*. New York: Walker, 1973.

Creel, George. *How We Advertised America*. New York: Harper, 1920.

d'Elvert, Christian Ritter. *Beiträge zur Geschichte der Rebellion, Reformation, des dreissigjährigen Krieges und der Neugestaltung Mährens im siebzehnten Jahrhundert*. 4 vols. Brünn: A. Nitsch, 1867–1878.

Fischer, Fritz. *Krieg der Illusionen: Die deutsche Politik von 1911 bis 1914*. Düsseldorf: Droste Verlag, 1969.

Frauendienst, Werner. "Das Kriegsschuldreferat des Auswärtigen Amtes." *Berliner Monatshefte* 15 (March 1937).

Gatzke, Hans W. *Germany's Drive to the West (Drang nach Westen): A Study of Germany's Western War Aims during the First World War*. Baltimore: Johns Hopkins Press, 1950.

Gollwitzer, Heinz. "Der erste Karlistenkrieg und das Problem der internationalen Parteigängerschaft." *Historische Zeitschrift* 176, no. 3 (1953).

Grappin, Pierre. *Le Bund Neues Vaterland (1914–1916): Ses rapports avec Romain Rolland*. Bibliothèque de la Société des études germaniques, vol. 7. Lyon-Paris: Imprimerie artistique en couleurs, 1952.

Guttmann, Bernhard. "Lichnowskys Erinnerungen." *Frankfurter Zeitung*, 17 Jan. 1928.

Haller, Johannes. *Aus dem Leben des Fürsten Philipp zu Eulenburg-Hertefeld*. Berlin: Gebrüder Paetel, 1924.

Hantsch, Hugo. *Leopold Graf Berchtold: Grandseigneur und Staatsmann*, 2 vols. Graz-Vienna-Cologne: Styria Verlag, 1963.

Harden, Maximilian. Special articles in *Die Zukunft:* "Die Töchter der Nacht," 23 March 1918; "Der alte Sauerteig," 30 March 1918; "Diplomatarium," 6 Apr. 1918; "Wider Lichnowsky," 27 Apr. 1918.

Hayes, Bascom Barry. "The German *Reich* and the 'Austrian Question,' 1871–1914." Diss. Yale 1963.

Helmreich, Ernst C. *The Diplomacy of the Balkan Wars, 1912–1913*, Cambridge, Mass.: Harvard University Press, 1938.

Herre, Paul. "Fürst Lichnowsky und die Kriegsschuldfrage." *Die Kriegsschuldfrage* 6, no. 2 (Feb. 1928).

Heuss, Theodor. *Friedrich Naumann: Der Mann, das Werk, die Zeit.* 2nd ed., Stuttgart: Deutsche Verlagsanstalt, 1949.

Hiller von Gaertringen, Friedrich Freiherr. *Fürst Bülows Denkwürdig-keiten: Untersuchungen zu ihrer Entstehungsgeschichte und ihrer Kritik.* Tübingen: J. C. B. Mohr (Paul Siebeck), 1956.

Hindenburg, Herbert von. "Der Grandseigneur als Diplomat. Erin-nerungen und Bemerkungen zum Fall Lichnowsky." *Frankfurter Zeitung,* 25 Nov. 1928.

Igálffy-Igály, Ludwig. "Stammtafel der Ritter, Freiherrn, Grafen und Fürsten Lichnowsky v. Woszczyc vom 14. Jahrhundert bis zur Gegen-wart." *Adler: Zeitschrift für Genealogie und Heraldik* 3 (17), no. 9/10 (May–Aug. 1954).

Jarausch, Konrad H. *The Enigmatic Chancellor: Bethmann Hollweg and the Hubris of Imperial Germany.* New Haven and London: Yale University Press, 1973.

————. "The Illusion of Limited War: Chancellor Bethmann Holl-weg's Calculated Risk, July 1914." *Central European History* 2, no. 1 (March 1969).

Kahlden, Eberhard von. "Die Herrschaft Kuchelna: Ein Oberschles-ischer Grossgrundbesitz Sr. Durchlaucht des Fürsten Lichnowsky: Reisebericht." *Landwirtschaftliche Jahrbücher* 29 (1900).

Kantorowicz, Hermann. *Gutachten zur Kriegsschuldfrage 1914.* Edited by Imanuel Geiss. Frankfurt/Main: Europäische Verlagsanstalt, 1967.

Kardorff, Siegfried von. *Wilhelm von Kardorff: Ein nationaler Parla-mentarier im Zeitalter Bismarcks und Wilhelm II. 1828–1907.* Ber-lin: E. S. Mittler, 1936.

Kirchner, Richard. "Die Berichte Lichnowskys." *Frankfurter Zeitung,* Erstes Morgenblatt, 22, 25, 27, 29 Feb. 1920.

Kobold, Karl. *Beethoven: Seine Beziehungen zu Wiens Kunst und Kultur, Gesellschaft und Landschaft.* Zurich-Leipzig-Vienna: Alma-thea-Verlag, 1946.

Korostovetz, Wladimir v. "Graf Alexander Konstantinowitsch Benck-endorff." *Berliner Monatshefte* 14 (Nov. 1936).

Kritt, Robert. "Die Londoner Botschafter Konferenz 1912–1913." Diss. Vienna 1961.

Kühlmann, Richard von. "Reichsgraf Paul Wolff Metternich zur Gracht." *Berliner Monatshefte* 13, no. 1 (Jan. 1935).

Lehmann-Russbüldt, Otto. *Der Kampf der Deutschen Liga für Men-schenrechte vormals Bund Neues Vaterland für den Weltfrieden 1914–1927.* Berlin: Hensel, 1927.

Ley, Stephan. "Schloss Grätz: Beethoven und die fürstliche Familie Lichnowsky." *Atlantis* 9 (Jan. 1937).

Lichnowsky, Eduard Marie. *Geschichte des Hauses Habsburg.* 8 vols. Vienna: Schaumburg, 1836-1844.

Ludwig, Emil. "Der Fürst Lichnowsky." *Die Weltbühne,* 20 March 1928.

———. "Ehrenrettung eines Toten." *Vossische Zeitung,* Abend-Ausgabe, 28 March 1928.

———. *Wilhelm der Zweite.* Berlin: Ernst Rowohlt Verlag, 1926.

Maenner, Ludwig. *Prinz Heinrich zu Schönaich-Carolath: Ein parlamentarisches Leben der wilhelminischen Zeit (1852–1920).* Stuttgart-Berlin: Deutsche Verlagsanstalt, 1931.

Mann, Golo. "Fürst Lichnowsky." *Du* 20, no. 9 (Sept. 1960). Reprinted in *Geschichte und Geschichten.* Frankfurt/Main: S. Fischer Verlag, 1962.

Matthias, Erich, and Morsey, Rudolf, ed. *Die Regierung des Prinzen Max von Baden.* Quellen zur Geschichte des Parlamentarismus und der politischen Parteien: Erste Reihe: Von der konstitutionellen Monarchie zur parlamentarischen Republik im Auftrage der Kommission für Geschichte des Parlamentarismus und der politischen Parteien. Edited by Werner Conze, Erich Matthias, and Georg Winter, vol. 2. Düsseldorf: Droste Verlag, 1962.

Meyer, Klaus. *Theodor Schiemann als politischer Publizist.* Frankfurt/Main: Rütten und Loening, 1956.

Michaelis, Herbert; Schraepler, Ernst; and Scheel, Günter, ed. *Ursachen und Folgen vom deutschen Zusammenbruch 1918 und 1945 bis zur staatlichen Neuordnung Deutschlands in der Gegenwart.* 5 vols. Berlin: Dokumenten-Verlag, 1958–1960.

Monger, George. *The End of Isolation: British Foreign Policy, 1900–1907.* London: Thomas Nelson, 1963.

Montgelas, Max Graf. "Persönliche Bemerkungen zu Fürst Lichnowskys 'Auf dem Wege zum Abgrund.' " *Die Kriegsschuldfrage* 5 (Nov. 1927).

Nicolson, Harold. *Sir Arthur Nicolson, Bart., First Lord Carnock: A Study in the Old Diplomacy.* London: Constable, 1930.

———. *King George V.* London: Constable, 1952.

Opočenský, Jan. "Documents: A War-Time Discussion of the Responsibility for the War." *Journal of Modern History* 4 (March-Dec. 1932).

Renouvin, Pierre. "L'Afrique centrale dans les relations anglo-allemandes en 1912–1914." *Etudes maghrébines: Mélanges Charles-André Julien.* Publications de la Faculté des lettres et Sciences

Humaines de Paris, Série "Etudes et Méthodes," vol. 11. Paris: Presses universitaires de France, 1964.

Rich, Norman. *Friedrich von Holstein: Politics and Diplomacy in the Era of Bismarck and Wilhelm II.* 2 vols. Cambridge: At the University Press, 1965.

Ritter, Gerhard. *Staatskunst und Kriegshandwerk: Das Problem des "Militarismus" in Deutschland.* 3rd ed. 4 vols. Munich: Verlag K. Oldenbourg, 1965–1968.

Röhl, John C. G. *Germany without Bismarck: The Crisis of Government in the Second Reich, 1890–1900.* Berkeley and Los Angeles: University of California Press, 1967.

Rolo, P. J. V. *Entente Cordiale: The Origins and Negotiations of the Anglo-French Agreements of 8 April 1904.* New York: Macmillan, St. Martin's Press, 1969.

Rosenberg, Alfred. *Novemberköpfe.* 2nd ed. Munich: Eher, 1939.

Schlesisches Güteradressbuch. Breslau: W. G. Korn, 1912.

Schmidt-Pauli, Edgar von. *Fürst Bülows Denk-Unwürdigkeiten: Ein Protest.* Berlin: Schlieffen-Verlag, 1931.

Schüssler, Wilhelm. *Deutschland zwischen Russland und England: Studien zur Aussenpolitik des Bismarck'schen Reiches.* Leipzig: Koehler und Amelang, 1940.

Schwertfeger, Bernhard. "Fürst Lichnowsky und das deutsch-englische Kolonialabkommen." *Tägliche Rundschau,* 29 Dec. 1927.

Spender, John Alfred, and Asquith, Cyril. *Life of Henry Asquith, Lord Oxford and Asquith.* 2 vols. London: Hutchinson, 1932.

Springborn, Arnold. *Englands Stellung zur deutschen Welt- und Kolonialpolitik in den Jahren 1911–1914.* Würzburg-Aumühle: Konrad Triltsch Verlag, 1939.

Stahl, Friedrich-Christian. "Botschafter Graf Wolff Metternich und die deutsch-englischen Beziehungen." Diss. Hamburg 1951.

Stein, Peter. *Die Neuorientierung der österreichisch-ungarischen Aussenpolitik 1895–1897: Ein Beitrag zur europäischen Bündnispolitik im ausgehenden Jahrhundert.* Göttinger Bausteine zur Geschichtswissenschaft, ed. by Prof. Goetting et al., vol. 44. Göttingen: Musterschmidt, 1972.

Steinberg, Jonathan. *Yesterday's Deterrent: Tirpitz and the Birth of the German Battle Fleet.* London: Macdonald, 1965.

Steiner, Zara S. *The Foreign Office and Foreign Policy, 1898–1914.* Cambridge: At the University Press, 1969.

Stern, Fritz. "Bethmann Hollweg and the War: The Limits of Responsibility," in *The Responsibility of Power: Historical Essays in*

Honor of Hajo Holborn. Edited by Leonard Krieger and Fritz Stern. Garden City, N.Y.: Doubleday, 1967.

Thilo, Charlotte. "Die Bevölkerungs-, Siedlungs- und Wirtschaftsverhältnisse im Hultschiner Ländchen," in *Beiträge zur schlesischen Landeskunde.* Edited by M. H. Friedrichsen. Breslau: Ferdinand Hirt, 1925.

Thimme, Friedrich. "Auf dem Wege zum Abgrund. Ein ehemaliger deutscher Botschafter wird zum Kronzeugen für Deutschlands Schuld." *Kölnische Zeitung,* zweite Sonntagsausgabe, 11 Dec. 1927.

————. "Die Antwort des Fürsten Lichnowsky." *Kölnische Zeitung,* 30 Dec. 1927.

————. " 'Die grosse Politik der europäischen Kabinette 1871–1914': Persönliche Erinnerungen." *Berliner Monatshefte* 5 (March 1937).

————. "Ehrenrettung des Fürsten Lichnowsky?" *Berliner Börsen-Zeitung,* 31 March 1928.

————. "Fürst Lichnowskys 'Memoirenwerk.' " *Archiv für Politik und Geschichte* 7, no. 1 (1928).

————. "Fürst Lichnowskys Ressentiments." *Die Kriegsschuldfrage* 6, no. 3 (March 1928).

————. "Wer rettet Emil Ludwig? Das Ergebnis einer 'Ehrenrettung.' " *Berliner Börsen-Zeitung,* 31 March 1928.

————, ed. *Front Wider Bülow: Staatsmänner, Diplomaten und Forscher zu seinen Denkwürdigkeiten.* Munich: F. Bruckmann, 1931.

Thimme, Hans. *Weltkrieg ohne Waffen: Die Propaganda der Westmächte gegen Deutschland, ihre Wirkung und ihre Abwehr.* Stuttgart-Berlin: Cotta, 1932.

Vietsch, Eberhard von. *Bethmann Hollweg: Staatsmann zwischen Macht und Ethos.* Boppard am Rhein: Harald Boldt Verlag, 1969.

Wagner, Walter. "Kaiser Franz Josef und das Deutsche Reich von 1871–1914." Diss. Vienna 1950.

Waltz, Jean Jacques, and Tonnelat, Ernest. *A travers les lignes ennemies: Trois années d'offensive contre le moral allemand.* Paris: Payot, 1922.

Wegerer, Alfred von. *Der Ausbruch des Weltkrieges 1914.* 2 vols. Hamburg: Hanseatische Verlagsanstalt, 1939.

————. "Weitere Irrtümer des Fürsten Bülow über den Kriegsausbruch." *Berliner Monatshefte* 9, no. 4 (Apr. 1931).

Wernecke, Klaus. *Der Wille zur Weltgeltung: Aussenpolitik und Öffentlichkeit im Kaiserreich am Vorabend des Ersten Weltkrieges.* Düsseldorf: Droste Verlag, 1970.

Willequet, Jacques. "Anglo-German Rivalry in Belgian and Portuguese Africa," in *Britain and Germany in Africa.* Edited by Prosser

Gifford and W. R. Louis. New Haven: Yale University Press, 1967.

———. *Le Congo belge et la Weltpolitik.* Brussels: Universitaire libre de Bruxelles, 1962.

Williamson, John G. *Karl Helfferich 1892–1924: Economist, Financier, Politician.* Princeton: Princeton University Press, 1971.

Witt, Peter-Christian. *Die Finanzpolitik des deutschen Reiches von 1903 bis 1913: Eine Studie zur Innenpolitik des Wilhelminischen Deutschland.* Lübeck and Hamburg: Matthiesen Verlag, 1970.

Wolf, J. B. *The Diplomatic History of the Bagdad Railroad.* Univerversity of Missouri Studies: A Quarterly of Research 11, 1 Apr. 1936.

Wolff, Theodor. "Fürst Lichnowsky." *Berliner Tageblatt,* 28 Feb. 1928.

———. "Fürst Lichnowsky Botschafter in London." *Berliner Tageblatt,* 17 Oct. 1912.

———. "Das Telegramm des Fürsten Lichnowsky." *Berliner Tageblatt,* Abend Ausgabe, 21 Aug. 1914.

———. *Das Vorspiel.* Munich: Verlag für Kulturpolitik, 1924.

———. *Der Krieg des Pontius Pilatus.* Zurich: Verlag Oprecht and Helbling, 1934.

———. *Der Marsch durch zwei Jahrzehnte.* Amsterdam: Albert de Lange, 1936.

———. "Nicht einer." *Berliner Tageblatt,* 8 Apr. 1910.

Wolfstieg, August. "Die Anfänge der freikonservativen Partei," in *Delbrück-Festschrift: Gesammelte Aufsätze zu seinem sechzigsten Geburtstage (11. November 1908) dargebracht von Freunden und Schülern.* Edited by Emil Daniels, K. Lehmann, and G. Roloff. Berlin: Georg Stilke, 1908.

Young, Harry F. *Maximilian Harden, Censor Germaniae: Ein Publizist im Widerstreit von 1892 bis 1927.* Dialog der Gesellschaft: Schriftenreihe für Publizistik- und Kommunikationswissenschaft. Edited by Henk Prakke, Vol. 6. Münster: Verlag Regensberg, 1971.

Zechlin, Egmont. "Bethmann Hollweg, Kriegsrisiko und SPD 1914." *Der Monat* 18, no. 208 (Jan. 1966).

———. "Deutschland zwischen Kabinettskrieg und Wirtschaftskrieg." *Historische Zeitschrift* 199, no. 2 (Oct. 1964).

———. "Die Illusion vom begrenzten Krieg." *Die Zeit,* 21 Sept. 1965.

———. "Motive und Taktik der Reichsleitung 1914." *Der Monat* 18, no. 209.

Zmarzlik, Hans-Günter. *Bethmann Hollweg als Reichskanzler: Studien zu Möglichkeiten und Grenzen seiner innerpolitischen Machtstellung.* Beiträge zur Geschichte des Parlamentarismus und der politischen Parteien, vol. 2. Düsseldorf: Droste Verlag, 1957.

Index